Victorian Forerunner

Victorian Forerunner

The later career of
Thomas Hood

by

John Clubbe

1968
Duke University Press
Durham, N.C.

PRINTED IN THE UNITED STATES OF AMERICA
BY KINGSPORT PRESS, INC., KINGSPORT, TENN.

pour ma mère et mon père
for my mother and my father

Preface

Everyone thinks of Thomas Hood either as a romantic poet *manqué* or as a comic punster. He would have disliked either categorization. Today, looking back over the Victorian era, we see its literary figures in clearer perspective. The versatility of Hood's talent has become increasingly recognized, and he has, of late, been getting something more like his just due. His poetry, often misunderstood since his own time, once again finds discerning admirers. Already in 1930 William Empson had lauded its amazing technical virtuosity. More recently, W. H. Auden, reevaluating his comic poems, judged Hood a major poet.

Few would contest that during the last decade of his life (the years from 1835 to 1845) Hood wrote many of the poems that have established his surest claim to remembrance, and a reinterpretation of this period is desirable from both a biographical and a critical point of view. First, a sizable amount of new material—unpublished letters and doctoral dissertations—is now available, material ignored or unused by previous biographers; easily four-fifths of the unpublished letters date from the last ten years. Moreover, no previous study has adequately taken into account the importance of the personal crisis in Hood's life that took place during the winter of 1834–1835: it clearly determined the course the remainder of his life would take. From his own despair Hood looked upon the injustice prevalent within English society with newly opened eyes.

Second, the writings of the last decade of Hood's life have not received adequate critical interpretation. Deeply troubled by the widening rift between the "two Englands," Hood sought through his humanitarian poems to bring about some kind of reconciliation "between Rich and Poor," between "Hate on the one side and Fear on the other." This study examines in detail his interest in social and humanitarian causes and shows that it did not arise suddenly late in 1843 with the publication in *Punch* of "The Song of the Shirt," but was, on the contrary, an interest of many years standing. It also traces later developments in Hood's rich vein of grotesque poetry, known for its abrupt undercutting of the dramatic illusion, and explores the all-important influence of German romanticism—an influence hitherto ignored—upon these poems. Nor has anyone recognized the extent to which many of Hood's poems, to borrow Johnson's phrase, "point a moral." "One use of Victorian laughter . . . ," observes a recent critic, "was to ridicule in order to correct, or at least to unsettle, things and ideas which those who laugh take very seriously." [1] This was Hood's intent in what I call his "poems of moral humor." The detailed interpretations of all three of these themes—the humanitarian, the grotesque, the moral—are, I believe, basically new.

Linked together, biography and criticism can be mutually illuminating. A man of many-sided interests, Hood reflects important currents of English life in the years following Victoria's accession. In his career as poet, as in his interest in society, he indeed became a "Victorian forerunner."

Any study such as this builds heavily upon previous scholarship. Much as I would like to do so, it is impossible to name all those who have helped. But two chief debts I acknowledge with pleasure. One is to the Reverend Cornelius M. Cuyler, S.S., whose doctoral dissertation, "Thomas Hood: An Illustration of the Transition from the Romantic to the Victorian Era" (1943), examines Hood as a poetic bridge between the two ages. His main thesis, while convincing, does not negate my claim for the greater importance of the later writings. The other is to Alvin Whitley, whose dissertation, "Thomas Hood" (1950), is in matters of biography the modern pioneering study. Professor Whitley has, moreover, given generously to me of his unique store of knowledge about Hood. Besides the rich hoard of interpretation and information in these dissertations, two books also deserve mention: Walter Jerrold's 1907 biography, *Thomas Hood: His Life and Times,* a delight to read but out of date biographically and critically; and J. C. Reid's recent (1963) *Thomas Hood.* Often stimulating in its critical discussions, Professor Reid's study is especially valuable for its setting of Hood against the background of his age; but it slights what I consider most characteristic—and most important—in his work after 1835.

Much assistance of other kinds has been forthcoming. Of those who have read my manuscript at various stages, in whole or in part, I wish to thank Professor Carl Woodring of Columbia University for his care and for his patience, both apparently limitless; Professor James L. Clifford, also of Columbia, for his comments on style and on the art of biography; and, for much else, Professors Joseph P. Bauke, James D. Merriman, Helen M. Mustard, and Leonard M. Trawick, all of Columbia, and William H. Irving and Lionel Stevenson of Duke University.

Others, friends and scholars alike, have been helpful in many ways. Robert E. Cameron of Portland, Oregon, has never stinted in his generosity in lending or giving me rare items from his superb collection of Hood. In England I spent a pleasant afternoon with Jocelyn Brooke of Bishopsbourne, Kent, discussing Hood and his circle over a bottle of Riesling. To his great-grandfather, the Reverend Joseph Hewlett, Hood addressed many confidential letters during his last three years. The thirty-eight in Mr. Brooke's possession, the longest unbroken series of Hood letters to any one correspondent, constitute an invaluable aid. Both Mr. Brooke and Mr. Cameron have given me complete freedom in quoting from material in their possession.

Libraries in the United States and Great Britain have unfailingly greeted my requests for information with the sincere wish to be of help. In the Bibliography I acknowledge permission to quote from those libraries which hold unpublished Hood letters and manuscripts, but I wish here to express my gratitude to the many courteous librarians who have facilitated my researches, especially to the reference staff of the Columbia University Library. In addition, the Duke University Council on Research has aided publication of this book through a generous grant. Dorothy Roberts and Mary Taylor L. Garrity have exercised vigilance in the reading of proof. Lastly, thanks are due to Ashbel G. Brice and to the members of the Duke University Press for much help and good sense. Errors, which I hope are few, I accept as inevitable.

The author wishes to thank the Trustees of the British Museum for permission to reproduce Hood's engraving "The Progress of Cant."

J. C.

Durham, N.C.

Contents

Illustrations

Victorian Forerunner

Introduction

If Thomas Hood had died in 1835, he would be classified today as another minor romantic poet, like Darley and Beddoes, illustrative of the transition from the romantic to the Victorian era. He would be remembered for his work on the *London Magazine* and for his association with Charles Lamb. He would also be remembered as the first and closest disciple of Keats, as a poet who essayed with modest success a volume of poems in the sensuous Keatsian style, *The Plea of the Midsummer Fairies*. Most of all, Hood would be remembered as a comic poet and punster of genuine skill, though modern taste, disliking puns, has endorsed Samuel Johnson's "great contempt for that species of wit." By 1835 his personality and his work had not, however, made much impact upon the literary world.

But Thomas Hood lived ten years more. In that decade he wrote many of the poems that established his contemporary and posthumous fame. Poems like "The Song of the Shirt" and "The Bridge of Sighs" did not, as most critics have assumed, spring full-grown from his mind, but embody beliefs and passions that had long lain deep in his spirit. The financial reverses of 1834 and the profound personal disillusionment he experienced during the winter of 1834–1835 forced him to reassess his life and beliefs. Parallel to this reassessment ran a gradually heightening awareness of the distressed condition of English society and of his fellow man.

Hood's life span (1799–1845) embraced three periods of English literary culture. While neoclassic ideals still prevailed at his birth and were to continue in favor with the general public and the leading critical journals for three decades to come, Wordsworth and Coleridge had published in 1798 their *Lyrical Ballads*. In the nineteenth century's second decade, moreover, new poets began

3

to appear on the literary horizon; but Hood never met them. Of the three near-contemporaries to whom he owed his greatest poetic debt, Shelley and Byron had long left England when he came to maturity; the closest he got to Keats, last-born of the second romantic generation, was through frequenting the home of the Reynolds family in Little Britain. Nor did he ever meet a poet born two years after him, Thomas Lovell Beddoes. When in the early 1820's Hood underwent a literary apprenticeship on the *London Magazine,* he experienced the one close association he was to form in his lifetime with literary men of genius. But it was as "the baby of the house" [1]—not as their equal—that he looked up admiringly to men fifteen, twenty years older than he: Lamb, Hazlitt, De Quincey. Significantly, his one close literary friend among near-contemporaries, John Hamilton Reynolds, had exhausted his romantic vein by the time Hood got to know him well and soon abandoned literature for the law. Romanticism, as Hood knew it from his own experience, had already receded into the past. From first effusions to his poems of the 1840's, Hood's romantic poetry was, on the whole, imitative: imitative because he needed to gain a living by other kinds of writing and, more important, because he was unconcerned with formulating his own artistic creed. Only the early Victorians did he get to know as equals. When he died in 1845, a new generation of writers—in fiction, Thackeray and Dickens, in poetry, Browning and Tennyson —had begun to gain recognition. Thomas Hood, hovering between two worlds, two different conceptions of literature, felt at home in neither.

"The early Victorian poet," writes Jerome Hamilton Buckley, "sometimes no more certain than his contemporaries, was expected to furnish instruction as well as amusement." [2] Hood would have agreed. The "highest office" of literary men was, he wrote in 1837, "to make the world wiser and better; their lowest, to entertain and amuse it without making it worse." [3] Hood attempted to perform the two offices: through his poems of moral humor the mature poet attempted both to reform the world and to entertain it. The enormous appeal of his poetry throughout the nineteenth century lay in this humor tinged with a morality that reflected contemporary standards. The Victorian middle and lower middle classes, where he found the great mass of his readers, relished the domestic sentiment and the puns that pointed a moral. Hood's Victorian popularity also suggests a principal reason for his relative neglect today: the twentieth century prefers its humor without a moral attached.

But moral humor is only one of many factors in a consideration of Hood as a "Victorian forerunner," indeed as the first Victorian poet. Another, as important, is his groping for an understanding of the problems that beset a rapidly changing society. He took up— indirectly at least—most of the social and political questions that aroused man's interest at that time. More easily comprehensible to the Victorians than to us, Hood's poems dealing with contemporary issues are necessarily topical in nature; and this topicality— often difficult to fathom as the issues fade into obscurity—suggests a second reason for his present neglect. Issues the early Victorians faced with such direct courage seem, in today's hindsight, far more complex than those living in the dawn of a new era could have suspected. That Hood did propose specific remedies for immediate problems separates him from the second generation of romantics, whose writings about society, recent feats of scholarship to the contrary, often appear utopian or devoid of common sense.

Each of the major romantic poets felt at some stage in his career the intoxication of revolutionary principles and of unorthodox religion. But of the poets of the "interregnum" (the twenty years between the death of Byron and the emergence of Tennyson)— Darley, Wells, Clare, Procter, Beddoes, Reynolds—none, except Wells and Beddoes, gives evidence of either radical ideas or unorthodox religious beliefs. Their poetic reality lay elsewhere. Hood belonged to this group of poets, most of whom were born a few years on either side of 1800. He became the only one of them who evinced a genuine response to the changing life of a changing England.

Hood also reveals himself as herald of things to come in the development of his vein of romantic poetry. In the early 1820's he took as models first Byron, afterwards Shelley, before finally submerging himself in Keats. This imitative verse, patterned in the manner of the younger romantics (though with echoes of most English poets since the Elizabethans), marks him as predecessor to Tennyson and Browning, whose poetry passed through similar if not exactly parallel stages of influence. With him submersion in the romantics did not preclude—as it also did not with Tennyson and Browning—the later development of a distinct personal idiom. Yet though the lilt of Hood's lyrics was, as Harold Nicolson has noted,[4] to echo in the poetry of Tennyson, parallels extend beyond lyrical development. Both poets shared, although from differing standpoints, a deep concern with the life of their society. In their political views both evinced a distrust of party; both refused, in their desire to further a national policy, to support either the Tories or the Liberals.

If Browning's political stance, unlike Tennyson's, bears little resemblance to that of Hood, his debt to Hood's poetry is greater —and far different. "Thomas Hood's apprenticeship to the music hall," observes J. M. Cohen,

> his writing of sketches and songs to be presented by the popular comedian Charles Matthews [*sic*], vastly extended the vocabulary, the metres and the allusiveness of nineteenth-century poetry. This new capital, of which Hood himself lived to make very little use, was taken over by Browning for such a poem as the "Pied Piper," and finally developed into a medium capable of expresssing far greater psychological accuracy, of referring to far more things in a far less "poetical" way than any other Victorian poet could achieve.[5]

Poets of previous centuries had of course written "unpoetical" poetry—Samuel Butler, for intance, using a style that constantly shifted back and forth between the burlesque and the grotesque, had travestied the customs of his contemporaries in *Hudibras*. A half-century after Butler, John Gay in *The Beggar's Opera* was the last English poet before Hood to explore the possibilities of writing verse based on the rhythms of popular songs. Hood revived this tradition. While the intrinsic merit of his poems influenced by the popular stage and the music hall may not be high, one quality in them—easily overlooked—remains of utmost importance: newness.

Hood was scrupulous to keep every word, every image within the narrowing bounds of the feminine sensibility of the age—in this way also a "Victorian forerunner." Indelicacy was his abhorrence. "I have at least been a decent writer," he wrote in his literary manifesto of 1837; "I feel some honest pride in remembering that the reproach of impurity has never been cast upon me by my judges." [6] Hardly a typical "romantic" trait, this desire to keep his poetry fit reading for the whole family reflects the dominant Evangelical influence upon the Victorian *Weltansicht*. Moreover, one of Hood's main contributions to English verse—the manipulation of the pun within a dazzling range of meters—lies, in the main, outside the province of the romantic poets.

During his lifetime Hood received few sound criticisms. In the 1820's members of the *London* circle—"Barry Cornwall," Allan Cunningham, Lamb, Hartley Coleridge—all misjudged his poetic gift. Almost without exception, they urged him not to forsake his romantic, "serious" muse, where they considered his talent lay, to frolic amidst the pastures of comic verse. Subsequent writers—e.g., S. C. Hall in *The Book of Gems*—have enshrined for later generations the image of Hood as a mere pauper who pined to compose "serious" poetry for the ages, but whom Stern Necessity forced to write volumes of comic verse to keep the bill collector from the door. When told that Hall thought him a romantic poet gone awry, Hood was amused and attributed the characterization to Hall's not knowing him well: "my methodist face took him in." [7] Even Thackeray, throwing a retrospective glance over his own career in the *Roundabout Papers*, deplored Hood's forced labor. But insofar as we know his opinions about his métier, Hood never did.

This consideration of Hood as a dedicated poet led astray by necessity and by his "misguided" inclination to comic writing has now few adherents—and, I believe, rightly. After all, as Cornelius

M. Cuyler has pointed out, of the thirty years during which Hood wrote verse, 1815–1845, he devoted not more than two or three of them—and then not exclusively—to "romantic" poetry.[8] Once he had tired of or exhausted his Keatsian vein, he felt but slight inclination in later years to revive it. Only his *Plea of the Midsummer Fairies* falls within the Romantic Achievement; but the poems there, with few exceptions, rarely become more than pale copies of themes and techniques no longer vital.

If Hood is to retain our attention today, he will not do so as a "late" or "delayed" romantic; nor even, in W. M. Rossetti's attempt to define an artificial generation, as "the finest English poet between the generation of Shelley and the generation of Tennyson";[9] but rather he will survive as the first Victorian poet—a poet who anticipated many trends in modern poetry. Not in his romantic echoing of an outdated poetic fashion, but rather in his acceptance of a society becoming industrialized, in his comic grotesquerie combined with technical virtuosity, and in his moral humor—therein lie the deeper currents in the career of Thomas Hood.

> How sublime a thing it is
> To suffer and be strong.

These two lines from Longfellow, thought Hood's children, summed up the life of their father. Like Pope, he could well term his life "this long disease," but he managed somehow to build out of it a happy marriage, to raise two adoring children, and to obtain in his chosen field, literature, both popularity and critical esteem. In nearly forty-six years of adversity he achieved, if never health, at least happiness of an enviable kind. Financial security, unfortunately, eluded him always. He valued literature, as he did his good wife, more as an object to be prized and respected than as a mistress whose extravagant claims he need indulge. Content with modest success, he did not presume to seek the stars. A literary professional in the fullest sense, he always insisted on the worth and dignity of those who gained their living by the pen. And the profession of letters brought, Thomas Hood well knew, both its blessings and its heartbreaks.

Hood was born on May 23, 1799, in the Poultry, a district in the heart of London. Except for five years of enforced exile on the Continent, the mature man always evinced a decided preference for life in or near the capital. He was the second son and third child of Thomas Hood, a leading bookseller and partner in the firm of Vernor and Hood, and of Elizabeth Hood, née Sands. Like many a Scot, the elder Hood had taken the high road down from Scotland in his youth to try his fortune in London. He met with admirable success. Young Thomas had a brother older by several years, James, reputedly gifted beyond the rest of the family, but who, the *Memorials* records, "died at an early age, a victim to consumption, which ultimately carried off his mother and two sisters." [10] Two other sisters survived to maturity. In the year of James's death, 1811, Thomas's father died "of a malignant fever, originating from the effects of the night air in travelling...." [11] After his death the family fell into relative poverty; two years later, when about fourteen, Thomas, to help out his mother and sisters, left off his schooling and began work as a clerk in a counting house.

He had derived only mixed benefits from his school experiences. Despite the witty, caustic remarks in his "Literary Reminiscences" about its being time wasted, he developed in school a taste for literature and he won a Latin prize. He also mastered French well enough, he affirmed, to edit a translation of *Paul et Virginie*, but no one has traced it, nor the two novels claimed by him for his father. Throughout his youth he devoured all the books he got his hands on. Though in later life he read a good deal less, his poetry gives evidence of wide reading, especially in seventeenth- and eighteenth-century literature, and of an apt memory that recalled when wanted an appropriate quotation.

Instead of concentrating on the figures before him, Thomas found his thoughts in the counting house unaccountably straying to his favorite authors. Worse, bent over a table all day, he damaged his health. Happily, uncles on his mother's side took an interest in him. First under the patronage of James, later of Robert Sands, he served an apprenticeship as engraver; afterwards he worked for one of the well-known Le Keux brothers. Since his health still did not improve, he bade fair, in the language of the day, to "submit to a decline."

Doctors recommended fresh air and exercise, so off he went in 1815 to Scotland, where at Dundee and neighboring villages lived aunts and uncles on his father's side. There, for two years young Hood reveled in new-found freedom. Installed first in a boarding house, later in his Dundee aunt's home, he soon made the acquaintance of several young men whose interests complemented his own. Early endowed with an expanding wonder at life, Thomas continued to draw and to read voraciously, began to write poetry, even sent several prose contributions to local newspapers, none of which we can with certainty identify. Nor did the carefree invalid forget the ostensible purpose of his Scottish sojourn: to get well. He swam, took rambles through the countryside, and became a devotee of the rod and tackle, a pastime he treasured throughout life. Moderate health recovered, he returned in the fall of 1817 to London.[12]

During the three to four years following, Hood continued, first as apprentice, then on his own, his work as engraver. His commissions being such that he could do them at home, he began work on the plate in hand at about nine, labored through the morning, lunched, and with a break for tea continued to work through the afternoon. Evenings he relaxed with his mother and sisters in their suburban Islington home. The later hours Hood read or sketched. He always loved to draw and the hundreds of comic woodcuts scattered through his many volumes testify to a genuine talent in art. Often his mind did not cease its restless activity until the morning's early hours. Though strengthened by his stay in Scotland, at no period in his life did Hood achieve good health. Even his playing the flute eventually had to be given up because the effort placed too great a strain on his lungs.

Toward 1820 he joined a Literary Society, composed mainly of prim young ladies who encouraged him to read his original verse. He had already begun to write poetry in Dundee: his earliest long poem, "The Dundee Guide," a satire in couplets, bared the grave limitations of Dundee and its inhabitants, much in the manner that its model, Christopher Anstey's *New Bath Guide,* had ridiculed those of Bath. Of this poem only a few passages, printed in the *Memorials* from letters, survive; they show him already a highly perceptive critic of society, indignant at the "strict bigoted tenets" of Scottish Calvinism. In his next effort, "The Bandit," Hood molded his irresolute "Chieftain" on various romantic heroes, finally showing preference for the robust, hugely popular Conrad of Lord Byron. Before the Literary Society he read several new poems, including one more within his range and temperament, the already Keatsian "Departure of Summer."

Although the society's gatherings had quickened his interest in literature, it was not until John Taylor, who remembered with gratitude the interest the elder Hood had taken in him as a boy, offered him a position on the *London Magazine* that Hood conceived a change in occupation possible. He accepted the offer with evident joy, and, as a "sort of sub-editor," came to know the magazine's famed contributors: John Clare, Reynolds, "Barry Cornwall," De Quincey, Lamb, Hazlitt, Allan Cunningham. At first his tasks consisted of hardly more than the proofreading of articles, but Taylor and James Hessey, his partner, early recognized his talent and entrusted to him the answers-to-correspondents column, "The Lion's Head." From punning retorts to readers Hood soon passed to poetry. Contributing to the magazine over a two-year span (July, 1821, to June, 1823), he came during this time to first and final maturity as a "serious" poet in the style of Keats. In the pages of the *London* he first published the poems that appeared, with revisions, in 1827 under the title of *The Plea of the Midsummer Fairies.* On *The Plea,* his only collection of "serious" poems, rests Hood's claim to recognition as a romantic poet.

Critical journals accorded the volume a mixed reception. Though most of Hood's *London* friends responded to it warmly, the general public did not buy. Perhaps fortunately so. Had financial success crowned this venture into Keats's magic casements, Hood might never have developed his genuine talent for poetry of other kinds, but squandered it on more of the same—for him surely an aesthetic cul-de-sac. As George Gilfillan noted in 1850, one weakness in "Hood's more elaborate poetical pieces" stands out as paramount: "We find in [them] . . . no effective story, none that can bear the weight of his subtle and beautiful imagery." In the title poem especially, "Hood has not been able to infuse human interest into his fairy or mythological creations." [13]

Despite oppressive Keatsian echoes, apparent even in the titles, several shorter poems—the three "Autumn" lyrics, "Ruth," the "Ode to Melancholy"—succeed as imitations. If the memory of Keats's poem has dimmed, a first reading of Hood's "Ode: Autumn" may impress; if we keep Keats's ode in mind, however, Hood's seems little more than a thematic variation, too imbued with the poetic vocabulary of his older contemporary to rise to genuine originality. Keats constructs his ode "To Autumn" upon a series of images of "mellow fruitfulness"; in all three of Hood's poems it is the sadness and decay of this season that prevails. "Ruth" and the "Ode to Melancholy," poems written even later in the romantic afternoon, reveal only wistful discontent, not the deep understanding of life that Keats expressed when he wrote, ". . . in the very temple of delight, / Veil'd melancholy has her sovran shrine. . . ." Brooding over each image of decay with morbid sweetness of tone, Hood never rises further than the recognition that "There's not a string attun'd to mirth, / But has a chord in Melancholy." Only one poem, more genuinely Hood's, resists the Keatsian overtones: the sonnet "Silence"—a magical evocation of the desolation of solitude. William Sharp affirmed that, among sonnets, it takes a "place in the very front rank." [14]

Hood's Keatsian poems founder, I believe, largely because the poet did not regard this kind of poetry with instinctive sympathy. In the 1820's he did not have a temperament that took seriously either life or art; certainly he never found, as had his master Keats, deep meaning in the world of myth. His letters do not illuminate, as Keats's do, the nature and kinds of poetry. Nor does Hood speak of the poet's role as creator; "unlike Keats," writes Elizabeth Jennings, "he never felt the need to work out a personal aesthetic for the writing of verse." [15] Gilfillan saw the failure in plot construction and in creating living beings. But Hood's discomfort in the imitative Keatsian style shows up in other weaknesses: uncertain and never fully mastered technique; digressions that wander off and fail to return, as in Byron, for augmented effect; flaccid vocabulary and "Cockneyisms"; above all, too great a reliance on the phraseology of the Elizabethans refined as it is through the sensuous ears of their romantic disciple, John Keats. In Hood criticism today the poems of *The Plea of the Midsummer Fairies* do not rank high. J. C. Reid dismisses them as "faint carbons." And Laurence Brander is equally positive: "It is impossible to disagree with the judgement of the time that the 1827 volume of serious verse was very minor. Hood was going to write genuine poetry later in his life, but everything here is Romantic imitation." [16]

By 1824 Hood had abandoned hope for a career as romantic poet. Neither impulse nor dedication had ever been strong. Comic verse he learned to write facilely, recognized that it earned him a living, and never voiced regrets. During the rest of his life Hood produced few romantic poems of importance. He had not yet struck his true poetic vein.

More successful than *The Plea* from a commercial point of view was Hood's first volume of comic verse, co-authored with John Hamilton Reynolds: the *Odes and Addresses to Great People* (1825). Styled after James and Horace Smith's *Rejected Addresses*, the volume enjoyed a decent popularity and by the next year had run through three editions. Already Hood's concern for the betterment of English society stamps several of the poems. In "A *Friendly* Address to Mrs. Fry *in* Newgate" he admonishes the well-known Quaker prison reformer for not trying to inculcate morality in the poor *before* they are sent to prison, to educate them *before,* as he so happily puts it, "Sin seats / Her wicked self in the Professor's chair":

> O save the vulgar soul before it's spoil'd!
>   Set up your mounted sign *without* the gate—
> And there inform the mind before 'tis soil'd!
>
> . . . .
>
> Come out of Newgate, Mrs. Fry! Repair
>   Abroad, and find your pupils in the streets.
> O, come abroad into the wholesome air,
>   And take your moral place, before Sin seats
> Her wicked self in the Professor's chair.[17]

Throughout his career Hood manifested distinct preference for preventive reforms and remedies. Though puns explode in bewildering succession in "A *Friendly* Address," the poet, underneath the brilliant wordplay, did moralize his song. Much as he came to dislike rabid manifestations of Evangelical faith, he knew the great effect sermons had on many; behind the façade of his comic verse he learned early to conceal a "sermon" or "moral."

In a second poem, "An Address to the Steam Washing Company," Hood demonstrates the hardship that the new steam machines will bring to washerwomen. Not a literary Luddite, he makes his plea on humanitarian grounds: "Ah, look at the laundress, before you begrudge / Her hard daily bread to that laudable drudge. . . ." After drawing a pathetic portrait of the dispossessed washerwoman, "all haggard and pinch'd," Hood has her draw up a "Letter of Remonstrance . . . to the Noblemen and Gentlemen forming the Washing Committee." Scribbled down "in some moment of despair, / When linen got scarce, and her washing grew rare," her "Remonstrance" at automation, "Too angry for grammar, too lofty for prose," begins:

> It's a shame, so it is—men can't Let alone
> Jobs as is Woman's right to do—and go about there Own—
> Theirs Reforms enuff Alreddy without your new schools
> For washing to sit Up,—and push the Old Tubs from their
>   stools!

But your just like the Raddicals,—for upsetting of the Sudds
When the world wagg'd well enuff—and Wommen wash'd
  your old dirty duds.[18]

Again, the humorous style clothes a serious core. In the 1820's
few of Hood's poems contain a "moral"; after 1835, many do.

The year 1825 also marks Hood's marriage to Jane Reynolds,
eldest of the Reynolds sisters. He had been engaged to her since
the fall of 1822. Seven and a half years older than her husband,
Jane Hood proved an ideal wife: her maturity lent her the patience
to deal with his whimsical temperament and her own background of ill health gave her the sympathy necessary to nurse him
through his frequent illnesses. Mutual dependence and love
formed the cornerstone of twenty years of married happiness.
Upon the rare occasions of separation Hood wrote her letters of
remarkable tenderness. Of firm yet pliable character, Jane Hood
made a good wife to her husband, a good mother to her children.
Hood's happy domestic life, first at his mother's home, later as
husband and father, contrasts sharply with the failure of the
romantic poets—Coleridge, Keats, Shelley, Byron—ever to still
their longing for an idealized relationship and find happiness in
married love. From this background of domestic harmony and
his deep sense of the domestic virtues, Hood was to become a
favorite "family author" of Victorian England.

A girl was born to the Hoods in 1827, but soon after birth she
died. Her death moved Charles Lamb to write his best poem, "On
an Infant Dying as Soon as Born." The saddened father wrapped
a wisp of golden hair in the following lines:

> Little eyes that scarce did see,
>   Little lips that never smiled;
>   Alas! my little dear dead child,
> Death is thy father, and not me,
>   I but embraced thee, soon as he! [19]

Another child was born in 1830, and she lived. Christened Frances
Freeling in honor of Hood's friend, the Postmaster-General, she
soon became known to all as "Fanny."

In formal society Hood always remained reserved, naturally shy; but in his family and among close friends he relaxed and became a delightful host. Partial deafness, from which he suffered the whole of his adult life, would alone explain his quietness at social gatherings. Mary Balmanno describes him at one such gathering in 1827 at the home of Charles and Mary Lamb:

> In outward appearance Hood conveyed the idea of a clergyman. His figure slight, and invariably dressed in black; his face pallid; the complexion delicate, and features regular; his countenance bespeaking sympathy by its sweet expression of melancholy and suffering.

And Jane:

> Mrs. Hood was a most amiable woman—of excellent manners, and full of sincerity and goodness. She perfectly adored her husband, tending him like a child, whilst he with unbounded affection seemed to delight to yield up himself to her guidance. Nevertheless, true to his humourous nature, he loved to tease her with jokes and whimsical accusations and assertions which were only responded to by, "Hood, Hood, how can you run on so?" [20]

Punning was inveterate to Hood's nature. Both in speaking and in writing he punned continually and, it would seem, compulsively. His punning indicates that his mind possessed a fundamental, unresolved dichotomy: he perceived the comic in the tragic and the tragic in the comic. But this discovery of incongruity caused in him distinct unease. Since equivocation came easily to his nature, Hood was, through puns, provided with a defense mechanism by which he could shy away from the full implications of his vision. In his social poems his marked reluctance to affirm in a straightforward manner his beliefs on controversial subjects reveals a basic insecurity; through punning, the outlet his gifts permitted him, he reconciled his embarrassment before unease. Rarely did he stare boldly in the face of a problem, social, political, or other —hence the puns and anticlimactic endings of so many works.

He felt he could work best behind his comic mask. Tomfoolery by itself would not do; but neither would leaving a wholly serious implication. Consequently, a compromise—presenting a "moral" in comic verse—seemed, for the greater part of his career at least, the most adequate solution.

In 1825 Hood also published his "Hogarthian engraving," "The progress before the eyes of the scorner." [21] A well-composed tab-this title," wrote Lamb, "in which he marshalleth all the projected improvements of the age, and maketh them take their fantastic progress before the eyes of the scorner." [21] A well-composed tableau, "The Progress of Cant" chides those who hold reactionary attitudes on matters of national significance: Ireland, the theater, removal of Catholic disabilities, the new London university. But for man's hypocrisy and his inhumanity to his fellow man Hood reserves a harsher satire, a satire that justifies Lamb's calling him "that half-Hogarth." An overplump clergyman carries a sign, "No fat livings"; the Devil waves a banner, "Freedom for the Blacks"; one lad batters down another holding a flag, "Peace to the World"; a buxom matron struts along in a dress "Made by the Females in Newgate"; a grim-looking beadle, "Vagrant Act" embroidered on his belt sash, shoulders a hypocrite proclaiming "Goodwill to Man." Hood focused on no single abuse in "The Progress of Cant," nor could he advocate remedies; but the engraving does show his concern early in life with the world elsewhere. It would seem that over the next two decades cant, especially religious cant, progressed by leaps and bounds. Hood's awareness of it, at least, did so progress.

Not only as engraver, but as popular playwright Hood began to attract attention. Three months in 1826 of writing a weekly column for a new periodical, the *Atlas*, aroused his interest in the stage. During the late 1820's he wrote in all perhaps half a dozen plays of all kinds—farce, pantomime, musical comedy, even a "comic burletta"—for the comedians Charles Mathews and Frederick Henry Yates. Of those extant none are read or are readable today.[22] Indeed, the literary merit of the surviving fragments and songs leaves no reason to bemoan Hood's turning away from the drama after several years of varying success. But his writing for the stage did lead him to experiment with vocabulary and meter: onto the traditional meters of English poetry he learned to graft the rhythms of popular songs. Again, he had widened his literary experience.

Whims and Oddities, Hood's first volume of comic verse of a kind that was to become synonymous with his name, appeared in 1826. It enjoyed immediate popularity and the public soon called for new editions. To meet the demand Hood published in 1827 *Whims and Oddities*, "Second Series." These two volumes established him as the leading comic poet of his day and represent the high point of his career as a humorist. In his comic ballads Hood used the traditional ballad stanza to parody serious themes. All of them dramatize love and death: the lover returning to find his sweetheart untrue and killing himself—"Faithless Sally Brown" and "Faithless Nelly Gray"; the ghost of the beloved paying a midnight visit to her lover—"Mary's Ghost"; the demon lover enticing a human victim to destruction—"The Mermaid of Margate"; the disillusioned husband murdering his new bride—"Tim Turpin." Besides the comic ballads, Hood's temperamental fondness for writing about disease and death in grotesque forms shows up in several verse narratives, notably "Jack Hall" and "The Last Man." The latter holds its own with treatments of the same subject by Byron, Campbell, Beddoes, and Mrs. Shelley. The charnel house, gravediggers and body-snatchers, human decay and decay in nature, demons and ghosts: all fascinated Hood. Early developed, this *Galgenhumor*—the depicting of the Horrible as the Natural—stayed with him throughout his career.

Hood was above all an imitative writer. Confronted by the Romantic Achievement, he opted for one of two alternatives, occasionally, even in the same poem, for both: he consciously imitated another poet's style, or he consciously parodied a romantic theme. Though Keats dominates most of *The Plea*, other poems in that volume carry marked echoes of Wordsworth ("I remember, I remember") and of Shelley ("The Two Peacocks of Bedfont"). *Odes and Addresses* makes no attempt to disguise its borrowings from the Smiths' *Rejected Addresses.* "The Sea-Spell" and "The Demon-Ship" of *Whims and Oddities,* as well as "The Dream of Eugene Aram" of a few years later, reveal the pervasive, if more subtle, influence of Coleridge's "The Rime of the Ancient Mariner." The novellas in *National Tales,* a volume published in 1827, recall Boccaccio. Indebtedness extends even more to eighteenth-century models: Swift, Sterne, Smollett, Shenstone, and Dr. Johnson. While a Hood imitation is often in its own right a successful poem, we remain conscious that another writer's work stands behind his. Experimenting in many styles, Hood had not yet found his own. Only in the mid-1830's did he begin to acquire the experience of life that enabled him to transcend the superficialities of imitation.

Assuming in 1828 the editorship of an annual, *The Gem,* Hood succeeded in attracting distinguished contributors: Lamb, Bernard Barton, Hartley Coleridge, even the star attraction of the Annual trade, Sir Walter Scott. In its pages he inserted several poems of his own, including his Coleridgean tale of a man's sin and remorse, "The Dream of Eugene Aram." The next year saw the publication of *The Epping Hunt,* a long, punning poem that ran into a second edition by 1830. In this year he also published *Comic Melodies,* songs from his plays set to music by Jonathan Blewitt.

Success with *The Gem* encouraged Hood to edit his own annual. When at the end of 1829 his readers saw the first *Comic Annual,* they learned in the preface that they might consider it a "Third Series of 'Whims & Oddities.'" For ten consecutive years (1830–1839) the poet was to turn out an annual volume of fun. Surveying the series as a whole, the critic in the *London and Westminster Review* for April, 1838, found that "the contents . . . make them, independent of their own intrinsic worth, . . . valuable as a Pantagruelian commentary upon the follies, fancies, and manners of the world we live in." Although others contributed articles and poems to the first *Comic Annual,* in succeeding volumes Hood did proportionately more of the writing, as he also did proportionately more of the comic woodcuts. During the

1830's, aside from occasional reviewing and poems contributed to periodicals, the greater part of his income depended upon the financial success of his yearly volume. A survey of the ten *Comics*, however, leads irresistibly to the conclusion that they show a decided fall-off in creativity within his comic vein. While many poems amuse, few have the imaginative power of the best in the two *Whims*.

In mid-1833, after five years of interrupted labor and frequent delays, Hood completed his first novel. Published in three volumes at the end of 1834, *Tylney Hall* is somewhat better than the complete oblivion into which it has fallen would suggest. In its day it obtained, with the exception of the vituperative *Fraser's*, generally favorable critiques and mild popularity. Lamb's judgment is perceptive: "a medley, without confusion, of farce, melodrama, pantomime, comedy, tragedy, punchery, what not?" [23] "In attempting fiction," comments Alfred Ainger, "Hood was in truth using his left hand. His types of character, at least in middle-class life, are for the most part conventional, and fail to convince." [24] Though minor characters entertain and some scenes sparkle with gentle wit, Hood had little skill in constructing an extended narrative. The novel does not cohere.

The year of crisis 1835—the point of commencement of this study—began inauspiciously. It marks the turning point in the career of Thomas Hood, for in the beginning of this year he formed the decisions that guided him during the ten remaining years of his life. The crisis was both financial and personal. Though his finances collapsed completely only in late 1834, at no time in his life can they be considered promising. Hood's annual income, varying with the uncertain success of his comic volumes, never became stabilized. As early as 1829 creditors pressed him to discharge his debts. [25] While his income fluctuated widely over the years that followed, he never did get out of debt. In 1834, he severed dealings with his publisher of several years, Charles Tilt.

Though Tilt did agree to publish the 1834 *Comic*, the apparent cause of the break—besides the chronic money disputes that destroyed Hood's relationships with all his publishers—lay in Tilt's refusal to accept for publication the nearly finished *Tylney Hall*.[26] Preferring to limit his dealings to one house, the poet let A. H. Baily publish both *Tylney Hall* and the 1835 *Comic Annual*. His break with Tilt constitutes, however, but the prelude to a series of events whose causes and sequence still remain, in part, conjectural.

Two immediate causes for Hood's financial collapse stand out: first, either the failure in late 1833 or in 1834 of the engraving firm of Robert Branston and John Wright, or the dissolution in early 1835 of the partnership between Wright and Branston's successor in the firm, W. A. Folkard. A good friend of Wright's, Hood had a share in one of these businesses. He lost heavily. Second, several witnesses concur that the poet lived at Lake House, Wanstead, his home since 1832, in a style well beyond his income.

Proceeding concurrently with the crisis in Hood's finances was a series of personal calamities that included the rupture of ties with his wife's family, the Reynoldses. On January 19, 1835, Jane Hood gave birth at Lake House to a son, Tom; Charles Wentworth Dilke stood godfather. Jane had been ill after each of her other births, and this time she came close to death. For ten days— Hood described them as "The Most Terrible Ten Days of my Life"—he despaired of her life. Night after night he watched by the bedside holding her hand; twice from extreme exhaustion he pitched headlong from his chair. Without the devoted care given Jane by Dr. William Elliot, Hood believed she would not have survived her ordeal. Two of Jane's sisters, Charlotte and Marianne, along with Marianne's husband, H. G. Green, their two sons, and Reynolds *père et mère* were staying at Lake House. Fearing that Jane would soon die, they severely reproached Hood for his improvident manner of life; moreover, they blamed him for Jane's miserable state. In an outburst of anger the poet ordered them to leave his home; only Mrs. Reynolds, who, "if sometimes wrong headed ... is always right-hearted," remained.

The worry, tension, and day-to-day pressures of his increasingly untenable position severely weakened Hood's health, always as sensitive to mental as to physical strain. Creditors pressed him; local merchants refused him necessities of life; furthermore, humiliation before impending destitution increased his frustration. He was mentally exhausted from having completed both *Tylney Hall* and the 1835 *Comic Annual*. In addition, two deaths had recently saddened him: on December 27, 1834, his much-loved friend Charles Lamb had died; Hood was one of the small band of mourners at the funeral ceremony. He sympathized, too, with John Hamilton Reynolds—the one member of the family besides Mrs. Reynolds with whom he remained on good terms during the crisis—who had just lost his only daughter, aged ten. To make Hood's misery complete his own daughter Fanny came down with a severe case of the measles. Laboring under the triple burden of his own weak health, his wife's grave illness, and his uncertain future, Hood truly went through the most soul-searching moments of his life. At no other time did his fortunes ebb lower. Later he was to be in weaker health, in even more embarrassing financial straits, but never did despair assume such awesome proportions as it did in the early months of 1835. The six weeks after Tom's birth until Hood's departure for Germany on March 4 mark the dark night of his soul.

Despair prompted him early in February to write a long letter to Dilke, his strength and prop during the crisis. After bemoaning his disillusionment at the conduct of the Reynolds family, he voices his personal agony. Extremely painful to read, this letter is a key document for an understanding of Hood's later career. Nowhere else does he bare with such frankness his innermost feelings. Hood writes as a man deeply, suddenly upset, yet as a man who could still smile amidst infinite pain. "My dear Dilke," he begins,

Here I sit, solus, in that large drawing-room, with a sick wife upstairs,—a sick child in the next room to this … and a fly-load of company has just departed. … What was done to oppress me in my sore time of trouble I cannot forgive or forget. … I believe I shall be an altered man—more of a philosopher

—scorning the hollow & enjoying the real in joy or grief. . . .
My views in life are changed—& would have been whether
Jane lived or died, as you know. . . . In some ways my eyes
are opened & my heart is shut. I disdain hypocrisy. Toward
Jane I must feel more devoutly loving than on that dear day
that made me her husband. . . . My eyes have been widely
opened—to the present, the past, & the future. . . . Think me
not mad, my dear Dilke, but I am writing of things words
cannot reach. Horrors, horrible, most horrible, must have
been her portion. . . . And now you know more of T. Hood
than you could gather from a Comic Annual, or the whole
series, or the Whims, or anything I have ever written, saving
this letter. . . .²⁷

Now that he saw life through different eyes, a bitter resignation,
long in coming, settled over him. As he nursed his wife back to an
unhoped-for recovery, Hood recognized the extent to which his
happiness depended on her. At the same time that he solidified
one friendship he made another: Charles Wentworth Dilke and
Dr. William Elliot would serve him well in years to come.

Two postscripts as long as the original letter tell of his changed
attitude toward life; in the second the tone approaches hysteria.

I mean what I write. The *realities* of life have come so home
to me that I will not put up with its humbugs. This is hence-
forth the motto of yours ever. T. H. . . . I am not mad most
noble Dilke, but speak the words of truth & soberness—It is
no splenetic misanthropic mood against all the world. . . .
Have no care for me. My mind which has stood firm throughout will not fail me *now*. But there are times in a man's life
when his thoughts become intensified, so as to review a past
life & project a future in a few short hours. Such has been my
case. Jane's illness will be a marked aera to me,—& will have
much influence on what is to come. The exigency of the time
has called forth a decision I knew not belonged to me, & I
mean to cherish it. It has been a great comfort to me to think
& know that I have true friends who will feel with and for me,

—who will appreciate my motives & give me credit for right feeling, & consequent right conduct, in the most critical & trying crisis of my life.[28]

As the upshot of the crisis, Hood decided to leave England of his own volition. In debt—the amount he owed his creditors was between £200 and £300—and without immediate hopes of repayment, he thought to economize by living on the Continent. He may even have feared imprisonment for debt. As the sum was

A PAUPER IN HIGH RELIEF.

not great and as he had before earned in one year an amount equal to his debts, he preferred to work his way out of his difficulties. With the example of Sir Walter Scott before him, he refused to avail himself of the bankruptcy courts.

Certainly the English scene did not hold pleasant prospects for him: health and future uncertain; his wife seriously ill; perpetual harassment by creditors and tradesmen; quarrels with in-laws. Life abroad, under almost any circumstances, might well seem more promising. Although the decision to settle in Germany appears, in the light of subsequent events, unfortunate, it also appears unavoidable. He had to leave England. His honor, and Hood was proud, required it. So "with these views, leaving every shilling behind him derived from the sale of his effects, the means he carried with him being an advance upon his future labours, he voluntarily expatriated himself, and bade his native land good night." [29]

Chapter 1

Life Along the Rhine

Germany in the year 1835 seemed in many respects an ideal place for Hood to settle and work. Few persons ever set out for a foreign land with higher hopes. Jane, still too ill to travel six weeks after the birth of Tom, was to stay behind in England until he found suitable lodgings. On the fourth of March he left England for Rotterdam aboard the steamer *Lord Melville*. A great storm arose that night; at its height, as Hood subsequently learned, eleven vessels, among them a Dutch East Indiaman, foundered off the Holland coast. For Hood this storm constituted a lasting experience: he became for the first time terribly afraid of the sea. In letters and in published writings of succeeding months and years he retold the terror of that memorable night. Whereas the narrative in *Up the Rhine*, his epistolary novel based on his experiences in Germany, will satisfy the seeker after vivid though hardly exaggerated detail, the account he wrote home to a startled Jane gains in being at once more matter-of-fact and more immediate.

I had a dreadful passage to Rotterdam: Wednesday night was an awful storm, and Thursday morning was worse. I was *sea-sick* and *frightened* at sea for the first time: so you will suppose it was no trifle: in fact, it was unusually severe. I went up at midnight and found *four* men at the helm, hint enough for me, so I went down again, and in the morning a terrific sea tore the whole four from the helm, threw the captain as far as the funnel (twenty paces), and the three after him. Had it not come *direct aft*, it would have swept them into the sea, boat, skylights, and everything in short, and have left us a complete wreck.[1]

Hood arrived in Rotterdam Thursday night, March 5, dined with an English couple whose acquaintance he had made on board ship, and the following day proceeded up the Rhine to Nijmegen. Leaving at five the next morning, he passed an uncomfortable Saturday night aboard the Rhine steamer making its way slowly upstream, and on Sunday he arrived in Cologne. Although he had become quite ill during the difficult Channel crossing, his mind remained active and alert to the impressions of travel, and he took copious notes for later use, storing up incidents that would find their way into a work then not conceived, *Up the Rhine*. Obliged to stay over in Cologne until Tuesday morning—the steamer had broken a paddle—he had ample time to admire the magnificent choir of the unfinished cathedral, symbol to German romantics of the gothic grandeur of medieval Germany. Tuesday night brought him to Coblenz; Wednesday to Mayence, where he passed the next day. After returning to Coblenz, Hood wrote his wife that if she felt well enough for the voyage with the children, she could join him. Situated at the confluence of the Rhine and Moselle, Coblenz had been strongly recommended to him by his good friend Dilke. He considered it, after a look through the nearby villages, by far the most suitable place to stay. Still very weak and tired from having to get up almost every day at five to catch the steamer, Hood kept in fine spirits; his letters, bubbling with future plans, exude in every line optimism and confidence.[2]

The Rhine landscapes were magnificent, prices low, the cares of England far away. At first Hood liked living among a foreign people: he was exhilarated by strange customs and the quaint towns, awed by the grandeur of the scenery. Like most foreigners who arrive in an unknown land with few narrow preconceptions, he thoroughly enjoyed himself during the first months of immersion in the new and unfamiliar. Relief from care is the most plausible explanation for the joy he felt in his first weeks in Holland and in the Rhine provinces—then part of Prussia. Intensely English Hood certainly was, yet his British insularity did not hamper him from entering, as far as his limited command of the

German language and the restricted opportunities for social inter-
course in Coblenz permitted, into the life of the country. Although he remained a foreigner in an alien society, his impressions
of people and customs were—during the early part of his stay—
often favorable. The inconveniences of the moment he transmuted
into "incidents" and recalled them amusingly in letters home.

After a few days in Coblenz, Hood managed with the aid of
English friends to find furnished lodgings, "commodious and
pleasant," at 372, Castor Hof: three little rooms in a house almost
at the juncture of the Rhine and Moselle. The back room commanded a fine view of the Moselle, the sloping vineyards, and the
blue mountains beyond. Coblenz in 1835 was a bustling, lively
town of about fifteen thousand inhabitants; soldiers of the Prussian army garrison quartered at the fortress of Ehrenbreitstein
across the Rhine came over daily. Bands played martial tunes while
gaily uniformed troops enlivened the scene with parades. Like
others who experience the high spirits that a first long voyage in
a foreign land brings, Hood delighted in sending home much
practical advice—on hotels, steamers, dining customs, on what to
do and what to see. He took excursions up the neighboring heights
of Ehrenbreitstein and marveled at the panorama that stretched
before him: below, the Rhine racing to the sea; farther away,
villages dotting a countryside of orchards, cornfields, and vineyards;
in the distance, mountains crested with ruined castles. Aglow over
the beauty of the Rhine and its scenery, Hood gloated to his wife
in England, "I am become quite a citizen of the world, I talk
to every one in English, broken French, and bad German, and
have the vanity to think I make friends wherever I go." [3]

In 1835, as in the four or five years previous, English tourists
went up the Rhine during the summer months in droves. The
popularity of the extended trip to Italy, the fashion among the
aristocracy and the educated in the fifteen years after Waterloo,
had waned and given way in the 1830's to the voyage up the
Rhine into romantic Germany.[4] As a result of the great influx of
English tourists, Hood estimated that in the last two years prices
along the Rhine had increased 50 per cent; yet living expenses, he

averred, still came to considerably less than a comparable existence in England demanded.

Jane Hood left England on March 29. After a wearying voyage of five days with the children, she was met by her husband at Cologne. Cologne in this epoch was known for the evil-smelling odors that pervaded its streets; to counteract them, if we may believe Coleridge, *eau de Cologne* was invented. Varnhagen von Ense, the German diplomat, found the town reduced to an "ominous nest of priests, mired in grime, bigotry, and prejudice." [5] Of former splendor remained a declining port, a decadent bishopric, and hordes of beggars who stationed themselves around the portals of churches and fought over the best spots—spots so lucrative that the mendicants valued them as suitable dowry for their daughters. But none of this bothered the Hoods in their happy sightseeing as they wandered through and often lost themselves in the narrow, winding streets. Going to the cathedral together, they looked with wonder at the light, elegant thirteenth-century choir, the scultpures in ivory, the tapestries woven from designs by Rubens, and the stained glass windows.

Coblenz delighted Jane: houses solid, "the streets wide, airy, and clean, with here and there a bit of pavement in the English style...." [6] Lodged near St. Castor's church, the Hoods often had occasion to pass the ironic inscription in front of the fountain:

Anno 1812.
Mémorable par la Campagne contre les Russes,
sous la Préfecture de Jules Douzan.
Vu et approuvé, par nous Commandant Russe
de la Ville de Coblentz, le 1er Janvier, 1814. [7]

Lovely as Jane found the town, she viewed the surrounding countryside with even greater pleasure; with her husband she went on the walks and excursions his letters had already enthusiastically described to her. One somber note intruded, however: Hood's health. It daily worsened. On May 6, almost two months from the day he had first set out, Hood "was seized with most frightful spasms in the chest." [8] After Jane summoned a doctor, Hood improved, though the next day found him as weak as a child. The weeks that followed brought other, less severe attacks, but under Jane's careful supervision he gradually recovered some measure of health.

Except for the precarious state of her husband's health, Jane Hood rejoiced in her new home. Because she "understood English wants," the servant "Gradle," inherited from their now-departed English friends, proved satisfactory. While "Gradle" (an anglicization of "Gretel," a diminutive of Margaret) did the general cooking, the mistress of the house essayed an occasional English dish; the Hoods could thus give up eating at a hotel *table d'hôte* and dine more cheaply at home. Food, especially vegetables, fruit, and nuts, was inexpensive and plentiful; with mutton only "3 groschen a pound, about three pence halfpenny," and other meats at like prices, the Hoods could maintain the flesh diet that foreign visitors to England found so startling. Hochheimer wine, Bavarian beers, and Westphalian hams delighted Hood, while the superb roasted coffee made him forget—if only for a time—English tea. Unfortunately, as he later discovered, the "specialties" of the German cuisine were not always available. One difficulty soon presented itself and stayed with the Hoods their entire time abroad: having to order by dictionary and with their faulty pronunciation, they occasionally got "onions for turnips, and radishes for carrots." Although linguistic difficulties led to dozens of minor misunderstandings, they were—for the most part—amicably resolved.

In late May or early June the Hoods made the acquaintance of Philip von Franck, an Anglo-German lieutenant, already fourteen years in the Prussian service.[9] When the Lieutenant heard that an English couple now resided in Coblenz, he took great pains to get himself introduced in order to meet a fellow countryman and to improve his now faltering English. Franck, whose mother was English and who had received part of his education in England, always regarded himself as a true Englishman. On this premise he and Hood got on famously. Helping them in innumerable ways, Franck proved a godsend to the Hoods: he explained German customs and guided them through the impossible language; he knew how to deal with servants and shopkeepers; and, by often coming over in the evening for a game of cribbage, he alleviated their social isolation. When Hood could find time off from the necessity for work—which seems often enough—he and Franck went off along the Moselle or Lahn on a fishing ramble. "He is really a treasure to us, thoroughly English, unpresuming, gentlemanly, and full of good sense, fond of a joke withal," wrote Hood to John Wright when, a few months later, Franck had become part of the family. "Between him and the children it is quite a mutual flame; on their side, sometimes, so as to be laughable." [10] While Franck's 19th Polish regiment remained stationed at Ehrenbreitstein, Hood rarely lacked companionship, and, minor mishaps allowed for, enjoyed life at Coblenz. The Lieutenant's presence kept the long months of exile reasonably gay.

With frequent outings into the countryside, the Hoods passed one of their happiest summers. Ideas for poems and sketches for the *Comic Annual* of 1836 came "without being laboured for." Moreover, Franck gave him good hints for German stories. Though his health continued precarious, Hood had almost completely regained his appetite. Indeed, the whole family prospered. Fanny, taking walks and skipping rope, found herself trailed by German children, curious at her dress. Already she had begun to pick up the language. Young Tom, Jane described as a "little fat arch rogue." After undergoing compulsory vaccination, he recovered rapidly and was soon, plump and "brown as a berry," in riotously good health. Only Jane Hood, though in most ways content, regretted English comforts.

In late August Dr. and Mrs. William Elliot, traveling up the Rhine, arrived for a visit. First met when he had tended Mrs. Hood through her near-fatal illness after the birth of Tom, Dr. Elliot was to become Hood's medical advisor and lifelong friend. In after years, close ties between the two families continued with the Hoods' and their children. Since Hood lacked all faith in German doctors—he often compared them to the quack Sangrado in *Gil Blas*—he felt reassured after the English doctor had examined him. As long as he lived on the Continent, Hood recounted in long passages of his letters to Dr. Elliot—passages frequently excised by his children in the *Memorials* and understandably so—

the details of his latest symptoms and attacks, while the doctor, for his part, gave the best epistolary diagnoses he could. For an idea of medical practice in the mid-nineteenth century and the extreme generality of all diagnoses, a student of the history of medicine would find few more illuminating accounts than this correspondence.

Germany definitely broke Hood's health: never after was he a well man. The years covered in this study coincide exactly with this decline in health. In a consideration of his achievements and failures, Hood's health is a vital factor to come to terms with. It remains, in the end, the factor hardest to assess. Rarely is it possible to overlook the personal sufferings, at times intense, of the man. He had in his youth a severe attack of scarlet fever; rheumatic fever felled him in the winter of 1823–1824, and he suffered intermittently from it thereafter. Tuberculosis was prevalent on his mother's side, for, besides his mother, two of his sisters and a brother succumbed to the disease. Walter Jerrold, his first biographer, followed the traditional nineteenth-century view that the poet "inherited the fatal scourge of consumption" from his mother. More recently, J. C. Reid has asserted that Hood suffered from "rheumatic heart disease." A modern diagnosis, based in part on materials not used by either Jerrold or Reid, sees Hood suffering from an increasingly severe case of "pulmonary edema," with syphilis, perhaps contracted prenatally, as the main disease.[11] In any case, at no time in his life could Hood be considered robust, even normally healthy. After 1835 his illnesses frequently kept him bedridden for long stretches of time. In Dr. Elliot's diagnoses Hood believed he got the best medical advice then available, and probably he did. More interesting than the maladies themselves is Hood's reaction to them, how they affected his life, and, more important, his poetry. Between his decline in health and his awakening consciousness of society's injustices there exists a close parallel.

When Franck's regiment was transferred to Posen in the beginning of October for what turned out to be an absence of less than three months, Hood's sense of isolation grew. His Coblenz acquaintanceships narrowed themselves to a M. Ramponi (or "Rampone"—Hood spelled his name variously), an Italian "teacher of languages," who dropped in regularly on Sunday afternoons. Long conversations conducted in faulty French ensued; marveling at the extent of the Italian's ignorance of England, Hood fought over with him the Battle of Waterloo and told him about English life. In a November reply to a letter from John Wright, the personal as well as business friend who took care of the mechanical side of preparing the *Comic Annuals* until his death late in 1839, Hood reveals incipient homesickness: "I can almost talk German, I shall be glad to come back to England." [12] His desire to return to his native land needed two years for fulfilment; three more elapsed after the first visit before the final return. In regard to his speaking German, the "almost" is optimistic; though he did come to read German well enough to struggle through the local newspapers, Hood never succeeded, despite many attempts, in speaking the language with any fluency. In addition, partial deafness impeded him from picking up correctly the sounds of the guttural Rhineland dialect.

On Christmas Day, celebrated in German fashion and enlivened by the newly returned Franck's presence, Jane treated the whole family to an English plum pudding. Though Hood wished to introduce into England the German custom of a decorated Christmas tree with candles, not until its advocacy by the Prince Consort, Albert, did Victorian England and later, the United States, find the custom congenial. One of the highlights of Hood's stay in Germany occurred a few days after Christmas: the New Year's Ball, attended by "all the rank, beauty, and fashion of Coblenz." Everybody came: the commander of all the Rhenish provinces as well as Hood's tailor, a mixture of classes that surprised the poet, as did seeing "at the ball a score or two in the uniform of common soldiers offering their partnership to the ladies"—that is, until he realized that "some of them were the sons of barons." All present danced "waltzes, gallopades, and contredanses." In Germany the waltz had led a respectable life longer than in England, where its introduction over twenty years before had incited a lame noble-

man to apostrophize it as the "Voluptuous Waltz!" The enchant-
ing melodies, to which even the most proper girls danced,
captivated Hood, as they had finally led to toleration from Byron.
A small cannon went off at the stroke of twelve, the waltz immediately ceased, and dancers of all ages scampered to greet each
other with hugs and embraces to the chorus of *Prosit Neujahr!*
After shaking hands with the regimental officers he knew, Hood
consoled himself with congratulating a few ladies met long ago at
the *table d'hôte*. All in all, he noted wryly, "a funny scene."

The *Comic Annual* for 1836 constitutes Hood's literary achievement for the year 1835. Having taken longer than usual to complete it, he found, unlike most years previous, no time to write
anything else. Both the excitement that accompanied his change
of residence and his health, a "sad hindrance," forbade the additional effort. Unfortunately, miscalculating the size of the volume,
he wrote too much, and thus wasted precious strength. Hood had
published his first *Comic Annual* in 1830. Several competitors,
capitalizing on his success, soon had entered the field, among them
the *New Comic Annual* and Louisa Sheridan's *Comic Offering, or
Ladies Mélange of Literary Mirth*; but by 1835 most of his rivals
had dropped out. Running to about 180 pages—no mean amount
of humor to turn out each year—Hood's little duodecimo volumes,
priced at twelve shillings, had from the first dominated all others
in quality.

The punning poems and humorous sketches that delighted
thousands Hood brought forth only at the cost of great physical
anguish. After years of struggling to churn out the requisite humor,
he remarked bitterly in 1840 that "no gentleman alive has written
so much Comic and spitten so much blood within six consecutive
years." "His own family never enjoyed his quaint and humorous
fancies," wrote his daughter, "for they were all associated with
memories of illness and anxiety." [13] He not only wrote the whole
of the *Comic* himself, but he also had to prepare nearly all of the

humorous woodcuts—deemed worthy by A. H. Baily, Hood's publisher from 1834 to 1839, of separate publication. Not the least attraction of these volumes and often misplaced or omitted in later editions, Hood's woodcuts are vital for a correct understanding of the written text; some of them, moreover, evince a fine eye for externals and a genuine skill in grotesque art. Others embody a pun. All show him as a visual Mayhew to his age. "It will be seen from the illustrations of the present work," Hood wrote modestly in the preface to *Whims and Oddities*, "that the Inventor is no artist;—in fact, he was never 'meant to draw.'. . ." [14] But he never pretended to correctness. Rather, except for their vigor and pointed effect, his drawings purposely resemble those of a child.

Hood generally worked in the quiet of night after the rest of the family had gone to bed. That he was frequently dilatory in his work no one denies, though the comment by William Tegg, a pupil of Messrs. Branston and Wright, the engravers of most of the woodcuts in the *Comic Annuals* to 1833, seems overstated: "He put off everything till the last moment; he never supplied copy or drawing till about December. . . . Nothing would move him to work till he was forced by the necessity of the occasion, and then he made himself ill. It was not that he was an idle man, but a dreamy one." [15]

Although several poems in the 1836 *Comic Annual* deal with social questions, two poems in the *Comic* of the year previous show that Hood had already turned, almost for the first time since the *Odes and Addresses* of 1825, to themes which reveal his dissatisfaction with English society. Anticipating his later humanitarian verse, these poems reveal a deepened awareness of life; they remind us that Hood never lost his strong empathy with human misery. Like other poets of social protest in the 1830's, he condemned less the sweeping changes overtaking society than the evils and abuses resultant. The circumstances of his life—his health especially—often dictated the kind of poetry he composed. In the five years before the 1835 *Comic*, the most carefree of his existence, Hood had felt impelled to write few poems that manifest concern with

society's injustices.[16] But when, in the latter part of 1834, he wrote
"A Lay of Real Life" and "The Sweep's Complaint," he knew
whereof he spoke. With personal and financial woes nearly overwhelming him, he reveals in these two poems a deepening insecurity.

If ever environment determined present misery, it did to the
hero of "A Lay of Real Life." Not once does humor relieve the
intensity of oppression, nor the presence of an ominous doom.
The speaker narrates his fate simply and with quiet stoicism:

> Who ruined me ere I was born,
> Sold every acre, grass or corn,
> And left the next heir all forlorn?
> > My Grandfather.
>
> Who said my mother was no nurse,
> And physicked me and made me worse,
> Till infancy became a curse?
> > My Grandmother.
>
> Who left me in my seventh year,
> A comfort to my mother dear,
> And Mr. Pope, the overseer?
> > My Father.
>
> Who let me starve, to buy her gin,
> Till all my bones came through my skin,
> Then called me "ugly little sin?"
> > My Mother.
>
> .   .   .   .
>
> Who, gratis, shared my social glass,
> But when misfortune came to pass,
> Referr'd me to the pump? Alas!
> > My Friend.
>
> Through all this weary world, in brief,
> Who ever sympathised with grief,
> Or shared my joy—my sole relief?
> > Myself.[17]

If he who suffered "Real Life" could still see life steadily, the London chimney sweeps in Hood's "The Sweep's Complaint" knew not even this slight comfort. Fifty years before their plight had roused Blake to angry passion. Negro slaves had been manumitted in the colonies in 1833; why, Hood asks, tolerate at home similar if not worse conditions of slavery? "To place this gross partiality in the strongest light and shade," he observes in an essay also inspired by the sweeps' plight, "The Black and White Question," "let the servitude of the born Blacks be compared with that of those 'Africans of our own growth,' as Elia calls them, who derive their nigritude not from nature but from soot." [18] Citing the "Act for the Better Regulation of Chimney Sweepers and their Apprentices" of 1834, Hood condemns the laxity in it that permits masters to obtain apprentices easily and to abuse them just as easily. Since with the connivance of local parish authorities they could twist or evade each article of the Act, he urges that it "undergo rigorous revision" or "be immediately repealed." But the general injustice he depicted in the essay served only as prelude to the poem with its more ready sympathy for the individual sweep.

"The Sweep's Complaint" Hood wrote soon after the above-mentioned Act had forbidden sweeps "to call or hawk in the streets." Because the Act prevented sweeps from calling out their trade, it worsened rather than improved their lot; but it did relieve the consciences of their employers, who no longer had to hear misery proclaimed publicly. The poem begins with a sentimental picture of the silent sweep roaming the London streets in search of work:

> One morning ere my usual time
> I rose, about the seventh chime,
> When little stunted boys that climb
>   Still linger in the street:
> And as I walked, I saw indeed
> A sample of the sooty breed,
> Though he was rather run to seed,
>   In height above five feet.

Not able to cry his employment, he becomes a miserable, baffled creature:

> And while he sought the dingy job,
> His lab'ring breast appear'd to throb
> And half a hiccup half a sob
>   Betray'd internal woe.
> To cry the cry he had by rote
> He yearn'd, but law forbade the note. . . .[19]

The sweep asks: "God help us if we don't not cry, how are we to pursue our callings?" And further: "Every thing, except the sweeps I think, is to be allowed to keep themselves!" [20] Parliament had, in effect, refused the sweeps the possibility of earning their living; new laws, instead of bringing alleviation, only made a hard task harder. One of man's inalienable rights, Hood believed, was the right to gain a livelihood. That right was being denied. By letting the sweep present his plight in the first person, he makes his point clear without having explicitly to state his moral intent. Using the "language of common men," Hood extends his indictment of specific injustice to dramatize the misery of *all* the poor:

> I only wish Mr. Wilberforce or some of them that
>   pities the niggers,
> Would take a peep down in our cellars, and look at our
>   miserable starving figures,
> A-sitting idle on our empty sacks, and all ready to
>   eat each other,
> And a brood of little ones crying for bread to a
>   heart-breaking Father and Mother.
> They haven't a rag of clothes to mend, if their
>   mothers had thread and needles,
> But crawl naked about the cellars, poor things, like
>   a swarm of common black beadles.
> If they'd only inquired before passing the Act and
>   taken a few such peeps,
> I don't think that any real gentleman would have set
>   his face against sweeps.[21]

Poems like "A Lay of Real Life" and "The Sweep's Complaint" reveal Hood in a role other than that of funnyman. I do not mean to imply that these poems are typical of Hood's work during the 1830's. They are not. A many-sided individual, he rarely let one sentiment or one kind of poetry dominate his thought for long. On the whole, though, he deserves a re-evaluation—if not for the quality of his work, for much of it was, everyone admits, hack work—then certainly for its purpose. Misread since his own day as pleasant trifling, his comic verse deserves recognition for its serious ethical tenor. Many of Hood's readers enjoyed this moral bent. And most of them enjoyed it all the more not realizing it was there.

For the *Comic Annual* of 1836 Hood wrote "Poetry, Prose, and Worse" and "Sudden Death." Both poem and prose sketch reflect his awakened interest in society's ills. Although "Poetry, Prose, and Worse," ostensibly inspired by an *Athenaeum* review of a book on Turkish literature, purports to comment on Turkish customs, Hood, in fact, uses Turkey only to consider the home situation:

> O! would that we copied from Turkey
> In this little Isle of our own,
> Where the times are so muddy and murky,
> We want a poetical tone! [22]

Humorously, he suggests poetry as a mitigating influence and urges just application of the Golden Rule, especially to the less fortunate. We could then counteract "Our Laws," "the dryest / That earth in its compass can show!" In all of his humanitarian writings Hood pleaded for justice, usually not legal justice, but human justice tempered with mercy. Strict legal justice, in view of England's archaic laws, he thought cruel, inadequate, too inhumane to help those who most needed help.

"Poetry, Prose, and Worse" deserves mention not because of its poetic merit—which is slight—but because the themes Hood treated in it half-humorously partook in later years of overriding seriousness. Taking up specific injustices, he asks that poetry allay the effects of "new measures before us, / As bills for the sabbath or poor"; that poetry urge clemency on bailiffs; that warrants and bills for debtors appear in poetry; that the harsh criminal code be softened. Its central stanzas suddenly becoming earnest in tone, "Poetry, Prose, and Worse" gauges Hood's developing interest in social questions even—perhaps because—away from the English scene. His years in Germany gave him both detachment from and a new interest in English life. Through his observance of foreign social customs and ways of life, he came to realize that the injustice and squalor of his native land had largely eluded him hitherto. Without full consciousness of the stand he took and almost always in humorous disguise, Hood interjected with increasing frequency in his comic writings themes wholly serious. He still wrote the earlier kind of comic poem, but increasingly as the years went by it becomes, in greater or lesser measure, a serious poem. Though in the *Comic Annuals* of 1835 and 1836 such poems are few, they are nonetheless significant: they constitute the transition to the wholly serious poems of social protest of Hood's last year.

"Sudden Death" was the latest in the series of "Sketches on the Road," a popular feature of his recent annuals. With a fondness for picturesque detail that recalls Dickens, another admirer of the fast vanishing way of life represented by the stagecoach, Hood narrates incidents along the English highways involving colorful eccentrics. One contemporary admirer of these sketches, finding Hood "a faithful chronicler of what is actual and tangible," praises the "cleverness" by which "the most familiar incidents of every-day journeying are . . . made notable and important in the best style of Dutch painting." [23] "Sudden Death" ridicules age-old aristocratic attitudes in the face of unexpected change. Miss Norman, a lady of tenuously ancient family, is predisposed to regard "Pedestrianism" as "a very vulgar exercise . . . a bodily exertion very derogatory to persons of birth and breeding" [24]—and definitely not in the family tradition. When her carriage horse collapses and dies fifty yards short of her home, she haughtily refuses to borrow another except one belonging to a properly aristocratic family. There matters stand until an aspiring pig butcher, "Sam the Sticker," seizes her, drops her in his tumbril, and trundles her through the village to her utter but deserved mortification. Moral (one usually peeks out in Hood): excessive pride in birth and station will bring about a fittingly self-induced fall.

Three exceptions aside, the volume's other contents require only brief notice. The long extravaganza "Love and Lunacy" relates a "lunatic" misunderstanding between two lovers. Though written in Spenserian stanzas, the poem reminds us continually of Byron's *Beppo* in its theme and in its gay parody of romantic conventions. Its jingling stanzas and unconcern for plot recall the occasional truth in Jane Hood's exasperated admonition—"Hood, Hood, how can you run on so?" With "The Quakers' Converzatione," where he pokes inoffensive fun at this sect, and "The Ocean, Considered per Se," a fantasy of nonsense whose title gives a fair indication of its fun content, Hood rounded out the light side of his volume.

Hood deemed his "last book . . . a good one." Though he included the whole of the 1836 *Comic Annual* in *Hood's Own*, the selection of the best from the *Comics* published in 1839, still its poems and prose sketches evade distinction. Curiously, the *Comic* for 1836 does not reflect—one story excepted—his German experiences. Several reasons for this omission suggest themselves: Hood wrote, first of all, for English readers, and English readers before the Christmas fireside would prefer English to German domestic scenes. Second, he wished to save the German material for his "German book," *Up the Rhine*. A third, yet more crucial factor is simply that despite Franck's aid and insights, he never could quite immerse himself in German society. When he criticized German customs in *Up the Rhine*, he did so from the point of view—necessarily limited—of an outsider. To be convincing, domestic fiction needs successful empathy with a milieu, precisely what is lacking in the one German story of the 1836 *Comic*, "The Domestic Dilemma: A True Story, from the German of Jean Paul Nemand." Nemand is the poet's intentional misspelling of *niemand*, German for "no one." The story revolves around German beds, whose shortness and discomfort were always a favorite butt of Hood's humor. As detailed parallels to Jean Paul's writings are unlikely, "The Domestic Dilemma" is best considered as a good-natured spoof of his idyllic domestic depictions and of German life in general.

Neither the *Edinburgh* nor the *Quarterly* deemed the *Comic Annuals* important enough to review. *Blackwood's,* after John Wilson's enthusiastic greeting of the first *Whims and Oddities* in January, 1827, maintained a largely unbroken silence. Popular appeal, rather than serious intellectual or artistic appraisal, caused the frequent, usually enthusiastic notices in the monthlies and weeklies. Typical of the critical attention Hood received are the lengthy reviews in the *Athenaeum.* Often written by the editor, Dilke, they consisted of a few lines of warm praise interspersed amid columns of extracts. Indeed, the generally held assumption of the age seems to have been that the "public will prefer extract to opinion." Though here motivated by personal friendship rather than financial gain, these reviews serve as excellent examples of the "puffing" the upright editor so readily deplored in competitive journals. In the second of two notices (December 19, 1835) the reviewer—John Hamilton Reynolds on this occasion—quoted with approval long excerpts from "The Domestic Dilemma" and "Sudden Death." Not surprisingly, he found them illustrative of "wit of the best class." Hood could not ask for more.

Thomas Hood gradually became disillusioned with German ways. As his stay lengthened from weeks to months and years, the novelty of the new faded. His native Englishness reasserted itself, and Hood's comments on German society evince growing bitterness and alienation. He began to find himself, as W. M. Rossetti once put it, "a good deal of an Englishman, and his surroundings vexaciously German." [25] Nothing pleased him any more. Continual skirmishes with the landlady led to a change of lodgings—to 752, Alten Graben—in the spring; "Gradle" the maid, because of dishonesty, had to be dismissed and replaced. Foreign customs, at first relished, he found increasingly repugnant and barbaric. Isolation from all except his immediate family brought about a longing for home—or at least for removal from Coblenz. Worsening health clinched the disillusionment. Still, assertions by biographers that Hood viewed the German scene with total disgust from the first telescope the impressions of two years: first impressions were distinctly favorable.

To the Dilkes, John Wright, and Dr. Elliot, Hood sent long, familiar letters—letters that reveal him at his informal best. To some, Hood's letters are the most attractive of his prose writings. Their gossip and imagined dialogues served him, as he realized himself, in lieu of the English conversation he sorely missed in whiling away the long hours. Always a sensitive correspondent, he instinctively adopted the correct tone, whether it was the familiar jocularity apparent in his letters to the Dilkes or the manifest respect in those to Sir Robert Peel. His correspondence with the editor of the *Athenaeum* exhibits the stamp of an alert mind that viewed its German surroundings occasionally with a wistful humor, more frequently with the kind of disillusionment that comes only from personal experience. In sum, Hood never quite adapted himself to life away from England. He tried first to achieve detachment from his environment by taking on the kind of cosmopolitan outlook displayed by a Byron or a Browning. When he found this attitude of detached tolerance difficult to hold in the face of constant chicanery, he adopted the more congenial one of detached —and strongly adverse—criticism.

In a surge of bitterness Hood wrote Dilke in January, 1836, that "Coblenz is dearer than it was,—& will be cheaper." [26] From a financial point of view, nonetheless, he still felt fairly satisfied with his experiment of living abroad. "Lastly experience has had to be paid for," a resigned Hood concluded; "I speak advisedly & from full knowledge." [27] He wrote, admittedly, "with his bristles up."

In calmer moments Hood differentiated between "the honest, conscientious, liberal, warm-hearted, intellectual Germans we give the country just credit for" [28]—a breed, however, of which he found distressingly few specimens—and the Germans among whom he lived. In these, few or none of these attributes were evident. The supposed German intellectualism he found rarely **in evidence,** although his knowledge of Germany was, he granted readily, confined to the Rhineland. But for that region he claimed the right to speak with the knowledge of a resident. Particularly distressing in his view was the obstinacy with which Rhineland Germans persisted in viewing the English as legitimate objects for plunder. He saw the unwary English traveler, misled by the German reputation for honesty, fleeced everywhere. At seeing his countrymen charged by hotel owners at least twice the going rate for natives his rage kindled. "But I want fair play for my countrymen," he observed with disgust to Dilke, "against whom there is much illiberal feeling, which is the more annoying, because Germans from other parts, who think well of us, are surprised to find opinion against us on the Rhine where it would be presumed we are so well known." [29] Though tempered slightly in *Up the Rhine,* his views there—sweet revenge for his own experiences—present a decidedly unflattering portrayal of life along the Rhine.

Between farmers, whom he thought truthful and fundamentally decent, and townsmen, whom he thought deceitful and mean-spirited, Hood distinguished sharply. The townsmen passed the daylight hours in questionable commercial activity and the evenings silently puffing away on their pipes, enveloped in increasingly thick clouds of smoke. Since the Prussian government forbade smoking on the streets, pipe-smoking indoors was the one characteristic of German society upon which all foreign travelers commented. In his essay "On Noise" Schopenhauer diagnosed the effect on Germans of excessive smoking: smoking did not disturb them in reading or thinking simply because they did not think. Smoking had become a substitute for thought. Uncharitable in old age to his fellow countrymen, the author of *The World as Will and Idea* warmly seconded Hood's observation in *Up the Rhine* about noise: "for a musical people," the poet complained there, "they are the most noisy I ever met with." [30]

Though Hood at times succeeded in getting hold of a few nondescript English newspapers that managed to pass the strict Prussian censorship, Dilke's *Athenaeum* had to serve as his chief source of news about the world outside. Local German newspapers supplemented it on occasion. The *Rhein und Moselle Zeitung* he considered typical, since it had "standing articles, therefore favourite ones" on beet-root, sugar, and the railroads. As with the natives, thus with their newspapers: proudly displayed extracts headed "Distress in Rich England" told of paupers in London streets; political articles paraded the familiar continental jargon about "the haughty Isle of shop-keepers." Hood attributed this ill-natured envy to jealousy of England's wealth and resentment of her political influence.

The long, cold, wet spring of 1836 turned abruptly into a torrid summer. For relief the Hoods took several excursions into the surrounding mountains. They particularly enjoyed a visit to the Laacher See, which lay within an extinct crater and had on its banks a ruined monastery and cloister. The wild countryside, although on a larger scale and more "diversely wooded," reminded Hood of "some of the romantic parts" of Scotland. Returning by Tönnenstein, the Hoods drank the spring water there; "with wine and sugar, it drinks like champagne," observed the poet, "but it is good neat." Whenever free, he went fishing with Franck; sometimes Jane and the children accompanied them. His description of one outing well exemplifies the unstudied charm of his letters:

Whilst we were fishing, all of a sudden I missed De Franck,— but spied him at last up to his neck in the middle of two rocks between which he had slipped in jumping from one to another. He made a strange figure when he came out,—the best lay figure for a Rivergod imaginable,—for German sporting jackets have an infinity of pockets, and there was a separate jet of water from every one, as well as from his sleeves, trousers, and each spout of his drowned moustachios (N.B. they're very long). He did not seem much improved, when, having gone to the Inn, he returned in a suit of the landlord's, who, though twice as tall, was not half so stout. However, we did not care for appearances, for we thought nobody would notice him, as it was not a holiday, and there was no company. But we were mistaken. The landlord's dog sniffed a robbery, and knowing his master's clothes again, insisted on stripping the counterfeit, and was obliged to be pulled off *vi et armis*. The landlord was very much distressed, and made a thousand apologies; and, to do him justice, was a very obliging, honest, reasonable fellow, and certainly deserved to be paid better than *with his own money, out of his own waistcoat pocket*. . . .

As Hood extricated his hapless friend, Jane and a lady companion scrambled up to the ruined castle of Lahneck and their own adventure.

Having seen everything on its old ground-floor, female curiosity, prevailing even over female fear, tempted them up a dilapidated staircase to one of the mouldering attics; and then, how unfortunately fortunate! some half-dozen of the topmost stairs caught the contagion of curiosity, and paid a visit to the cellars. You may imagine the duet that ensued *in a very high key*—but as you know I am deaf and De Franck was more intent on the *perch below*, than on the *perch above*, it was, consequently, a long hour (Jane says six) before they were rescued, heartily sick, you may be sure, of the local and the vocal.[31]

While excursions and fishing jaunts improved Hood's health, summer, always his best season, brought warmth to his body, optimism to his spirits. Urging the Dilkes to venture up the Rhine for their annual vacation, he finally enticed them to come with the news that in September the Prussian army would hold a grand review. The King himself might be present. Soon after the Dilkes' arrival Coblenz and the neighboring villages began to fill up with troops and officers. The review, though not favored with good weather, left everyone impressed. On the last day but one the whole party, except Dilke, who had become ill with an inflammatory disorder, set out to see the "taking" of Bassenheimer, a village eight miles off. From an excellent vantage point they watched one army outmaneuver the other in a sham battle lent verisimilitude by the beating of drums and the firing of muskets.

In October, while Dilke still convalesced, Lieutenant von Franck offered Hood the opportunity to march across Germany with his regiment, ordered to Bromberg. Happy over the news, Jane Hood summed up to Mrs. Elliot the advantages for her husband: "As it was his intention to travel for his German book, this affords the best opportunity. He would see parts of the country which are not common to travellers; he would have the advantage of very pleasant companions, and the help of Mr. De Franck's German. . . ." [32] Popular with the regiment's officers, many of whom had expressed pleasure at the handsome invitation extended him by their colonel, Hood gratefully accepted. He knew the marches would be long and grueling: fifteen to twenty miles per day for three days, one day of rest, and then on again. On account of the Dilkes he did not leave with the regiment, but planned to catch up with it by coach. Jane decided to accompany him for part of the journey. Mishaps dogged their route, the first taking place even before departure when the servant failed to awaken them for the 6:00 A.M. coach. Hood, by chance, woke up at 5:30. A frantic half hour ensued. Though the Hoods just caught their coach, Hood left behind in the rush important papers having to do with the new *Comic*, which, dilatory as ever, he had not finished before departure.

The Hoods left Coblenz on October 11. They arrived via the "Bads" of Nassau the same evening in Frankfort, whereupon they took the night coach for Eisenach, reaching it on the thirteenth. The next morning they proceeded on to Langensalza, and found the jovial lieutenant comfortably quartered in a nearby village. During the night ride in a carriage stifling with heat and odors, Hood, unperceived by Jane, had fainted. Coming to, he let down the window to enjoy the night air, which "seemed like a breeze through the branches and blossoms of the tree of life." From this celestial breeze, however, he caught a "severe cold on the chest" that forced him to remain a few days at Gotha. Not wishing to leave the Dilkes too long to themselves, Jane Hood left him there. Later, after a physical collapse upon his return to Coblenz, Hood assumed that the acute pains he felt in his chest as a result of the cold air had affected his lungs. A year and a half after the Channel crossing, the night ride on the Eisenach road marked the second turning point in his health's decline.

After a few days of rest at Gotha, Hood rejoined the regiment at Halle, reached on the twenty-second after a tedious journey by *Beiwagen*. The first day he rode with the regiment was the first he arose without pain. The horse he had bought proved quite gentle, for he noted with pride that he fell off only twice the first day and thereafter rarely. Sleeping and eating well, he felt himself "getting better every mile." The cordial welcome by the officers of the 19th had greatly cheered him; with those who spoke French, still his best foreign language, he enjoyed spirited conversation. Ever sensitive to his environment, Hood expected from the desolateness of the vast plains around Leipzig to see a forlorn seacoast; the Saxon inhabitants, cheerful and honest, "the reverse of Rhinelanders," he genuinely liked.

A passage which his children later excised from his letter to his wife of October 23 underscores the trip's importance for Hood's state of mind: "I seriously think it will save me—for I was going into a low bad way, irritable in body & mind—a plague to you and a curse to myself. But that is past. . . ." [33] Reaffirming his love for Jane, a love resistant to time, he expressed his intention to go on beyond Berlin "as far as I can consistent with certainty of getting back." Hood knew that during the last weeks at Coblenz he had acted irritably. He also knew why: he drank too much.

Drinking suggests a major reason for Hood's temperamental instability vis-à-vis publishers and friends. Continually tested by hardship, emotional and financial, he sought relief in drink when pressures came to a head. Though fundamentally an upright person, he remained highly suspicious of the motives of others. Consequently he was ever on the defensive, unwilling to compromise. If he had led an easier life, his character would have shown to greater advantage; but again, if pressure had not forced him to work, we would have been the poorer in poetry. While Hood believed sincerely that alcohol—wine chiefly—fortified his health, its effects made him at times a trying person to get along with.[34]

The march was fun: up promptly at four, Hood walked in the dark until five or five-thirty, leading his horse until he saw the road. At breakfast, which consisted of the previous day's foragings, he joined the officers. Each amused the others in recounting the hazards of the night's lodgings. Hood, Franck, and a Polish officer usually drew the same quarters; whenever there were but two beds, the lieutenant, good-naturedly wishing to spare his friend discomfort, regularly bedded down "on the straw." Though Hood was thus quite fortunate, others besides Franck fared less well: "One officer had such a tumble-down hut assigned to him, that his very dog put his tail between his legs and howled at it; a second had slept in a pigeon-house, and was obliged to have the birds driven out before he could dress in the morning; and our friend Von C., by some mistake, was billeted on the whole wide world!" [35] After an eight-hour march came relaxation in the evening. At dinner, the officers chatted with their hosts and Hood told tall stories, including one to a gullible *Frau* that he "had come 50,000 miles, was married at 14, and had 17 children."

At Wittenberg, rich in memories of Luther, Hood went sightseeing. The Reformer's statue in the market place "represents a sturdy brawny friar," he wrote in *Up the Rhine*, "with a two-storey chin, and a neck and throat like a bull's." He could not resist commenting: "To the reader of Rabelais there cannot be a truer effigy of his jolly fighting, toping, praying Friar John; a personage who, I have little doubt, was intended by the author for Luther." [36] After crossing the bleak, sandy heaths of Brandenburg, the regiment reached Potsdam, on the outskirts of Berlin, where the King reviewed it. At last, on October 28, they arrived at Berlin itself, then a rapidly growing but unlovely city of a quarter of a million inhabitants. When a friend of Franck's, Prince Radziwill, invited the lieutenant to stay over for a few weeks, Hood's pretext for continuing with the regiment disappeared. It left without him the next day.

For the experience of the past days on the road Hood felt gratitude. While he appreciated the unfailing hospitality and kindness he had met everywhere, he regretted most that he would never again see the friends whose lives he had, if only for a brief moment, shared. "Thus ended my practical connection with the gallant Nineteenth," he recorded in *Up the Rhine*.

> But I shall often recall my chance quarters—my provident morning foragings against a jour maigre—when a *searching* wind might have found a roll of bread-and-butter in one pocket, and mayhap a brace of cold pigeons in the other— the cheerful rendezvous—the friendly greetings—and the picnic by the road-side:—I shall often hear in fancy the national "Am Rhein! Am Rhein!" chorused by a hundred voices—the exciting charge, beaten at the steep hill or deep ground—and the spirit-stirring bugle ringing amidst the vast pine-woods of Germany! [37]

Lodgings in a third-rate hotel aside, Hood enjoyed his Berlin stay. He did not neglect to visit the usual sights: the Old Bridge, the Brandenburg Gate, and the art museums; but because he found the "vituperative eloquence" of the men in the Berlin Fishmarket equal to that of their rough-tongued counterparts in Billingsgate, his visit there proved the highlight of his stay. England's reality became, for a moment, actual. Another day Franck introduced him to the aristocratic Radziwill family, at whose home he spent a pleasant afternoon.

A week's stay in the Prussian capital satisfied Hood. Deciding not to tarry longer from his family, he began the long journey home by the most direct routes. On the way an accident to the *Eilwagen* resulted in a delay of six hours and "the first of my cold"; "a night journey from Frankfort in an *open* coupe confirmed it." Arriving in Coblenz "ruddy as a ploughboy," he turned white the next day and developed an alarming cough. It ended in his spitting blood. Bled, he stopped coughing, but remained weak for long months after. "I suspect this time it was a touch on the lungs," a saddened Hood wrote to the now-departed Dilkes, "which were never touched before, being indeed my strongest point." [38] Though still unwell at the time of his departure, Dilke had decided to quit Coblenz rather than risk the onset of cold weather. "To make things better," Hood noted in a letter to Franck, "I had not sent enough for the 'Comic,' and was obliged to set to work again, willy-nilly, well or illy" [39]—another strength-sapping effort. Truly a sick man, he faced with courage a life in which "not only are my marching days over, but I fear I shall never be able to travel again." A sobering thought for a man not thirty-eight.

A few days before Christmas, Hood received a letter from Dilke felicitating him on the new *Comic Annual*. The *Athenaeum* reviews of December 17 and 24 had rated the eighth in the series, as ever, highly. After a few weeks' hard labor in November had finished it and very nearly Hood as well, Baily had gotten it out rapidly and sent it off to the booksellers just in time for the Christmas trade. Hood had found work slow on the new annual, doubly so as he wanted to reserve his sketches and poems on German life for *Up the Rhine*. Regretting his absence from native soil, he thought that by the time he wrote it up topical material about the English scene would have become stale. The volume's preface relates in punning prose the "ifs" of his dilemma:

> I might have been getting up an urgent call for the Repeal of the Corn Laws—when the Corn Laws had been regularly outlawed, at the poetical petition of Ebenezer Elliott and Corney Webbe. . . . I might have been insisting on a fairer mode of Registration—when the whole system had been Rumfordized and the Books ordered to be kept on the principle of Cobbett's Register. . . . A Work on the Working of the New Poor Laws might have turned out a work of supererogation— there being no Poor for Laws to work upon, the Philanthropic Party having transformed all paupers, at their own expense, into Poor Gentlemen. And, finally, how foolish I should have looked with my "Remarks on the Franchise," or the "Complaint of a Ten Pound Voter a shilling short"—if in the meantime voters were admitted by avoirdupois, as a test of their weight in the Country! [40]

Other political and social subjects tempted Hood as well: dissenters' rights to marry according to their own forms, flogging in the army, Hebrew Emancipation, the Irish Church, extinction of tithes and sinecures, free trade. He also stated his disapproval of Evangelical-supported Sabbath bills and of "Bull-baiting" in Exeter Hall, a building heinous to him because in the spring Evangelical groups held annual meetings in it. Since in 1835 an Act of Parliament had forbidden bull-baiting, Hood punned on the anti-Catholic, "Bull-baiting" atmosphere of the more bigoted Evangelical gatherings. A favorite hope, to which he soon returned, was to write a "Modest Plea for the better Protection of Copyright. . . ." [41]

Hood took a stand in the preface to the 1837 *Comic Annual* that revealed his deep concern with the fabric of English society—a stand that placed him well in the forefront of even professedly liberal opinion of his age. When a few years later his brother-in-law Reynolds wrote him, "You are so removed—and have been removed so long; that your sympathies with matters here are below zero," [42] he made a serious misjudgment. At no time in his five-year exile did Hood lack interest about affairs in England; every English newspaper he got his hands on he devoured. As he thrived on topical events, only with a knowledge of them do many of his poems become intelligible. Not only do the political and humanitarian topics mentioned in the preface to the 1837 *Comic* show close familiarity with the English scene, but the preface also serves as a reminder that not all his work for the *Comics* was of a nature "to furnish forth a little harmless amusement for the Christmas Fireside." Even his son Tom, editing his father's collected works in the 1860's, expressed surprise at the "numerous articles, some more or less of a political tendency—an unusual quality in my father's writings." [43] In actual fact, despite the preface's boldness, only a few poems deal directly with a political or social theme.

"Agricultural Distress" is a most unfunny poem. Drawing on the *Athenaeum's* reports about the series of bad harvests that culminated in 1836, Hood hoped that "like the report of a gun, . . . [it] will serve to startle the deep silence that has brooded over the

Parliamentary Enquiry on the same subject." [44] He graphically
depicts the injustices farm laborers and tenant farmers had to
undergo: gentry ruining the fields by hunting in the harvest season, cattle let to graze in the wheat, pigs given hay to eat, victimi-
zation by shrewd townsmen in selling farm products. For balance,
Hood includes a few merely humorous "distresses." But none of
the indignities match in humiliation the ultimate "distress" that
surpasses and comprises them all: the *"Farming of the Poor!"*

Besides "Agricultural Distress," several other poems in the 1837
Comic Annual reveal Hood's unease: "Drinking Song" and "Ode
to Doctor Hahnemann, The Homœopathist." "Drinking Song, by
a Member of the Temperance Society . . ." parades a hearty use of
traditional drinking-song themes and meters—but apostrophizes
water. In it temperance society cant receives rough handling. From
boisterous German *Trinklieder* heard in the Coblenz streets, Hood
no doubt drew inspiration:

> Come, pass round the pail, boys, and give it no quarter,
> Drink deep, and drink oft, and replenish your jugs.
>
>   .   .   .   .
>
> See drinkers of water, their wits never lacking,
> Direct as a railroad and smooth in their gaits;
> But look at the bibbers of wine, they go tacking,
> Like ships that have met a foul wind in the *straits.*
>   Then hey for a bucket, a bucket, a bucket,
>   Then hey for a bucket, filled up to the brim!
> Or, best of all notions, let's have it by oceans,
> With plenty of room for a sink or a swim! [45]

Nor was this the first occasion that Hood and temperance reformers had crossed swords. A poem in the 1833 *Comic Annual,*
the "Ode to Admiral Lord Gambier, G.C.B.," had in a good-
humored yet essentially serious way attacked the reformers of the
Temperance Society. Undistinguished in his naval career, Gambier
had shown new zeal in the cause of temperance reform. The "Ode"
was undoubtedly inspired by this observation—Hood cited it as
one of the poem's mottoes—in the *Temperance Society's Herald:*

"Well, if you reclaim such as Hood, your Society will deserve the thanks of the country." [46] Not the man to take kindly to slurs on his personal habits, Hood responded coyly: "Oh! Admiral Gam— I dare not mention *bier* / In such a temperate ear. . . ." [47] Two years later the poet returned to the attack in the *Comic Annual* of 1835 with the "Ode to J. S. Buckingham, Esq., M.P. On the Report of the Committee on Drunkenness." Complete with an elaborate set of footnotes, the poem ends thanking "the Committee for their Report. . . ." The "moral" Hood draws states his future position:

> *That men are brothers,*
> *And those who make a fuss,*
> *About their Temperance thus,*
> *Are not so much more temperate than others.* [48]

It was a battle of long standing.

Though Hood, a wine-devotee, recognized that everyone should have freedom to determine his life's beliefs, still, excess, even in relatively harmless forms, always irritated him. He reacted strongly to infractions of the "mean"—a mean dictated by common sense— in regard to drink, religion, medicine, and politics. The reaction varied: humorous in "Drinking Song," ironic in the odes to Gambier and Buckingham, uncompromisingly earnest in the "Ode to Rae Wilson, Esq." of the next year. Furthermore, a combination of several factors determined the kind of poem he wrote: the nature of the offense against "moderation," the extent of its nuisance to him, lastly, the journal in which he published his protest.

The "Ode to Doctor Hahnemann, The Homœopathist" treats morbid aspects of disease and death. Always sick himself, Hood could not be unaware of medical incompetence. After condemning what he thought was quackery, the poet exhorts the medical "tribe" to approach the human body *"with serious fear, / By hands made pure, and hearts of faith severe. . . ."* [49] Near the close of this professedly humorous poem Hood finally admits to "Inserting a few serious words by stealth," and this admission—and practice—

holds true for many other works written during the last decade. Still, most readers would have missed the "moral." The reviewer for the *London and Westminster Review* cites this poem as one "which nineteen out of twenty readers have read merely for the sake of [its] . . . rich fun." [50]

Without "moral" but with characteristic restraint, a poem and a prose tale in the 1837 *Comic Annual* give evidence of Hood's penchant for grotesquerie. "The Desert-Born," one of his many dream poems, plays with the horror or Hoodian pseudo-horror of the grotesque. Fond of using "romantic irony," the poet yet uses it in a way, so far as I know, unique. "The Desert-Born" features a double anticlimax. Although the opening verse paragraphs imply that the narrator is to be awarded an exotic, "desert-born" Arabian maiden, the sad reality is that he gets only a magnificent "mare of milky white!" Taking a wild ride through the desert, horse and rider fail to clear a huge rock and go under:

> Wild shriek'd the headlong Desert-Born—or else 'twas
>   demon's mirth,
> One second more, and Man and Mare roll'd breathless
>   on the earth!

Whether the horse actually "shriek'd," or whether " 'twas demon's mirth"—German supernaturalism would have influenced him here —the reader never learns. At the end the narrator awakes:

> I cursed the hour that brought me first within this
>   world of strife—
> A sore and heavy sin it is to scorn the gift of life—
> But who hath felt a horse's weight oppress his
>   labouring breast?
> Why any who has had, like me, the NIGHT MARE on his
>   chest.[51]

The pun at the close again undercuts the poem's "reality."

In *Don Juan* Byron's romantic irony cut both ways: he developed with care a comic situation, in the midst of which he brought the reader up short with a sober reflection; more often—and Hood is close to him here—he undercut the reality of a serious scene with a final, comic twist. Although Ian Jack suggests that "one of the ways [Hood] uses puns may be regarded as a mode of Tieck's 'romantic irony,' " [52] I find the reference misleading. Tieck in his early novel *William Lovell,* for instance, often addressed the reader in person, wondered if he felt confused at the unexpected entrance of a character, and reminded him he had first introduced the character in a previous scene. Hood's use of romantic irony, however, remains invariably the same: after presenting an apparently

IT'S A MERE FLEA-BITE.

serious poem, often one with supernatural, social, or humanitarian overtones, he undercuts, by a quick pirouette, its reality either with a pun or with a revelation that all has been a dream—or, as in "The Desert-Born," with both. He had a pathological fear of being taken at face value.

In the prose tale "Hitchin Hall" Hood gleefully narrates the adventures of a family who have unknowingly moved into a house ruled by insects. Particularly horrifying is the accompanying wood-cut bearing the caption, "It's a Mere Flea-bite," showing one of the family about to be bitten by a flea the size of the metamorphosed Gregor Samsa in Kafka's *Die Verwandlung*.[53] Like "The Desert-Born," this *comédie noire* tale comes equipped with a "reasonable" ending; it did not, however, as the poem apparently did, have its origin in one of the poet's own vivid dreams.

Spending much of his time working on *Up the Rhine*, Hood faced the prospect of another long winter in Coblenz with gloom. He recuperated slowly from his attacks of spitting blood and hardly stirred from the house. Attacks came at about six-month intervals: the first had come upon him in August of 1835; he had a second, more severe, in February of 1836, eight months before the march to Berlin; a third felled him upon his return; in February of the next year, 1837, came still another. The vicissitudes of the Rhineland climate, freezing winters that melted rapidly into torrid summers, proved his severest trial. In addition, the draft-filled house gave him rheumatism. The poor health that pursued Hood throughout the long winter months ended the hope he once had of visiting Franck in Bromberg. In a melancholy mood he reminisced to his old comrade-in-arms of past trout campaigns: "It is miserable work . . . to be such a shattered old fellow as I am. . . ." [54] All exertion brought pain; he could hardly summon up the strength to write old friends. Looking back upon his fishing expeditions with Franck and the glorious march to Berlin as dreams already well in the past, he became convinced that another winter and summer in Coblenz would finish him.

The last winter of his stay in Germany provided the occasion for Hood to write "Copyright and Copywrong," three long "letters" in favor of changes in the copyright laws. Published consecutively in the *Athenaeum* of April 15, 22, and 29, 1837, they lent support to bills introduced by Thomas Noon Talfourd in the House of Commons to obtain better legal protection for authors, including a sixty-year copyright.[55] Not able to move the House on this occasion, Talfourd failed in his attempt.

Hood's philosophy of fair play in all human relations shows to good advantage in his confident belief in the worth of the literary profession and in his resigned acceptance of its pitfalls. "Literary property," he affirmed, "is the lowest on the market. It is declared by law only worth so many years' purchase, after which the private right becomes common; and in the meantime, the state being notoriously infested with poachers, is as remarkably unprotected by game laws." [56] Both the lack of international copyright regulations and the insufficiency of legal protection within England to guard against literary pirates hurt a struggling author like Hood more than they did writers like Bulwer and, later, Dickens. Though affected by pirates, they still earned ample revenues from authorized editions of their works. Hood did not. If copyright protection had given him a fair share of the income from the American sales of his books, his financial position would have been greatly relieved.

Hood returned throughout the letters to a favorite theme: the need for literary men to maintain their independence. Although he praised the Literary Fund, set up to aid authors in financial straits (and he later would have recourse to its generosity), he implied that "the truly abject state of Literature may be gathered from the fact, that ... a proposal has lately been brought forward for the erection of almhouses for paupers of 'learning and genius,' who have fallen into the sere and yellow leaf, under the specious name of Literary *Retreats*." [57] Using the punning style never altogether absent from his serious work, he barely contained his sarcasm when he insisted that corrective measures would eliminate any need to establish such houses. "I do hope ... that the legislature will interfere, and endeavour to provide better for our sere and yellow leaves, by protecting our black and white ones. Let the law secure to us a fair chance of getting our own, and perhaps, with proper industry, we may be able—who knows?— to build little snuggeries for ourselves." [58] His long years spent earning a living for himself and his family by his pen had brought him, he believed, the understanding to speak with authority on the position of literary men.

The low status of literature in society led Hood to protest the "marked disproportion, as compared with other professions, in the number of literary men who are selected for public honors and employment" [59]—a neglect he traced solely to their being poor. After examining charges often leveled against authors—eccentricity, improvidence, "want of principle, and offences against morality and religion"—he refused to plead guilty. "Literary men, as a body," he claimed with rare boldness, "will bear comparison in point of conduct with any other class." [60]

As prose, "Copyright and Copywrong" is uneven, the argument more felt than logically thought out. Throughout, Hood wrote in the spirit of an independent, professional man of letters. In their idealism the Copyright Letters reveal his quixotic unconcern—or unawareness—that society runs on economic wheels. That in his sickbed he took time away from precious working hours to write them does indicate the importance he attached to a just copyright law. Although he did not expect the letters to have much effect, he noted with pleasure a few months later that they had "made quite a stir in the literary world of London." [61] A sincere believer in literature as a moral and educational force, Hood rises to eloquence when he comes to record his own debt,

a debt so immense, as not to be cancelled, like that of nature, by death itself. I owe to it something more than my earthly welfare. Adrift early in life upon the great waters—as pilotless as Wordsworth's blind boy on the turtle-shell—if I did not come to shipwreck, it was, that in default of paternal or fraternal guidance, I was rescued, like the ancient mariner, by guardian spirits, "each one a lovely light," who stood as beacons to my course. Infirm health, and a natural love of reading, happily threw me, instead of worse society, into the company of poets, philosophers, and sages—to me good angels and ministers of grace. From these silent instructors . . . I learned something of the divine, and more of the human religion. They were my interpreters in the House Beautiful of God, and my guides along the Delectable Mountains of Nature.[62]

During 1836 Jane and Thomas Hood had often expressed a desire to return in the next year to England. But several factors, while forcing a change of residence, combined to prevent the much hoped-for return home. Although the Hoods had economized in Coblenz, they had not saved enough to pay their English debts. Furthermore, during the unusually severe winter of 1836–1837, Hood's health suffered greatly. Never admitted as such, another, perhaps the determining factor—intellectual and social isolation—reinforced their decision to leave Coblenz. The Hoods, therefore, decided to seek a residence more economical and healthful—and closer to England. Their choice fell on Ostend. Only a day or two's distance by post from London, it also lay within easy traveling range. On the sea, from earliest youth a source of health, Hood felt confident of a more tonic climate. In a long letter to Dr. Elliot he depicted the twin agonies of conscience and malady that haunted the "eight month winter":

But meaning to do that which is honourable & right—with the consciousness of doing all I could—& the confidence that my case was not irretrievable my heart has never acquiesced in melancholy attacks—tho I have had to struggle against the want of society & books. It has been much against my rallying in health, that the attacks have so abridged my time that when tolerably well I have had to work unremittingly to make up for lost time—& this haste adds much to the mental wear & tear. Whilst every delay was a positive loss as to the sale of my books. The long passages of parcels to & fro on the Rhine were also sources of great vexation anxiety & urgency, six weeks, each way, cutting deeply into the time for drawing printing & engraving.[63]

Spring brought some cheer to the Hood household. Still weak from his illnesses, Hood yet walked and fished on sunny days. Now that he had more than a nodding acquaintance with horses, he occasionally went riding, though he did not dare attempt anything that demanded excessive strain. With three other lives dependent on his health and totally without provision should he die, Hood could not afford another relapse.

Although he several times expressed to John Wright his hope of publishing *Up the Rhine* by the end of the year, his optimism exceeded his capabilities. He reported in an April letter to Franck that "the materials of my book are in London, so let the Rhinelanders look out for squalls." [64] But as his "German book" did not come out until over two years later, the squalls remained on the horizon. Proposing for himself the goal of once and for all learning German, he set up an ambitious study program, but lacking energy and time he went no further than the taking of a few lessons. In the end, then, Hood never realized his hopes with German. If he ever knew the language well enough to read it with ease, he would have known it by the end of his two-year stay in the Rhineland. A letter to Wright of April 30, 1837, less than six weeks before he left Germany forever, records the failure:

> I have been trying to learn German, but it is very hard, I am too deaf to catch the pronunciation, and when I do, can't imitate it. And the grammar is hard, and the construction too. The Germans are fond of long-winded sentences; and as the verb comes at the end, you're very much bothered. [65]

Plans to leave Coblenz matured by late spring. Reluctant to abandon lodgings leased through July 15, the Hoods kept putting off their departure date. Last-minute vexations—settlements with the landlord, with rapacious local merchants, and with "Kätchen" the maid—led to Hood's final disenchantment, provoking him to exclaim, "I left not a single friend or acquaintance worth a sigh." [66]

The Hoods left Coblenz on June 10. After a steamer trip down the Rhine to Cologne, they took on the next day the coach to Aachen; the third day brought them to Liège in Belgium. "You will not be surprised to hear," wrote a gleeful Hood to Dr. Elliot, "that as soon as I found that we were out of Prussia I threw up all our caps hats & bonnets with a mental vow never to enter the dominions of Frederick William again.... Coblenz I was particularly glad to turn my back upon—for it was associated with nothing but illness, suffering, privation, disgust, & vexation of spirit." [67] But to the last, as much as he continued to find the people unbearable, his memories of the Rhine landscape retained the glory and the freshness of his first enthusiasm. "And yet, oh yet when I look at the Rhine, it *is* a lovely country, and I love the beautiful." [68]

The weather along the road proved excellent and the trip passed without mishap or severe inconvenience. At Liège, after a

COUNTRY QUARTERS.

long, hot day in the carriage, the Hoods rested at the home of a M. Nagelmacher, whose French-speaking household Hood described as "one of the most amiable and accomplished families I ever met with." [69] In two more days they reached Brussels. While their parents took a day's rest, Fanny and young Tom went to see the Gothic cathedral of St. Gudule. Spending the next night at Ghent, the Hoods, after passing through picturesque Bruges by barge, gained Ostend by nightfall of the nineteenth. Hood and Jane were greatly fatigued by their ten-day journey, but the children came through the experience "as fresh as larks." Too tired to go sight-seeing along the way, the poet yet retained vivid impressions of Flemish towns encircled by lush green countryside and long cherished a desire to explore Flanders at more leisure. Comfortably settled in lodgings at 39, rue Longue, relaxing in the bracing sea air, he summed up bitterly his two years on the Rhine: "In short with cheating & downright thieving I doubt whether we have economized much.... Indeed the last two years have been as twenty to me in effect, and I almost feel as if on the strength of my weakness, I could give advice & dictate to young men, who were born no later than myself." [70]

Chapter 2

Ostend

England's closeness reassured Hood, contributing in no small measure to his happiness. With two years of living in a foreign land behind him, he adjusted readily to the Belgian fishing port. For one thing he expected less. As his high hopes that life abroad would solve all problems had died their necessary death, he shed with pleasure the lightly worn mantle of cosmopolitanism of his first months in Coblenz. "There is a great deal of this Citizen of the worldship professed now a days," he wrote Dr. Elliot soon after arrival in Ostend, "in return for which I think the English only get ridiculed by foreigners as imbeciles & dupes. Overweening nationality is an absurdity—but the absence of it altogether is a sort of crime." [1] The poetry Hood wrote abroad suggests that his foreign sojourn intensified both his native Englishness and his interest in English society. "In the same circumstance of exile they reinforce their character by memories of the life they have left," wrote T. E. Lawrence of travelers like Charles M. Doughty in Arabia; "In reaction against their foreign surroundings they take refuge in the England that was theirs." [2] Hood's foreign stay, like Doughty's, brought out the most English side of his character. His conduct typifies that of a certain kind of Englishman abroad.

In late June, 1837, not only did balmy days and quick communications between Ostend and his native land hold forth the promise of hope, but Hood hoped also to recoup his fortunes. "To the present time," he wrote Dr. Elliot,

> I have only the negative comfort of not having receded in my circumstances—should the new Copyright Act pass I have perhaps acquired something though not immediately available—but as I have before now made as much in one year as would cancel all my liabilities, I see no reason to despair of yet returning to England (health allowing) in a year or two a free man. I feel sure but for illness I should ere now have been so

—& perhaps now the sea, as it has done formerly will give me strength. And if I could but once begin to *cancel*—I believe it would do more for me than climate diet or anything else. In the mean time I have English-like comforts round me—my wife's care never fails—& my children are an amusement & relaxation to me. I draw & write with relish when well enough—& have a decently clear conscience & an old reliance in Providence.[3]

Hood did not return to England because he could not; "the truth is," he affirmed, "I must not be in England but at the same time within easy & quick communication with it." If he returned, he would either have to pay his creditors or find men who would guarantee his financial integrity—or go to jail for debt. Pride insisted he attempt the first solution; a physical collapse in 1840 dictated the second; the third he hoped always to avoid. For the time being, unwilling and unable to face harassment by creditors, he found life abroad, even with its discomforts, preferable. And compared to the advantages, the discomforts hardly counted.

Hood was content in Ostend. Perhaps because "the natives" spoke English, he found them "civil and obliging, and not malicious, like the Rhinelanders." [4] Established in lodgings that, costing but £4 more per year than in Coblenz, provided "£50 worth more of English-like comforts, great and small," he relished daily the bracing sea breeze that had often in past times restored his health. "The Esplanade is very fine," he wrote John Wright, "and the sands famous for our brats, who delight in them extremely. We munch shrimps morning and night, as they are very abundant, and quite revel in the fish." [5] Famished to read English books after a two-year fast, both Hoods went through a local lending library's entire stock in a month. Even work was not forgotten. He recorded great strides on the new *Comic Annual* and, still hopeful for early publication, on *Up the Rhine*.

The "Ode to Rae Wilson, Esq." appeared in the *Athenaeum* of August 12, 1837, less than two months after Hood's arrival in

Ostend. A wealthy and pious Scot, Rae Wilson wrote up his travel experiences in windy, forgotten books that glorified the narrowest Protestantism. Delighting in using Hood's works as exemplars of the profaneness and ribaldry of the age, this self-appointed guardian of the public morality took especial offense at lines in "The Blue Boar" of Hood's last *Comic Annual*. They concern a sow from whose jaws "A sprout of cabbage, green and raw, / Protruded,—as the Dove, so stanch / For Peace, supports an olive branch. . . ." [6] Wilson, interpreting the "Dove" to represent the Divine Spirit, deemed the simile irreverent—another of Hood's "horribly indecent allusions to Holy Writ." [7] The poet claimed he meant the dove as "a lay representative of the peace of this world, and as such, [it] has figured time out of mind in allegorical pictures. . . ." [8] Though the simile itself is ridiculous and meant to be, the context supports Hood.

It was not the first time he had aroused Wilson's ire. Whenever a well-meant, yet hopelessly narrow-minded measure having to do with religious freedom was put before Parliament, Hood reacted by penning a poem or "ode" to its sponsor. Several poems of the 1830's—the "Ode to Sir Andrew Agnew, Bart.," the "Ode to Spencer Perceval, M.P.," and "A Charity Sermon"—serve as prelude to the "Ode to Rae Wilson, Esq.," which in turn looks forward to "An Open Question" of 1840. Paladin of Evangelicalism and Member of Parliament, Agnew four times sponsored a "Lord's Day Observance Bill," a bill that, designed "to prevent all manner of work on the Lord's day," would indirectly favor the well-to-do. For his religious intolerance Hood administers him a firm chiding in the "Ode to Sir Andrew Agnew, Bart.":

Religion one should never overdo:
Right glad I am no minister you be,
For you would say your service, sir, to me,
Till I should say, "My service, sir, to you."
Six days made all that is, you know, and then,
Came that of rest, by holy ordination,
As if to hint unto the sons of men,
After creation should come re-creation.

Right read this text, and do not further search
To make a Sunday Workhouse of the Church.[9]

This position of tolerance the poet held the rest of his life. The poem—especially the line, "After creation should come re-creation" —drew Wilson's fire in his *Records of a Route through France and Italy, with Sketches of Catholicism* (1835), where the Scot berated Hood thus: "I wonder what Johnson would have said of the man who could utter, not only so despicable, but so truly infamous a pun as that." [10] But in the 1834 *Comic Annual*, where the poem appeared, Hood had announced in the preface his intention, "as usual," of "mingling a little instruction with amusement." And he was as good as his word. Defending himself against the objection that his "pages swarm with puns," he affirmed his intention to "persist in using the double barrel as long as meanings will rise in coveys." [11]

The year before Spencer Perceval had been Hood's Evangelical bugbear. A Member of Parliament, Perceval had

made himself notorious by a motion in the House of Commons [January 26, 1832] for presenting an humble address to the King, to order a day for a general fast and humiliation. . . . Mr. Perceval delivered himself of an harangue, in which he denounced his brethren in the House as "infidels all"—denounced the "blasphemous proposition to admit the Jew into this House"—and predicted the fate of Sodom and Gomorrah upon all Christendom. He read copious extracts from the Bible in illustration of his views, and described himself as speaking in the name of the Lord.[12]

Hood, of course, could not let such an opportunity slip by. Wasting no time, he had soon "delivered himself," in turn, of the "Ode to Spencer Perceval, M.P.," published in the *Athenaeum* on February 18, 1832. Speaking in the name of common humanity, he concluded punningly but forcefully:

Whatever others do,—or don't,
I cannot—dare not—must not fast, and won't,

Unless by night your day you let me keep,
And *fast* asleep;
My constitution can't obey such censors:
must have meat
Three times a-day to eat;
My health's of such a sort,—
To say the truth, in short,
The *coats* of my stomach are not *Spencers!* [13]

In regard to both Agnew and Perceval silence would, perhaps, have
been the better part of discretion, but discretion was never Hood's

THE HOUSE OF COMMONS.

forte. And to make matters worse he published the Perceval ode
in the *Athenaeum*—"a journal which," Alfred Ainger notes, "had
uniformly rated Mr. Wilson's productions at their true value." [14]
When Wilson attacked again it seemed only natural that Hood
should turn once more to its hospitable pages.

Hood's writings, a random glance shows, manifest abundant disgust with cant, abundant hatred of bigotry. Deep-rooted, of long
standing, this disgust and hatred first arose when, living in his

youth in Scotland with his father's family, he had come into close, unpleasant association with the "unco guid." His Scottish aunt was an especially rabid Sabbatarian. Time had not tempered the smug belief of the "Rigidly Righteous," as Burns called them, in their absolute election—that inner assurance of salvation which another Scot, James Hogg, had satirized with such ferocity in *The Private Memoirs and Confessions of a Justified Sinner.* In later years, Hood's two surviving sisters, Jessie and Elizabeth, became infected with the Evangelical virus. But it was, Ainger observes, against a "vulgar Pharisaism," "a decadent species" of the Evangelical faith that he revolted; "he shared the mistake . . . of confounding the narrowest and most bigoted section of the party with the party as a whole." [15] Nor was Hood himself without prejudice: his Rhineland sojourn had turned him against Catholicism. But true *"divines"* he valued, he once averred to Mrs. Dilke, "especially if they are not attached to any particular church or chapel. . . ." [16] General disgust with Evangelicalism and "Christian Charity" prompted "A Charity Sermon." It reveals the depth of his disillusionment:

> Well, I've utterly done with Charity, though I us'd so to
>   preach about its finest fount;
> Charity may do for some that are more lucky, but *I* can't
>   turn it to any account—
> It goes so the very reverse way—even if one chirrups it up
>   with a dust of piety;
> That henceforth let it be understood, I take my name en-
>   tirely out of the List of Subscribers to the Humane
>   Society.
>   Oh, Charity will come home to roost—
>   Like curses and chickens is Charity.[17]

If Evangelical "Charity" led to Heaven's doors, if "Holy Willie's Prayer" found answer, Hood wanted his "name entirely out."

No contemporary vice aroused him more deeply than religious fanaticism. If high spirits dominate the volumes of the 1820's, they often gave way in the *Comic Annuals* of the 1830's to astringent social criticism. In "The Sweep's Complaint" the downtrodden sweep questions why "Christian laws should be ten times more hard than the old stone laws of Moses." [18] And in 1836, casting about for political and social topics, Hood thought of resurrecting old friends: "At the same hour, whilst I was writing in deprecation of Sabbath-Bills [Andrew Agnew], and Parliamentary Piety [Spencer Perceval]—Sir Andrew had, perchance, embraced Judaism, and exchanged Sunday for Saturday." [19] By 1837 the glass had darkened still further: long in genesis, serious in intent, the satire in the "Ode to Rae Wilson" takes on a somber hue. It is direct, uncompromising. Though Hood never approaches the *sæva Indignatio* or deep pessimism of a Swift, it was not because he did not despair; rather, his "sympathy with his fellow man was too deep." [20] Wilson's latest attack provided Hood's mind with the fillip it needed to crystallize: the "Ode" was the result.

The poem's strength lies in its clear-eyed depiction of the unsavory religious atmosphere:

> Censors who sniff out mortal taints
> And call the devil over his own coals—
> Those pseudo Privy Councillors of God.

A man of different stamp, Hood proudly declares, "Of such a character no single trace / Exists . . . in my fictitious face." He affirms his own credo:

> Well!—be the graceless lineaments confest!
> I do enjoy this bounteous beauteous earth;
>   And dote upon a jest
> "Within the limits of becoming mirth;"—
> No solemn sanctimonious face I pull,
> Nor think I'm pious when I'm only bilious—
> Nor study in my sanctum supercilious
> To frame a Sabbath Bill or forge a Bull.
> I pray for grace—repent each sinful act—
> Peruse, but underneath the rose, my Bible;
> And love my neighbour far too well, in fact,

To call and twit him with a godly tract
That's turn'd by application to a libel.
My heart ferments not with the bigot's leaven,
All creeds I view with toleration thorough,
And have a horror of regarding heaven
As anybody's rotten borough.[21]

Though "d—— canters" might wish otherwise, Hood insisted that
everyone should enjoy freedom of worship. Nor could one serve
both God and Mammon. "Rogue that I am," he has one "canter"
say, "I lie—I cheat—do anything for pelf, / But who on earth can
say I am not pious?" That Hood proclaimed wide toleration and
the right to have a personal relationship with God confers upon
him the mantle of a religious "liberal." And his "liberal" views undoubtedly gave his more pious contemporaries the impression they
had a freethinker on their hands, an unbeliever even. Thus the
many attacks he underwent from such "self-constituted saints" as
Rae Wilson. The following lines, innocent as they are, would have
struck many as unchristian:

Yet I am none of those, who think it odd
A man can pray unbidden from the cassock,
And, passing by the customary hassock,
Kneel down remote upon the simple sod,
And sue in formâ pauperis to God.[22]

Similarly in politics. Hood declared in "Rae Wilson": "no part
I take in party fray." But he only half meant it. Although in his
public utterances he refused to support the political goals of either
party, in his private correspondence he voiced views distinctly
"liberal." He frequently expressed the wish to see a national party
rule England. "For my part," he told Wright in October, 1837, "I
say, hang party!" "There wants a true *country party* to look singly
to the good of England—retrench and economise, reduce taxes,
and make it possible to live as cheap at home as abroad. *There*
would be patriotism, instead of a mere struggle of Ins and Outs
for place and pelf." [23]

Preaching of one kind or another distinguishes Victorian England; a moral earnestness accompanies all activity. "A Ruskin *preaches* art as well as industrial and economic morality," writes John Dodds. "Dickens is much concerned with the moral effect of his writing. Even a Thackeray can think of a novelist as a 'weekday preacher.' " [24] Sermons—listened to conscientiously, repeated at home, sometimes even memorized—influenced, in turn, Victorian literature. One poet, Thomas Cooper, even wrote "secular" hymns, modeled upon those sung at religious services, to further the Chartist cause.[25] Though no writer of hymns, Thomas Hood did believe in "lay" sermons. Many of his poems have an implicit ethical content, some close with an explicit moral. To clinch his argument in the "Ode to Rae Wilson, Esq.," he appends to it "a tale / Whereto is tied a moral." But for his "moral" poetry, tolerant Hood was, however, judged "immoral" by intolerant Evangelicals; "Rae Wilson" was, his son noted, "one of the results of a blind and unrelenting persecution, to which my father was life-long subjected, and which drew from him those few really bitter bursts of indignation at cant and hypocrisy. . . ." [26] And in their virulence Hood's "bitter bursts of indignation" scarcely yield to those of Blake, who, too, deplored the "thou shalt not" he found in the midst of "the Garden of Love."

Religion, because it pervaded all walks of Victorian society, caused untold personal anguish for many. But for many others, secure in the belief they were destined for Salvation, their faith led to sordid—though often unconscious—cultivation of hypocrisy. This hypocrisy and the resultant abuses disgusted Hood. He refused to let the narrow-minded impose their gloomy precepts upon all England. Belonging to the third of England that did not attend Sunday church services, he considered himself not less a Christian than those who did. Such a practice and a belief Evangelicals thought immoral. In many Victorian circles, the "proper test of the reality of a man's Christianity" in the century's second quarter, G. Kitson Clark observes, was to ascertain "whether he was a total abstainer and not whether he was charitable, or even just, to his opponents, or merciful to the fallen." [27] No "total abstainer" but always "charitable," Hood insisted on the primacy of justice and mercy. Fighting for them in "Rae Wilson," he affirmed there his belief that men of sense valued humane qualities above mechanical church attendance, above self-righteous indignation at humor, above the simple-minded belief that total abstention from alcohol marked the true believer. Hood's "Ode," though drawing from Wilson's attack its fire and point of focus, compels our interest for its sane defense of tolerance amidst Victorian intolerance. Successful in publicly humbling Wilson, the poem earned Hood recognition for the courage of his stand; even Baily, his publisher, wrote, "I have heard everywhere spoken of your . . . Rae Wilson." [28]

A month later Hood once again had to defend himself. *The Times* of September 12, 1837, provided him with diversion of a most exasperating kind: "Domestic Poetry: Petition to Her Majesty for Preserving the Royal Stud at Hampton Court," a satiric poem against the Whigs, reprinted from a magazine called *The Torch*, by "Thomas Hood." Not the author, Hood got "very much annoyed at that dammd Torch business." "It is too bad," he wrote Wright, "I that have not meddled with politics on my own account—& to be made to abuse *my own side!* . . ." [29] Unafraid of personal attacks from those Tories who "will sink of themselves at last from sheer want of character and principle," he yet felt dismay at both the forgery and the brazen use of his name.

> I like these money-turning Whigs, indeed;
> Who into coin change every thing they're able.
> You're [Queen Victoria] just installed, and they
>   would sell *the steed*—
> It doesn't make me think they're very *stable.*

The "dear lady" is then urged: "Kick out your Ministers and keep your bloods!" Favorable to the new queen,[30] Hood sent off with alacrity a denial—duly printed in the September 22 issue—of "one

of those forgeries which are a disgrace to the age and the country."
The Times's editor apologized, but claimed he had reprinted the
verses in good faith. Nor did he scruple to disparage: "The verses
in the *Torch* are as good as Mr. Hood usually produces of the
kind, while the puns in the above letter are not much worse than
those he is accustomed to publish with the sanction of his name."
A magnificent summer helped Hood rapidly complete the new
Comic Annual. The woodcuts finished "as easily as ever I did,"
manuscripts followed faster than Wright could acknowledge them.
For once the annual labor that was the *Comic* did not prostrate
him: "I am still fresh & full of running & in good spirits." By
November Wright had received all the manuscripts; the end of
the month found the new *Comic* on the bookstalls. In its second
notice (December 2) the *Athenaeum* reviewer found it, expectedly,
"as good as ever." Markedly different from its predecessor, the
1838 *Comic* reflects Hood's present happiness and health in
Ostend. No bitterness scars the humor; didacticism, "The Carnaby
Correspondence" excepted, comes rarely into evidence. Hood
amply redeems his pledge in the preface "to furnish forth a little
harmless amusement for the Christmas fireside." [31]

The lead article, "The Carnaby Correspondence," demonstrates
through a "factitious correspondence" "the inefficiency of certain establishments where Young Gentlemen are 'boarded, lodged,
and done for.' " Both it and another article, "Animal Magnetism,"
Hood wrote from "the same desire of being useful." [32] Aping with
verve the styles of an illiterate father, his eccentric sailor-brother,
a pompous schoolmaster hiding ignorance behind pedantry, and
the budding rake of a youngster himself, he spins a fascinating
yarn of educational and other incompetence. His "Literary Reminiscences," written the next year, shows that memories of his own
education still rankled. "The Carnaby Correspondence" he admitted he wrote "partly because the important subject of Education has become of prominent interest, and partly to hint that a
writer may often mean in earnest what he says in jest." [33] "Here,
to our thinking," wrote Henry Chorley in the *London and Westminster Review*, "is as pertinent and emphatic an argument for the

normal school system as many which have been spun out into pamphlets, or evaporated into speeches." One shocked reader, convinced by his didactic purpose, wrote the poet he had withdrawn his son from school. Hood had succeeded to an unlooked-for degree.

Year after year the *Comic Annuals* maintained a steady sale. After the first in 1830 had enjoyed exceptional success, sales of each successive volume of the English edition ran to a thousand or fifteen hundred copies. Yet, meant for a family audience, the *Comics* had a readership of at least several times that number. Though considerable, American sales—because of the lack of international copyright regulations—brought him nothing. A popular writer in an age that favored popular writers, Hood did not gain great fame until the publication in *Punch*'s Christmas, 1843, number of "The Song of the Shirt." Persons of responsibility often found his comic volumes pleasant reading: in England Sir Robert Peel told him he had read almost every one; in Germany the aristocratic Radziwill family, he learned, had enjoyed several of them and had even read *Tylney Hall*; in America his light verse helped Abraham Lincoln relax from presidential cares. A moralist to society, even if read primarily for his puns and domestic humor, the poet himself attached highest importance to what he said "in earnest."

"Pray congratulate Moxon for me on having an article on his sonnets in the 'Quarterly,'" Hood wrote Wright, "where I have never had a line though I write odes!" [34] Critical neglect from the arbiters of taste may have stemmed from the belief that he lacked seriousness. Nor did the uneven quality of his annual volumes facilitate the task of a reviewer disposed to attempt an evaluation. But that "the leading reviews, Whig and Tory," disdained to recognize his work, Hood always attributed to political prejudice. Unwilling throughout his career to associate his name with a political party, he accepted without complaint the consequences thereof. Refusal to review his work, he remarked to Franck in 1838, "is funny enough in professedly *literary* reviews, and shows they are practically political ones. And the result is, I am going, I under-

stand, to be reviewed by the *Radical* review, and, I hear, favourably." [35]

The *Comic* off his hands, Hood turned to a new project: *Hood's
Own*—"not my wife, but a reissue of the *Comic*." In October,
when Wright wrote suggesting to him a republication of the contents of past *Comics* "with an infusion of new blood," he had
pricked Hood's interest. "Such an idea as a periodical," replied
Hood, "it would have been impossible at Coblenz to entertain for
a moment," in view of the bad communications with London and
"from sheer mistrust of my health." [36] Though doubtful he could
get out the first of the monthly installments by January, Hood
considered the project sound—but only if his health bore the
monthly strain. Wright stilling his remaining doubts in a November trip to Ostend, Hood decided to come secretly to London
after Christmas to prepare the first numbers. "Please God I
be well the next year ensuing, the 'Comic' will take up but one-
quarter of my time, and I must have some work cut out for the
rest." [37] Hoping to attract the "tarnation powerful large class"
who would put down a shilling a month while hesitating to lay
down twelve at once for a *Comic Annual*, Hood hoped to recoup
both fortunes and native land. True to principle, he insisted quality
remain the determining factor: "I do not think I fall off, and have
no misgivings about over-writing myself; one cannot do too much
if it be well done; and I never care to turn out anything that does
not please myself." [38] Convinced he could do as well or better
than before, he faced his future with optimism.

Christmas Day he spent with his family; then he took the
packet for London—his first return to native soil in nearly three
years. There as the Dilkes' guest he completed final arrangements
for *Hood's Own*. Though up each morning until one or two preparing the first numbers with Wright and Baily, he led otherwise a cloistered existence, "never stirr[ing] out the whole time."
"The stake was so great," he wrote his sister Elizabeth after his

return to Ostend, "that the utmost secrecy was necessary." He feared recognition by creditors; but, in order not to give literary "pirates" advance notice, he also wanted to keep news of *Hood's Own* from getting afoot. "Arrangements are making to enable me to come over openly when business requires," he explained to "Betsy," "tho we shall continue to reside here, both to save money & to suit my health." The sale of the *Comic* just sufficing to cover yearly expenditure, he had not thus far been able to economize on the Continent. But in the interval, he noted with relief, "no fresh debt." [39]

Between preparing *Hood's Own* and going over three years' accounts with Baily, Hood found time to get a thorough examination from Dr. Elliot. Confirming a new diagnosis made by an Ostend doctor, Elliot identified the seat of trouble as an enlarged liver, not, as Hood had feared, the lungs. If the blood-spitting had come from the lungs, he told Franck, "my death-warrant was signed...." [40] Ill six months out of twelve since he came abroad, unwell the other six, Hood had until now reserved his full energy for the *Comic*. But upon his return from London he felt he could entertain ambitious plans in regard to both *Hood's Own* and the neglected *Up the Rhine*. Ostend's calm he appreciated more after the fatigue and strain he had undergone in London: "It must be something very tempting to make me go to London as yet; it would kill me in a month. Indeed I am better already for being back." [41]

The January and February numbers of *Hood's Own* came out on schedule and sold well. But the poet, seriously ill in February, failed to meet the March deadline. "All Tuesday [February 20] Hood had been in such an exhausted state he was obliged to go to bed," Jane Hood informed Mrs. Dilke,

but I was up all night, ready to write at his dictation if he felt able; but it was so utter a prostration of strength, that he could hardly speak, much less use his head at all. The doctor said it was extreme exhaustion, from the cold weather, want of air and exercise, acted upon by great anxiety of mind and nervousness.[42]

After the post had left, releasing the pressure on his mind, Hood's anguish ceased. Surviving a few late numbers, *Hood's Own* prospered. When he heard it got notices "frequent and favourable," Hood asked Wright if Baily had made efforts to push the sale. "There are plenty of English to buy *cheap* books," he claimed, "and with so many cuts, it cannot be pirated." [43]

"I only want health at present to be very comfortable," Hood wrote Dr. Elliot during the winter of 1837–1838, "and for the time being, I am better where I am than in London. I have as much cut out for me as I can do; and am quiet here, and beyond temptation of society and late hours, living well, and cheaply to boot." [44] A bottle of French wine a week brought ruddiness back to his cheeks, but he did not overindulge. Though friends sent him English books, most news about home he got either from the *Athenaeum* or from infrequent copies of *The Times*. Jane had had a miscarriage in November, 1837; severely ill for three weeks afterwards, she had now fully recovered. About this time George Robert Lewis came to Ostend to paint Hood's portrait. The poet liked the result; friends, sent copies of the engraving made from it, agreed with him that it was an excellent likeness. He is dressed in his usual black, and only the twinkling eyes and the smile twitching at the corners of his mouth indicate his humorous nature.

Despite Ostend's proximity to England the Hoods found themselves almost as isolated as in Coblenz. Along with other Channel ports, Ostend attracted goodly numbers of "dashing" Englishmen who could not pay their debts: "such English—broken English and bad English—scoundrelly English!" With such an unruly group gossip gyrated in ever larger orbits. "If I were but to put into a novel what passes here," Hood confided to Elliot, "what an outrageous work it would seem." [45] The domestic-minded Hoods, needless to say, kept to themselves.

Hood stayed indoors the whole winter. His lodgings proved adequate, if chilly; but for once landlord and landlady were not impossible. Bitter cold forced him to snuggle next to the fireplace in his snowshoes; "we all but stir the fire with our noses," he told Franck, "and sweep the hearths with our shoes." [46] At this time

Hood sent off two articles for the 1838 *Sporting*, an elegant annual published by Baily and edited by "Nimrod," Charles James Apperley; one he entitled "The Ass Race," the other, amusing testimony both to his admiration of Walton and to his favorite sport, "The Praise of Fishing." [47] During Ostend's carnival, "the Saturnalia of the lowest class," the maid, Mary, staggered home between seven and eight each morning in dismal condition—conduct which brought about her dismissal.

Bruges, fifteen miles distant, the Hoods visited in late spring. The rapidity of a relatively new means of transportation startled them: "We have been up the railway to Bruges in forty-six minutes, Brussels in six hours for nine francs!" [48] In June Jane left for a sojourn with her family in England. When she called on Dr. Elliot and told him Hood's latest symptoms, he confirmed the seriousness of the poet's condition: "But I shall never be strong again—Jane got the verdict of our friend Dr. Elliot, that the danger of the case was gone, but that as I had never been particularly strong and sturdy, I must not now expect to be more than a young old gentleman." [49] A cold, damp summer required a daily fire. Though often ill, several times Hood went out sailing; the fresh air did wonders for him. Once, after a shorter than usual sail in which Jane accompanied him, he reported laconically to Franck that his wife lacked enthusiasm for the sea: "Take me home—set me ashore directly! Oh, I'll never come out with you again! and so forth." [50] He should have remembered the occasion at Ramsgate in 1833: "The Jane (Mrs. Hood) on putting out to sea, was quite upset, and obliged to discharge." [51] Ten days of October sun prompted Hood to exclaim, "I *have not felt* SO WELL FROM THE 1ST JANUARY, *as during the last ten days*." [52] And as the year drew to a close, his health improved further. Both it and work on *Hood's Own* had hindered progress with the new *Comic Annual*, had hindered too "that quiet *fore*-thinking which provided me with subjects." "But," he felt, "I have done wonders on the whole." [53] And so he had.

Thirteen numbers of *Hood's Own*,[54] another *Comic Annual*, enough additional work on *Up the Rhine* that at year's end he

could announce (prematurely it turned out) its completion to
Mrs. Dilke—Hood had accomplished much in 1838. Whenever
he had worked well, new plans bubbled forth in abundance: a
sequel to the still incomplete *Up the Rhine*, a two-volume novel,
perhaps an opera. His health apart, nothing jarring upset him
during this year. But health, to a man who has constantly to suffer
from it, is all-important. The following stanzas in "The Vision,"
the poem that closes the 1839 *Comic Annual*, seem autobiographical:

> Scarce could I contain my rage—
> O'er the retrospective page,
> Looking back from date to date,
> What I owed to Thirty-Eight.
>
> Sickness here and sickness there,
> Pain and sorrow, constant care;
> Fifty-two long weeks to fall
> Nor a trump among them all! [55]

The *Comic Annual* was promised, the *Athenaeum* reported, for
December 29. Ill health, Hood claimed in his "Literary Reminiscences," had retarded it forty days; its completion he considered a
"*lay miracle.*" Staleness had impeded the free flow of ideas; "the
having done it for so many years, and having fired some 700 or 800
shots, makes the birds more rare, *i.e.* cuts and subjects." [56] "Nothing," the preface pointed out, "is more difficult than to address the
public perennially on the same subject." And by the late 1830's
the day of the annuals, introduced into England scarcely fifteen
years before by Ackermann's *Forget Me Not*, had almost waned.
Though in "capital spirits" over the *Comic's* continued success,
Hood doubted he would produce a successor.

The best article in this year's *Comic*, "The Corresponding Club,"
narrates the history of a presumed "revolutionary" group in England
modeled upon the corresponding societies of the early stages of the

French Revolution. In writings that either touched on supernatural themes or implied a questioning of religion we have seen that Hood shied away from facing issues directly. With a political subject we see a similar reluctance to commit himself; the social and political reforms he advocates here he undercuts with an anticlimactic ending. But it is the serious questioning of society found in the first twenty pages of the article that, in my reading, leaves the lasting impression; the final two pages merely reflect Hood's unease, his compulsion to equivocate. At least one contemporary saw the matter behind the "manner":

> We readily admit that the character of Mr. Hood's writings was fun and laughter, and that, as a writer, he was a most facetious one; but we deny that laughter was his only object. He amused the multitude in order to attract their attention; his aim was to make mankind wiser, better, happier; and he made use of his wit and his humour as vehicles wherewith to convey his wholesome and more lasting lessons of morality. The light laugh passed away, but the solid truth remained. Thus many imbibed lessons of kindness and charity, who would have turned away from the inculcator of principles presented with a serious aspect. In truth, Hood was most serious in his purpose when he was most comic in his manner. . . . Thus, in an age of reform, Hood was one of the most effectual of reformers.[57]

We can, therefore, take as valid for much of Hood's later work his own admission "that a writer may often mean in earnest what he says in jest." Realizing this enhances our comprehension of what he tried to do in the only way he knew. And that was, put simply, to focus the attention of his reading public on the injustice prevalent in England. While the narrative in "The Corresponding Club" of a revolt against the existing social and political order is fictitious, it gathers strength when we consider that Hood's advocacy of reform, even if here presented in humorous guise, basically reflects changes he wished for in his society. Though no "revolutionary" himself, he did feel deeply dissatisfied with present English society, and this dissatisfaction had long roots in the past. What differentiates the public poems of the 1840's—like "The Song of the Shirt"—from earlier writings on social questions is that, while in the earlier the "serious" message is often hidden under puns and layers of whimsy, in the later it is not. On every overriding social issue of the day, in the 1830's as well as in the 1840's, Hood expressed views that placed him in the forefront of liberal, on occasion, of radical thought.[58]

"The Corresponding Club"—ironically placed at Stoke Poges, setting of Gray's "Elegy"—opens with dissidents meeting at the local pub to discuss reform. They soon begin to protest the injustices of the times. Though presented humorously, all the protests contain a hard core of truth. One local worthy, noting that "the people had laid down long enough," suggests: "There was no sort of use in getting up petitions—they ought to get up themselves." Another espouses equality; a third defends the rights of the poor; to an enthusiastic audience he advocates two of the Chartist demands: "Short Commons and Universal Sufferage was the birthright of the poorest pauper on earth." A fourth urges: "The best way to get at the Exchequer was through the excise-office. Let them leave off everything as was taxed, direct or indirect." [59] Although malapropisms intrude everywhere and the humorous undercurrent tempers stronger outbursts, Hood's comic mirror reflects well the unrest and unease which the Chartist movement provoked in the late thirties.[60]

The tide of protest encompasses all man's activity: "Timothy Boltbee prescribed all existing evils to unperfect edication. He had gone among the lower classes on purpose to learn their ignorance, and they positively knowed nothing. He was for universal schools everywheres...." A Quaker suggests they gain control of "the Money Market, and the Cattle Market, the Coal Market, and the rest of the Markets...." If successful, "they might dictate their own terms to Ministers or any one else." Someone else finds the New Police obnoxious. A Mrs. Frisby brings the complaints to a vigorous climax. After urging more feminine influence on society, she closes out the meeting with a whole cluster of reforms: "There was still the Bastiles [popular slang for the Poor Houses] and the Tithes, and the Pensioning List, and the Factory Children, and Army Flogging, and 'Resting for Debt, and Law Reform, and Corporation Reform, and Church Reform, and Parliament Reform, and Police Reform, and all sorts of reforms to be gone through." [61]

Hood had resided for over three years away from England, but life in his native land constantly occupied his thoughts. While the literary merit of "The Corresponding Club" is not great, its value as an index to Hood's mind is. Underneath an increasingly thin icing of humor lay critical reflection of substance on social and political themes. That it was the fabric not the foundations of society that needed change Hood undoubtedly believed. But the innocence with which he presented his "revolutionists'" proposals should not delude us. While he may not have deemed all necessary, some were needed, he was convinced, to promote greater equality in English life. One surmises the attraction his work had for readers like Sir Robert Peel.

Hood's illnesses often determined what and how he wrote. When he was sick, his mind experienced a heightening of perception: he empathized with the plight of others. Yet, even if his sickness dictated subjects different from those he wrote about while in relative health, a one-to-one parallel would oversimplify matters crudely. If continual good health had been his lot, he would have written, one suspects, far less often in defense of the poor, the maltreated of society. While as "sincere" as most things written by this basically sincere man, his poems of protest were inspired as much by his own sick condition as by the sickness in society. Bad health plagued him continually during 1838. And it was in this year that he wrote "The Corresponding Club."

The Corresponding Club moves to action. Reports of a revolution circulate. "An infatuated mob with a banner inscribed 'Bred for Ever' had burned every baker's shop in the place, and was proceeding avowedly to set fire to Mrs. Grigg's water mill. . . . Another band also bearing a flag with the motto 'Vurk and Vages' had destroyed Mr. Grubbin's extensive manufactory, and great

fears were entertained for Mr. Trotter's. The Dragoons had been
ordered to charge in the High Street, and had gone over to the
other side." [62] When no Cromwell arises to lead them in their
glorious hour, Hood's "revolutionists" abandon the cause. The
uprising soon fizzles out.

But did a revolution take place at all? Apparently not, Hood
implies; and the "explanation"—expected—should not surprise.
"The formidable 'Corresponding Club,'" it turns out, "is simply
what is vulgarly called a Free and Easy, and the discontents of its
members are confined to the badness of the beer, the shortness
of the measures, the dearness of the charges...." An anticlimactic
ending once again undercuts the reality established; the reader is
left dissatisfied, uncertain of Hood's intent. He wishes to know
what he should take seriously, what he should not. But it is part
of Hood's skill as a writer that he leaves him with no ready-made
solution. And it is part of his skill as a moralist that he has preached
his "sermon" without its becoming conspicuous.

The "nonsense" ballad "A Plain Direction," also written for the
1839 *Comic Annual*, recounts with charm and simplicity a man's
search for an ideal England.

> In London once I lost my way
> In faring to and fro,
> And ask'd a little ragged boy
> The way that I should go;
> He gave a nod, and then a wink,
> And told me to get there
> "Straight down the Crooked Lane,
> And all round the Square."
>
> I box'd his little saucy ears,
> And then away I strode;
> But since I've found that weary path
> Is quite a common road.
> Utopia is a pleasant place,
> But how shall I get there?
> "Straight down [etc.]

*   *   *   *   *

I've heard about some happy Isle,
Where ev'ry man is free
And none can lie in bonds for life
For want of L. S. D.
Oh that's the land of Liberty!
But how [etc.]

I've dreamt about some blessed spot,
Beneath the blessed sky,
Where Bread and Justice never rise
Too dear for folks to buy.
It's cheaper than the Ward of Cheap,
But how [etc.]

  * * * * *

They say there is a Temple too,
Where Christians come to pray;
But canting knaves and hypocrites,
And bigots keep away.
O! that's the parish church for me!
But how [etc.]

  * * * * *

I've heard about a pleasant land
Where omelettes grow on trees,
And roasted pigs run, crying out,
"Come eat me, if you please."
My appetite is rather keen,
But how shall I get there?
"Straight down the Crooked Lane,
And all round the Square." [63]

Looking backward in its plainness of statement to lyrics of Blake and Wordsworth, "A Plain Direction" looks forward, more importantly, to the nonsense verse of Edward Lear, C. S. Calverley, W. S. Gilbert, J. K. Stephen, especially Lewis Carroll. Yet Hood gives his poem its own individuality. The first two stanzas, showing his quest for a "Utopia," serve as prelude to his wish for modest improvements in English society. The middle stanzas quoted score off three pet grievances: imprisonment for debt, "Bread and Justice" beyond the poor's reach, religious hypocrisy. Whimsy prevails in the last stanza, reminiscent of Lewis Carroll. But Hood differs from Carroll and other Victorian nonsense poets in that he makes pointed criticisms of society—criticisms, though, easily overlooked in the lilting ballad rhythms.

"A Plain Direction"—a Cinderella among Hood's poems—employs simple, at times colloquial speech. Preferring understatement and unadorned language to "poetic effects," Hood foreshadows trends in modern poetry. Both the everyday words and the relaxed syntax recall Auden and other English poets of the 1930's.[64] A hundred years after Hood, they too criticized the defects and injustices of their society, though the bleakness of hope during the "long weekend" forbade the humor and occasional optimism found in Hood. Balancing nicely the "real" with the "ideal," the serious with the not-so-serious, "A Plain Direction" typifies Hood's approach to poetry and to life.

Assistants to the London drapers, "oppress'd and discontented with [their] ... lot," complained that long working hours took away all evening leisure. Instead of having to stay on the job until ten—their present case—they wanted to leave work at seven. In "The Assistant Drapers' Petition," a poem preceded by a humorous but pointed introduction, Hood came to the defense; "it seems by the following poetical address," he wrote, "that they have rhyme, as well as reason, to offer in support of their resolution."

> Ah! who can tell the miseries of men
>   That serve the very cheapest shops in town?
> Till faint and weary, they leave off at ten,
>   Knock'd up by ladies beating of 'em down!
>
>   *   *   *   *   *   *   *
>
> O come then, gentle ladies, come in time,
>   O'erwhelm our counters, and unload our shelves;
> Torment us all until the seventh chime,
>   But let us have the remnant to ourselves!
>
>   *   *   *   *   *   *   *

Till sick with toil, and lassitude extreme,
    We often think, when we are dull and vapoury,
The bliss of Paradise was so supreme,
    Because that Adam did not deal in drapery.[65]

In "The Bachelor's Dream" happily-married Hood depicts the bachelor's most dreaded nightmare: finding himself enmeshed in the chains of matrimony and having to endure all its tortures. Such an "awful dream" must of course be quickly dispelled:

> Now was not that an awful dream
> For one who single is and snug—
> With Pussy in the elbow-chair
> And Tray reposing on the rug?—
> If I must totter down the hill,
> 'Tis safest done without a clog—
> What d'ye think of that, my Cat?
> What d'ye think of that, my Dog? [66]

"Rural Felicity," another poem, allows city-bred Hood to debunk with efficacy the "joys" of country life. Despite sundry illnesses and the work he did for *Hood's Own*, the quality of the work in the 1839 *Comic Annual* remains high.

In 1838 Hood wrote for *Hood's Own* his "Literary Reminiscences." Modesty preventing him from writing an extensive autobiography, he gave only the "circumstances that prepared, educated, and made me a literary man." [67] As Hood claimed to tell only "such anecdotes as a bad memory and a bad hearing might have retained of my literary friends and acquaintance," [68] he made no fetish of accuracy and wrote solely to provide his audience with a lively narrative. Furthermore, embarrassed to write about himself "from a shrinking nervousness about egotism," he attempts to cover up his discomfiture by an overly playful tone. Only in the fourth installment, a series of vivid pen portraits of the literary giants of the *London Magazine* in the twilight of English romanticism, does Hood, content to remain in the wings, write with unself-conscious verve. The punning style captures well the joyous atmosphere of the monthly *London* dinners, presided over by editors Taylor and Hessey. Around the table sat the magazine's contributors, among them Hazlitt, De Quincey, Clare, and Lamb. To their conversation young Hood listened with eager, respectful attention. He always acknowledged it as a literary apprenticeship for which he could be most grateful. Later, when Lamb and his sister moved to Colebrooke Cottage, his near neighbors and now good friends, Thomas and Jane Hood, often came over for an evening's chat. There Hood met Wordsworth and Coleridge. The last pages of the "Literary Reminiscences" evoke a moving recollection of Sir Walter Scott.

Hood prefaced the important fourth installment with an explanation why "I have promised much, projected still more, and done little." [69] His health, he affirmed, had been a sad hindrance to his ambitions. In self-defense he summoned up a *Rambler* essay, "The miseries of an infirm constitution," by a favorite author. "The time of such a man," claimed Dr. Johnson,

> is always spent in forming schemes, which a change of wind hinders him from executing, his powers fume away in projects and in hope, and the day of action never arrives. He lies down delighted with the thoughts of to-morrow.... But in the night the skies are overcast, the temper of the air is changed, he wakes in languor, impatience, and distraction, and has no longer any wish but for ease, nor any attention but to misery.[70]

Hood pleads sickness as an excuse for his lack of achievement. But the type of man Johnson had in mind, ostensibly a "valetudinarian" is, in fact, as much a procrastinator. His failure to do more, as in Hood's case, stemmed only in part from illness: he malingered. Though often prostrate, incapable of work, Hood did find, on occasion, "illness" a convenient excuse for "laziness."

Hood visited London, again as the Dilkes' guest, over the Christmas holidays and the first weeks of January, 1839. Not for the first time did he manifest marked unease over the trustworthiness of the accounts his publisher for five years, A. H. Baily, rendered him. Though he and Baily had always remained on terms of cordial reserve, Hood had never felt quite sure of him. As early as January, 1836, he voiced agreement with Dilke's low estimate of his character: "As to Baily you are right—but I am in his power—& I believe he in money matters to be safe—a most important point." [71] When Baily failed to visit him at the Dilkes, Hood's suspicions increased; but for the moment he could do nothing. He had never learned how to cope effectively with dishonesty, and mental anguish of this kind did not endear London to him. As in the year previous, he came back to Ostend "very willingly."

The winter months again passed uneventfully. In the spring of 1839 the Hoods moved to new lodgings, "La Rhétorique," on rue St. François, a noisy street filled with railway trucks and fish barrows. The Belgian climate suited him, he gradually became aware, scarcely better than had the German. Indeed it was worse. The North Sea fogs left humidity everywhere; "when it rains," Hood noted, "I sympathize with the damp like a salt-basket." [72] Producing in him "great lassitude and general torpor of the functions, circulation, and digestion especially," [73] the weather greatly reduced his capacity for work; at times, it prevented him from writing—or even thinking. "Another year will set me up, or knock me down," he wrote in a weary hour to Lieutenant Franck; lamenting "the wear and tear of my nerves, & c.," he thought he could not "last longer." [74]

Disillusionment came more slowly to the Hoods in Ostend than in Coblenz. But after the rays of hope had finally dissolved, it could hardly have been more complete. "We still have an undiminished liking to the place, which suits our quiet 'domestic habits,' " wrote Hood after a year, "though it is as notorious as dull, amongst the *notoriously* gay." [75] Ostend did indeed suit his tastes better than did Coblenz; yet after he had made a few fleeting trips back to England, its charm, too, palled. But if contemporaneous testimony is not heeded, Hood's later distaste for the Belgian fishing port and its Flemish population blurs the pleasant image of the first year and a half. As in Coblenz, time had slowly brought about a change of sentiment. Once again the familiar pattern repeats itself: longer residence and declining health gave rise to acerbity. The Belgians fared no better than the Germans. By 1840 the "civil goodhumoured & obliging" Flemish of the first year had metamorphosed into the "lucre-loving Ostenders"; by 1842, "I allude to the Belgians, the most sordid, illiberal, and huckstering tradespeople in Europe...." [76] In the spring of 1839 the wheel approached full circle.

On May 23, his birthday, Hood remembered Béranger's line, "Dans un grenier qu'on est bien à vingt ans!" "But then I am two score," the poet wrote Franck, "and sometimes am ready to call them the Forty Thieves, having stolen away all my youth and health." [77] In this spring Baily published in volume form *Hood's Own*. Lauding it as "the best parlour window book of its day," the *Athenaeum* of May 11 rated the six hundred closely-packed pages "A work, in its way, without example, [that] is the almost unaided labour of one man." A fair assessment, yet it hardly takes into consideration the agony and toil that lay behind the production of so much humor.

In October Jane Hood left for England to visit her family and to look after her husband's business affairs. When Baily was elusive, she wrote back, "I *fear* he is as fake as we think him." [78] To complicate matters further, John Wright, who had faithfully prepared the *Comic* for press during Hood's absence from England, died during Jane's visit. While she was away, a painful attack of rheumatism took Hood by surprise just as he was at last about to put the finishing touches on *Up the Rhine*. Telling Jane not to worry, he assured her he kept his spirits up. Friends dropped in regularly to cheer the invalid, but it was his devoted children who nursed him through the crisis. A resigned Hood sighed, "I am doomed to have this trial once a year."

By the spring of 1837 Hood had completed, except for minor changes and the woodcuts, work on *Up the Rhine*. But, in part because he miscalculated its plan, the book underwent a long delay in publication. When the first edition, dedicated to Dr. Elliot, finally came out just before Christmas, 1839, it was exhausted in a fortnight. Hood had set the price at 12s.—he later repented of it as too high—yet the volume's sale and reception justified his hopes. Thanking him for his copy, Dilke wrote that he found it "a book in many points of view excellent, & above all for the large spirit of human philosophy which pervades it." [79] The *Athenaeum* reviewer of December 7, seconding his chief, doubted whether "Mr. Hood had ever before presented himself before the public in an aspect more engaging." He judged particularly apt Hood's rendering of the "inimitable little touches of national manners and peculiarities which only a keen eye can see." Since he had no *Comic Annual* in the offing, Hood pinned all hopes for his next year's income upon the book's success. The thought that it might earn him enough money to pay his debts and get away from Ostend guaranteed him for the year's close, if not improved health, at least high spirits.

Up the Rhine Hood had originally conceived upon the lines of Sir Francis Bond Head's *Bubbles from the Brunnens of Nassau*, a lively account of fashionable life in the Nassau spas. While he admired *Bubbles*, the book he finally wrote does not much resemble it. A change of mind occurred, as he admitted in the preface, and he took as model Smollett's *The Expedition of Humphry Clinker*, though using "inferior materials, and on a much humbler scale." [80] Close parallels exist between the two novels in their character types and in their use of the epistolary form— parallels that led George Saintsbury to consider Hood's book "the best of all the children of *Humphry Clinker*." [81]

The literary ancestors of Hood's heterogeneous party of tourists derive directly from Smollett's pages: Richard Orchard, the hypochondriac uncle (Matthew Bramble in *Humphry*); his bumbling sister, Catherine Wilmot (Tabitha Bramble); the scatterbrained maid, Martha Penny (Winifred Jenkins); lastly, Frank Somerville, Orchard's nephew, who combines the reliability of Smollett's titular hero with Jeremy Melford's ironic wit. Parallels admitted, Hood's tourists are yet not exact copies of Smollett's. More finely does Smollett draw his characters, and he creates one character well beyond Hood's imitative skill—Lismahago. Though imagination went into giving each correspondent in *Up the Rhine* an individual style, here again Hood is Smollett's disciple. Original as comic and humanitarian poet, he remains, as writer of prose, too close to his model to rise to genuine creativity.

Up the Rhine, its characters and its continental setting aside, differs, however, in tone and structure from *Humphry Clinker*. As Hood takes his tourists from England to Holland, then up the Rhine, the book maintains a whimsical tone, uncharacteristic of *Humphry*, but characteristic of Head's *Bubbles* and of Hood's previous books.[82] Having before conceived the *Comic Annuals* as continuations of the two *Whims*, so he considered *Up the Rhine* too "a sort of outlandish *Whims & Oddities*." That Orchard's party decide to make an extended stopover at Coblenz should not surprise: they have stumbled upon "our old friend Markham," an English expatriate, obviously a persona for an ired Hood. Knowing what he wants to say about German society, Hood says it with energy and conviction. As the tone of the novel changes, the tempo of the prose quickens. Hard fact replaces whimsy. Asked a series of leading questions about German life, "Markham" delights to hold forth on the dozens of irritations he has suffered. In many instances he duplicates, even to the choice of words, incidents about Rhinelanders that had embittered Hood's letters to English friends. Though Hood had become increasingly soured as his stay had worn on, his observations do reveal alert interest about German life and customs in the *Vormärz*.[83]

After Markham's first torrent of abuse has subsided, enter Mrs. Markham, "a handsome, but careful-looking personage"—a description calculated to bring a smile to Jane Hood's lips. With her more even disposition, she "laugh[s] over" the "minor annoyances and inconveniences of living in a foreign country." [84] Markham, however, remains adamant. Only Saxons he likes. Fancying a resemblance to the English character, he asks, "Are we not Saxons too?" Not wishing to offend his readers, the poet tempers extreme judgments. Mrs. Markham interrupts one outburst, "Now he is too bad—isn't he?" Frank Somerville tempers another. Hood felt strongly what he gave Markham to say: he had said it so long himself. With such disclaimers he could vent his discontent, yet not disturb readers expecting a good-humored travelogue. The final pages, fairly straight autobiography, narrate Frank Somerville's march with a Prussian regiment to Berlin (we should read Hood with Franck's 19th). The march over, the narrative abruptly, awkwardly ends. In the preface to *Up the Rhine* Hood mentioned that if his book met with success a sequel would take the same family on a tour of Belgium. Fortunately, posterity was spared this tale of acrimony and personal sorrow.

Literary references in *Up the Rhine* are rare, though in the tales Hood intersperses among the letters he does make use of Rhine legends. Few direct parallels exist, but "German Romances" —his aggregate term for these stories, pale copies of German *novelle* and *Märchen*—supplied him with ideas for plots and settings, and, especially, reinforced his penchant for eerie atmosphere. If his reading in other fields is an accurate gauge, he read, more or less as they came to him, the better tales as well as those on the *Schundromantik* level. Besides translations of German tales, likely models for Hood's stories are also the literally thousands of imitations of German *diablerie* that flooded English periodicals. Revealing one side of the repressed Victorian subconscious, these mechanical English imitations—the springs of the Gothic imagination had by now run dry—form an important undercurrent of Victorian literature.

Two tales of *Up the Rhine*, "The Fatal Word: A Romance of Bonn" and "The Last of the Romans: A Tale of Ehrenbreitstein," demonstrate Hood's favorite—and now familiar—use of the supernatural: a sudden last-paragraph anticlimax, when the protagonist awakes from a dream, undermines the illusion of the story's "reality." By utilizing jarring anticlimaxes, Hood repudiated a common practice of German romantic writings; in Novalis's *Heinrich von Ofterdingen*, for instance, the hero's intuitions through dreams become more real to him than everyday experience, guiding him in his life's course. Afraid of his dreams and their power over him,

Hood reassures his readers at the end, as Mrs. Radcliffe had done
before him, of everyday reality. But his preferred technique, as
hers was not, lay in the anticlimactic ending or pun. From Hood
the public expected lighthearted fun; too skilled a professional
writer not to know how to make his point without giving offense,
he rarely failed expectations. For such an audience a serious questioning of everyday reality ("The Fatal Word") or of religion
("The Last of the Romans") had to be—and was—airily dissolved.

In January and February of 1840 Hood, accompanied by young
Tom, spent five weeks in London with the Dilkes. While invig-
orated by the change of scene and the visits of friends, he unfortunately did not see Dr. Elliot. "About a week after his return,"
Jane wrote the doctor in early March, "I am sorry to say he had
the worst attack of spitting blood that he has had since he left
Germany...." [85] Although the first attack she attributed to the
cold and to the damp climate, when over a ten- to twelve-day
period the attacks recurred, she became uneasy. In addition, having to go over the "very ill-kept and tardily-rendered accounts" he
had at last got from Baily in London further aggravated Hood's
condition. With Jane also unwell from anxiety and fatigue, he
decided to quit Ostend in the autumn: "another winter would
assuredly kill me."

Lying in bed during all of March, hardly speaking in order to
spare his lungs, his hands and feet always cold, Hood longed for
the fine weather that, he hoped, would restore his health and rid
him of his lassitude. As his desire for a settled existence grew
stronger, no practical alternative, he came to realize, existed for
him but to return to England. Although the original "mischief"
lay in the stomach or liver, now the infection, a new epistolary
diagnosis from Elliot indicated, had spread to the lungs. Inviting
him over for a visit and a consultation, the doctor offered him
the run of his spacious home, a garden for exercise, and anonymity:
"unless you were to appear in London among your friends no one

need know your name and quality." Once in England he could, Elliot wrote him, "negotiate some compromise advantageous to you and equally or much more so to others, because you would instantly become more productive. . . ." Under his care, he added, the poet "could find residence in England equal in your case to any in southern Europe; and within easy reach of your friends, with an easy mind, and plenty of mental food to digest, you might get into good condition and fit to work." [86]

Convinced, Hood accepted the kind invitation with gratitude. Arriving in London early in April, he stayed first a few days with the Dilkes. So that he might once again reside unafraid in England, he sought an equitable arrangement with his creditors. And it seems likely that he succeeded. In any event, he stayed in England, probably because he convinced his creditors they had a better chance of repayment than if he remained on the Continent.[87] Feeling unwell after a few days in London, Hood hastened to the Elliots' home. The first night there brought his severest bloodspitting attack since Coblenz. Elliot observed Hood's condition closely for a few days, then told an anxious Jane: "Your husband is suffering from organic disease of the heart . . . and from hemorrhage from the lungs, or spitting of blood, recurring very frequently. There is also disorder of the liver and stomach." [88] Although the doctor predicted that complete rest might bring about partial recovery, the diagnosis made Jane quaver.

Upon Elliot's urging, Hood decided to stay permanently in England, as it provided "the best climate for both mind and body." Surrounded by friends, "under an English roof in an English bed," he slowly recovered. On beautiful spring days he took strolls in the garden, where "the fresh air really seems fresh life to me." Most of all he regretted, as the idle days became weeks, the great sacrifice of time away from work. His heart he could not prevent from remaining in the Lowlands, but he justified his long recuperation to Jane by affirming it would do him *permanent* good." By avoiding mental strain and by acquiescing to the Elliots' gentle care, he ran less risk of a relapse. Jane wished to join him, but Hood feared that, if she did, it might have re-

percussions on their children. The decampment of several foreigners who owed large debts had already caused panic in Ostend.
Finally overcoming Hood's half-hearted protests, an anxious wife
joined her husband in mid-May.

Hood's financial position got worse daily. After meditating legal
proceedings against Baily for many months, he finally opened them
in the spring—a rash, ill-timed action. Since the immediate effect
was to freeze both the stock and profits of *Hood's Own* and *Up
the Rhine*, he thus senselessly cut himself off from his year's
anticipated income. John Hamilton Reynolds pressed the suit for
Hood, but with slight skill and less success. Reproaching Baily
that "more extraordinary accounts were never issued from a publishing house," [89] Reynolds yet could not force him either to compromise or to settle. His rupture with Baily compelled Hood to
look for a new publisher. He knew it took time to complete arrangements, also that, despite assertions to the contrary, a new
publisher would probably query Baily about *Up the Rhine*'s profits. That its stock had been impounded, thus ruining its sale for
the oncoming tourist season, weakened Hood's position. Its profits would have sufficed, he calculated, to get him through the year
easily; instead, *Up the Rhine*, which brought in only "a poor
£150," had turned out an "undeserved shipwreck." [90] Had the
profits mounted to £500 or 600 he believed Baily could not have
paid him; for "he is in a lead way & really has no money or he
would not let me go, so profitable as I must be to an *unscrupulous*
publisher." [91] Baily's countercharges Hood refuted in words of
self-righteous wrath: "But the truth is, I do not owe him a shilling
—as can be proved by his own accounts. . . . Seriously if you knew
all the wanton injury & suffering inflicted on me by that scoundrel
you would not only think that I ought to have redress but that
he ought to meet with punishment. But he is ripe for a full exposure, at the hands of . . . Thomas Hood." [92]

The *Athenaeum*'s pages record the final skirmish with Baily
in October. Hood wrote first, October 3, to disavow any "imputed
contributorship" to Baily's forthcoming *Sportsman's Oracle*. The
next week Baily replied. By publicly exposing Hood's poverty the

publisher hoped to embarrass him, but the poet riposted with irrefutable charges. Baily not having answered his accusations, Hood claimed the week after, October 17, that his "exposure" only underscored his own dishonor.[93] Perhaps it had; but Hood gained no more than the satisfaction of being in the right. Always sensitive to his good name, the poet once again displayed in his abrupt break with Baily a lack both of business sense and of common sense.

Friendship, or at least cordiality, followed by distrust marked Hood's arrangements with all his publishers: at the start, faith and confidence; at the end, wranglings and lawsuits. Baily was not the first publisher with whom he severed dealings precipitately; nor would he be the last. Hood's emotional instability, the roots of which lie deep in the obscurity of his youth, provoked continual vicissitudes. Essentially (perhaps excessively) upright, Hood never realized that the individual can, without conceding his integrity, yield on petty matters. Publishing was at this time a business in which few possessed integrity, and it is clear, from other sources than his own letters, that he worked with an especially seamy crew of publishers. But it was his own insecurity and nervous irritability, accentuated by the necessity of having to get things done by a certain time, that complicated even more the life of a man who, by nature, tended to let things slide. In this respect, though he never realized it, Hood became his own worst enemy. "Insufficiently disillusioned"—words applied with aptitude by C. S. Lewis to Shelley's youth—might well, with equal aptitude, apply to Hood's.

Throughout May, while Hood recuperated at the Elliots', Jane scurried about London searching for a home. She finally settled on a small cottage near Camberwell Green, chosen, undoubtedly, because of its proximity to Dr. Elliot's brother, Robert, also a physician. Having by June recovered some measure of strength, Hood began to concern himself with his children's fate. His premonitions proved correct. Fanny and Tom, held as "hostages," could not leave until their parents had discharged in full all debts contracted in Ostend—about £150. Selling to Richard Bentley the copyright of *Tylney Hall*, the novel to be in the popular series "Bentley's Standard Novels and Romances," was the only way Hood found to raise the necessary cash. He parted with his copyright *contre-coeur*, and only because he feared the copyright bill "dead and gone—or crushed to bits by party politics." [94] In mid-July he returned to Ostend with Jane to fetch the "hostages." The four-month separation having weighed heavily on all, it was a happy reunion.

CLOSE CORPORATIONS.

At the same time that he sought to regain his children Hood opened negotiations for several positions. He had promised Bentley an article for the June *Bentley's Miscellany*, but he could not fulfil his promise. Mental anguish over his children's fate, he told Bentley, prevented him from writing; nor could he make an arrangement to become a regular contributor. [95] The publishing firm of Fisher asked him to write a series of comic tales to accompany etchings by George Cruickshank, commissioned but not used for the standard edition of the Waverley novels, but for the same reason he did not accept this offer.[96] Nevertheless, as the "cruel position in which I have been placed by Mr. Baily" [97] made work of some kind imperative, Hood finally found a position to his liking. With Henry Colburn, Bentley's former business partner and now arch rival, he concluded in July a "capital arrangement." For Colburn's *New Monthly Magazine* he engaged to write articles, poems, and reviews, which the publisher stipulated to publish eventually in volume form.

Public journals had accorded Hood a gratifying welcome upon his return to English soil. Three months as a vegetarian, combined with total abstinence from alcohol, had re-established his health. As always after a "recovery," he radiated optimism: "I shall be all right now, health and everything." [98] Getting on with Colburn "very comfortably," he enjoyed his work, "hard work—which, like virtue, brings its own reward." [99] Few moments in the life of Thomas Hood did not permit him to summon up the strength to hope. *130980*

Chapter 3

The New Monthly *Years*

Hood did not enter the ranks of the *New Monthly Magazine & Humorist* as a stranger for in the 1820's he had occasionally contributed poems. Founded in 1814 by Colburn, the *New Monthly* had begun its rise in the literary world under Thomas Campbell's editorship (1821–1830) as the inheritor of the unfulfilled renown of the *London Magazine*. By a curious irony of literary history, Hood, who had assisted Taylor on the *London*, became twenty years later editor of the journal that had largely supplanted it. The *New Monthly* occupied a distinguished position in the roster of literary periodicals of the age. "Its succession of famous editors, and the large number of critical articles it contained," writes Walter Graham, "give the *New Monthly* a high place among the magazines of the century. Moreover, it contained many early examples of signed contributions; and in the original nature of its letterpress it was, from 1820 on, one of the most progressive of periodicals." [1]

Henry Colburn employed a well-known group of contributors: Theodore Hook, the present editor, whose last novel, *Fathers and Sons*, was being serialized in its pages; Laman Blanchard; the Countess of Blessington; Lady Morgan; Mrs. Frances Trollope; Charles James Apperley, "Nimrod"; and Douglas Jerrold, who in 1842 dedicated to Hood his *Cakes and Ale*. Another regular, the Reverend Joseph Hewlett, nicknamed from the title of his most popular book "Peter Priggins," usually had one of his humorous novels running in the *New Monthly*'s pages. While by name and by talent Hood stood above his fellow contributors, they claimed respectable rank in the literary world. The kinds of contributions solicited for the magazine were not meant to tax the minds of its largely middle-class readers: light, domestic fiction, sentimental poems, and informative digest articles predominated; travel nar-

ratives, as in most nineteenth-century "literary" magazines, enjoyed perennial popularity. Left a free hand in regard to contributions, Hood found the journal's pages hospitable.
His writings varied greatly in subject and tenor: imitation of
German *Galgenhumor* in "Diabolical Suggestions" and parody
of Schiller in "The Forge"; anger at Evangelical "charity" toward
the Negro in "A Black Job"; comic extravaganzas in prose like
"The Schoolmistress Abroad"; finally, the identification of death
in Nature with his own death in "The Elm Tree." Only a few
poems—"An Open Question" and "Miss Kilmansegg and Her
Precious Leg"—written soon after his return from Belgium under
the generic heading "Rhymes for the Times, and Reason for the
Season" display concern over society.

A bill before the House of Commons, sponsored by Sir Andrew
Agnew, proposed to close the London Zoo on Sunday. Hood,
champion of the underdog, fought the bill with a poem—"An
Open Question"—that demonstrates the obvious: the poor could
go to the zoo only on Sunday; closing it would deprive them of
one of their few places of recreation; most would never see the
animals. He could not conceal his outrage:

> What! shut the gardens! lock the latticed gate!
> Refuse the shilling and the fellow's ticket!
> And hang a wooden notice up to state,
> "On Sundays no admittance at this wicket!"
> The birds, the beasts, and all the reptile race
> Denied to friends and visitors till Monday!
> Now really, this appears the common case
> Of putting too much Sabbath into Sunday....

"What harm," he asks, would frequenting the zoo on Sunday
cause?

> What harm if men who burn the midnight-oil,
> Weary of frame, and worn and wan in feature,

> Seek once a-week their spirits to assoil,
>   And catch a glimpse of "Animated Nature?"

The same ironic refrain—"But what is your opinion, Mrs. Grundy?"—closes each stanza. Behind "the common case" stood none other than Hood's nemesis—the "saints":

> There are some moody fellows, not a few,
>   Who, turn'd by Nature with a gloomy bias,
> Renounce black devils to adopt the blue,
>   And think when they are dismal they are pious
> .   .   .   .
> Spirit of Kant! have we not had enough
>   To make religion sad, and sour, and snubbish,
> But saints zoological must cant their stuff,
>   As vessels cant their ballast—rattling rubbish!
> Once let the sect, triumphant to their text,
>   Shut Nero up from Saturday till Monday,
> And sure as fate they will deny us next
>   To see the dandelions on a Sunday—
> But what is your opinion, Mrs. Grundy? [2]

Characterized as "the serious set," "moody Fellows" and "saints," the Evangelicals, backers enthusiastic of the bill, get as rough a handling as they had gotten in the "Ode to Rae Wilson, Esq." In his anger Hood nearly forgot his immediate purpose—keeping the zoo open—to castigate the hypocrisy which, in his view, marked every act of these men and women of intense but narrow vision. "They constantly endeavored," writes Maurice J. Quinlan, "to make men more religious than it was consistent for human nature to be. Their hatred of pleasure caused them to be fearful of enjoying harmless pastimes. . . ." [3] Left to form society in their own image, these "moody Fellows" could become, thought Hood, even more than they already were, a blight on English life.

Most causes Hood fought for have now only historical interest. His poetry's topicality, usually unmixed, as in Dickens, with powerful treatment of the *"great human currents,"* [4] leaves many passages jejune reading. The reforms he supported having become law, his lines today lack compelling urgency, though then they aroused fierce controversy. Recognizing that "An Open Question" scattered its fire, Hood, to make clear the "moral," appended to the poem an explanatory prose note, in which he denounced "over-righteous sectarians" who fondly attributed all society's evils to breaking the Sabbath. He wrote a story ("A Tale of the Great Plague"), he once affirmed, in part "on account of the strangeness of the event, but also because it carries a moral pick-a-back, as a good story ought to do." [5] And to designate the purpose of a poem, "Etching Moralised," he quoted as motto Dr. Johnson's "To point a moral." [6] By tacking on an explicit *moralitas*—similar to the admonitory closing paragraph of medieval writers—to dozens of his apologues, Hood reveals his desire to instruct—and perhaps, too, some uncertainty whether he had, within the work itself, made clear the "moral."

The main point of "An Open Question" merits pausing over: Sunday could be—and was—used by the well-to-do to oppress the poor. Only the poor, Hood realized, would be victims of Sunday blue laws. Understanding this, Dickens in 1836 wrote an article, "Sunday under Three Heads," strongly critical of Sir Andrew Agnew's "Lord's Day Observance Bill" prohibiting Sunday labor. Only the death of King William prevented this bill, which had gone before Parliament four times before it secured a majority, from becoming law. Hood had already castigated Agnew in his 1834 "Ode to Sir Andrew Agnew, Esq." and he did in his "Ode" what Dickens was to do in his article two years later. Dickens's paper "contains nothing more effective," Humphry House writes, "than the demonstration how every single restriction—on traveling, shopping, amusements, etc.—that the Bill sought to impose was a restriction only on the poorer classes." [7]

Malthusian doctrines carried great weight in nineteenth-century English society. While the population multiplied by a geometrical ratio, the food supply—limited—was doomed forever to trail behind at an ever-increasing distance. Man, the Malthusians insisted, must soon multiply himself into starvation. Not only did this pessimistic belief underlie much Victorian thinking, but it influenced legislation brought before Commons. By closing the gin shops, by preventing those who labored six days from traveling on the seventh, by making "copulation even in marriage seem a sin," many upright individuals lent their names to causes like Sir Andrew's. They honestly believed they were doing the nation a public service. "It is difficult now to realize," House points out, that "thousands of good and sensible men ... believed his [Malthus's] principle of population to be exactly true—believed that as poverty was relieved and the standard of life raised, so surely there would be bred a new race hovering on the misery-line, on the edge of starvation." [8]

Hood assailed Malthusian doctrines in his letters and in his early "Ode to Mr. Malthus." Though humorous, light in tone, this poem methodically ridicules Malthus's ideas. Hood attacks, as always, from a humane point of view; human beings we must not subjugate to theories; humanity is, after all, a collection of individuals. He mocks by agreement:

> Oh Mr. Malthus, I agree
> In everything I read with thee!
> The world's too full, there is no doubt,
> And wants a deal of thinning out....
>   There are too many of all trades,
>   Too many bakers,
> Too many every-thing-makers,
> But not too many undertakers,—
>   Too many boys,—
> Too many hobby-de-hoys,—
> Too many girls, men, widows, wives and maids,—
> There is a dreadful surplus to demolish,
>   And yet some Wrongheads,
>   With thick not long heads,
>   Poor Metaphysicians!
>   Sign petitions
> Capital punishment to abolish;

And in the face of censuses such vast ones
    New hospitals contrive,
    For keeping life alive,
Laying first stones, the dolts! instead of last ones! [9]

Hood ironically proposes other victims: "My debtors ... / Who cannot or who will not pay," "all my creditors," neighborhood brats, Aldermen, foundling children, paupers—anyone, in short, who causes him discomfort or annoyance. And, in so doing, he points out the weakness of Malthus's case: who determines the "dreadful surplus"? The pious and wealthy, under the pretense of approving bills that will improve society, keep their social and economic inferiors from both multiplying and advancing up the economic ladder. And in the bargain they keep them in as miserable a state as possible. Every man his own Malthus.

"Miss Kilmansegg and Her Precious Leg," his longest, most ambitious, poem, Hood worked on over a six-month period. He wondered afterwards, if he had not "killed" his heroine, whether she would have killed him. The September, 1840, *New Monthly* carried the first installment; the last did not appear until February, 1841. During these six months Hood was often ill, always poor. In spite of its apparent facility, "Miss Kilmansegg," like the seemingly effortless puns in the *Comic Annuals*, provided many a difficult moment of composition. The rollicking stanzas which jingle along with increasing verve like a Strauss waltz in accelerating tempo amply demonstrate Hood's amazing metrical dexterity. Coupled with it, moreover, are the "sting of [the] rhymes and the crackle of [the] puns, perhaps the most accurate in the language"; [10] together they never permit the poem's pace to slacken, nor the reader's attention to flag.

Hood opens with an ironic account of the new heiress's pedigree to the Kilmansegg bullion. In "Her Pedigree" the word "gold" alone, or a variant ("golden," "Pactolian," "*oro*"), occurs at least once, often twice or thrice, in all but two of the first twelve stanzas. Used more sparingly in the course of the poem, "gold" adumbrates the gigantic final coda; by then, the word has become, R. E. Davies points out, more a dirge than a refrain.[11] Subtitled "A Golden Legend," the poem is, only in the most literal sense, a *legende dorée*. Rarely before had Hood orchestrated a verbal *leitmotif* with such frequency and force; wealth and the corruption it brings in its train become the poem's great theme. "Kil-mans-egg," the Dickensian family name, synopsizes the story: the bitterly competitive methods of gain of England's newly-affluent philistine plutocrats will not bear close scrutiny. From Miss Kilmansegg, golden "egg" of this latest generation of golden geese, "It wouldn't require much verbal strain / To trace Kill-man, perchance, to Cain." The description of the means by which the "Patriarch Kilmansegg" acquired his ill-begotten gains Hood, however, limits to "Tradition said he feather'd his nest / Through an Agricultural Interest. . . ." [12] While no actual model is known to exist for Miss Kilmansegg and her family, the poet undoubtedly had in mind the vulgarity displayed by this or that *nouveau riche* industrial leader or railway baron.

"Miss Kilmansegg" contrasts, implicitly when not explicitly, poverty and wealth: "What different lots our stars accord! / This babe to be hail'd and woo'd as a Lord! / And that to be shunn'd like a leper!" Although the irony of chance that determines rich and poor did not outrage Hood, it did lead him to draw a "moral": hazard of birth does not entitle the fortunate to demand or receive special privilege. Three stanzas, comparing those born to wealth with those born to poverty, prepare the way for Miss Kilmansegg—and anticipate "The Song of the Shirt":

> Not so with the infant Kilmansegg!
> She was not born to steal or beg,
>   Or gather cresses in ditches;
> To plait the straw, or bind the shoe,
> Or sit all day to hem and sew,
> As females must—and not a few—
>   To fill their insides with stitches! [13]

Neither the heroine—born, christened, brought up amidst luxury —nor her family, nor the idle entourage of hangers-on, arouses our sympathy. Hood did not mean us to sympathize. At the christening of the precious infant, he draws a portrait in acid of the proud father, Sir Jacob, as he "strutted and bow'd":

> He had roll'd in money like pigs in mud,
> Till it seem'd to have enter'd into his blood
>   By some occult projection:
> And his cheeks instead of a healthy hue,
> As yellow as any guinea grew. . . .

The disease without creates the disease within. The golden glitter in the Kilmansegg household leaves no object untouched, from the baptismal font to the baptismal presents, the "golden mugs and the golden jugs."

> Gold! and gold! and nothing but gold!
> The same auriferous shine behold
>   Wherever the eye could settle!
> On the walls—the sideboard—the ceiling-sky—
> On the gorgeous footmen standing by,
> In coats to delight a miner's eye
>   With seams of the precious metal.[14]

Succeeding stanzas recount the spoiled heiress's childhood, education, and the growth of her corrupted ideals: gold dominates them all. One day in Hyde Park her high-spirited Irish horse, "Banker," bred "by Bullion out of an Ingot mare," bolts in a fright. Carrying his mistress, Mazeppa-like, on his back, he races along in a "dead heat" that Hood compares—ominously—to that of "the Dead who ride so fast and fleet" in Bürger's "Leonore" ballad. The headlong pace of the verse, kaleidoscopic clusters of images hastening one after another, recalls the fantastic ride across the desert in "The Desert-Born." Hood, it seems, depicted speed and its associated "thrills" out of the sheer joy that he, sick and of necessity lethargic, felt at the thought of uncontrolled energy. So Kafka, death near, marveled at the sight of a man guzzling down a glass of beer; like Hood, he never ceased to be fascinated by life as he could not live it.

Through the streets of London clatters "Banker," until both horse and rider go under at none other than "Bond Street." Only at the cost of an amputated leg does Miss Kilmansegg survive her fall. Her parents unable to curb her strong will, she insists—to the consternation of all—that it be replaced by one of gold. With her "precious leg" she becomes the sensation of London: rich and poor alike find no other topic of conversation. Castigating those capable only of ogling the latest curiosity, Hood approaches a Swiftian universal satire that encompasses all mankind's foibles and vanities. Fiercely independent in his profession and in his life, he never scrupled to scorn mass conformity.

A "fancy ball" given in her honor by her parents climaxes Miss Kilmansegg's fame. Her fabulous leg, well-exposed, "tunic loop'd up ... / To show the Leg that was Golden!" captures everyone's attention:

> But what were Beauty, or Virtue, or Worth,
> Gentle manners, or gentle birth,
> Nay, what the most talented head on earth
>   To a Leg worth fifty Talents!

The irony would not have struck Miss Kilmansegg's admirers. Although more than an ornamental piece of gold, still the leg cannot be called a true symbol; few such exist in Hood's poetry. Rather, showing the vanity of man's desire for precious objects without real value, it serves to draw out the onlookers' innate greed: they see in it all they want in life. Miss Kilmansegg's admirers, Hood is at pains to insist, are mainly foreign fortune-hunters: grotesques, motivated by greed, who jostle the English "Gentry both new and old— / For people who stand on legs of gold, / Are sure to stand well with society." [15] If the leg were but of flesh and blood, the heroine but of modest fortune, she would get hardly a nod. Loosely, the leg represents an "objective correlative" to society's adoration before the latest Golden Calf, as

Miss Kilmansegg represents an "objective correlative" to a society made corrupt by Mammon-worship.

Hood balanced his poem with great skill: in each section a scene of calm succeeds one of great animation. "Her Dream" follows "Her Fancy Ball"; sleep, the balm of hurt minds, does not come to Miss Kilmansegg. Even the God-blessed poor find sleep difficult: "Pity, pity the wretches that weep, / For they must be wretched, who cannot sleep / When God himself draws the curtain!" No such mundane cares weigh the rest of Miss Kilmansegg, who "turn'd, and roll'd, and tumbled and toss'd"—the case, Hood claims, with those who "think too much, / Of the precious and glittering metal." [16] Dreaming visions of gold everywhere, she becomes at last a Golden Idol.

Suitors flock to demand the hand of the heiress. Her warped outlook on life leads her to choose the least worthy, a foreign count of cosmopolitan features and charm, a wily fortune-hunter in part based, as is Dickens's Smorltork in *Pickwick*, upon Prince Pückler-Muskau in his forays fifteen years before to snare a British heiress, but totally without any of the Prince's redeeming virtues. At her marriage "gold" again careers ubiquitously through the stanzas. Totally without sympathy for his heroine, Hood condemns her with uncommon hardness to a just fate. A Fortune needed a Title for "happiness"; but as the new Countess slowly, painfully discovers, the Title had even greater need of the Fortune. For a bride to whom "Gold, still gold, her standard of old, / All pastoral joys were tried by gold," nature's beauties at her country estate have little appeal. Without throngs to admire her she becomes depressed; her selfish vanity finds no consolation in an indifferent husband. The Count turns out to be a complete rake who, after working his way through her fortune, demands she sell her golden leg. When she refuses, he murders her. Death comes while "her mind was busy with early joys, / Her golden treasures and golden toys"; and she dies unredeemed. Because the Count killed her with her own leg, Hood ironically has the coroner's inquest bring in a verdict of suicide. The final section of this modern parable, "Her Moral," concludes with a crescendo of Gold:

Gold! Gold! Gold! Gold:
Good or bad a thousand-fold!
  How widely its agencies vary—
To save—to ruin—to curse—to bless—
As even its minted coins express,
Now stamp'd with the image of Good Queen Bess,
And now of a Bloody Mary.[17]

Criticism has meted out an uneven verdict on "Miss Kilmansegg," Hannah Lawrance, Hood's contemporary and lifelong friend, understood the poem's significance for her generation and understood that it was, basically, not a comic poem. "In its grim grotesqueness, 'Miss Kilmansegg,'" she observed,

> strongly reminds us of those strange and fantastic, but most powerful apologues of the middle-ages—"Reynard the Fox," "Piers Ploughman," and such like, where the bitterest satire mingles with the keenest humour, and where the writer, in the midst of the laughter he awakens, never suffers you to forget his terrible earnestness.[18]

A generation later, Arthur Symons thought the poem "mainly meaningless"; the manipulation of rhyme and pun, though skilled in the extreme, has "hardly more than a juggler's ability in its tap-tap of a ceaseless ball rising and falling like a shuttle-cock." [19] Today the wheel has come full turn: modern taste considers "Miss Kilmansegg" Hood's masterpiece.

"Miss Kilmansegg" develops Hood's central theme of man's relationship to his society. A "terrible earnestness," Miss Lawrance notes, prevails; he not only shows a new widening in his sympathy for the poor but a new severity in his indictment against the rich. (Miss Kilmansegg's father dies soon after her marriage; her mother goes insane.) The invective against Evangelical fanaticism that characterized the "Ode to Rae Wilson, Esq." and "An Open Question" gives way in "Miss Kilmansegg" to concern with all society. Hood returned to England ill, desperately poor. When he wrote "An Open Question" and "Miss Kilmansegg," he empathized with England's downtrodden, but the empathy lasted only as long as he remained poor himself. Ultimately, though always sympathetic to the underdog, he accepted life as he found it; he was not a born rebel. " 'As you like it,' is the great secret," Hood wrote Dr. Elliot in the midst of composing "Miss Kilmansegg," "and I like it well enough as it is." [20] When he had regained moderate affluence and health, he again could look obliquely at society's injustices. In the two and a half years following the publication of the last installment of "Miss Kilmansegg" (February, 1841), he wrote little that indicated anger at the lot of the English poor. Prosperity's balm would soothe—if only for a while—his nagging conscience.

Upon his return to England Hood faced—in addition to "law, literature, and illness"—a year of acute financial hardship. During the months he labored over "Miss Kilmansegg" his fortunes steadily worsened. Although he practiced the strictest economies in the tiny cottage near Camberwell Green, his earnings from his *New Monthly* contributions did not suffice to support himself and his family. These were difficult months. On January 13, 1841, without the usual solicitation, the Council of the Literary Fund took the unusual step and awarded him the largest sum they gave—£50. R. H. Barham, author of *The Ingoldsby Legends* and a friend, had brought his case to the Council's attention. Another friend, Dilke, citing in the official statement Hood's "extreme bad health" and consequent incapacity for work which left him "in want of even a few shillings," [21] confirmed his need. But the poet, after thanking the Literary Fund for its generosity, refused the grant. His intention stood firm. The reply he wrote reveals the quality of the man:

My embarrassment and bad health are of such standing that I am become, as it were, seasoned. For the last six years I have been engaged in the same struggle without seeking, receiving or requiring, any pecuniary assistance whatever. ... Fortunately since manhood I have been dependent solely on my own exertions—a condition which has exposed and inured me to vicissitudes; while it has nourished a pride which will fight on, & has yet some retrenchments to make ere it surrenders. . . .[22]

Further hardship descended upon the Hood household during the next few months. He had to yield, to rescind his decision. Capitulation came on May 25: "You may conceive," he wrote the Council, "the extreme pain with which I revoke my former decision." The Council renewed the grant on June 9 and Hood acknowledged his acceptance a few days afterwards: "It cannot but be gratifying to find that so many strangers are my friends, at a time when friends are proverbially apt to degenerate into acquaintance & acquaintance into strangers." The whole letter is eloquent testimony to the high worth he placed in the character of literary men. "My present cruel position," he was quick to note in a clear allusion to Baily, "is . . . due . . . to the fraudulent practices of a dishonest agent." [23] Though often badly in need of money during the next years, never again did he have to undergo the hand-to-mouth existence of his first year back in England.

During most of 1841 the Hoods continued to live in their cottage in Camberwell. After leading a placid existence on the Continent for five years, the poet found bewildering the rapid movement of English life. "Everything in England," he exclaimed to Franck, "goes at a pace unknown abroad." From his study window he marveled at the life bustling before him; each day he saw as many as fifty horse-drawn buses pass his door. "A buss goes as fast . . . as ten droskys," Franck learned, "and will take you three or four miles for sixpence, which is cheaper riding than at Berlin. To be sure, omnibusses, I suspect, kill horses, but droskys kill time!" [24] Unstable health forced him, not to his reluctance, to lead a quiet life. Life in England entailed fewer expenses and he spent less money than abroad. The English climate strengthened him, though he continued to suffer from three years' exposure to Ostend's malarial air: "I have regular bad days (Tuesday and Friday), with an extreme sympathy with wet weather, when I *give* like an old salt basket. This pleasant tendency," he told Franck, "I shall most likely enjoy for the rest of my days." [25] The Hoods took great pride in their children's precocity. Under Jane's direction, young Tom worked hard at mastering the "fairy work" of A *Midsummer Night's Dream*—surely advanced reading for a six-year-old. Fanny also showing a literary turn, Hood found on his hands two gentle critics, aged six and ten. Already he saw in them adumbrations of traits that in the 1860's led Tom to become editor of *Fun Magazine*, Fanny a writer of children's books. "He and Fanny are full of odds and ends," a happy father wrote Lieutenant Franck, "fairy tales, and plays, and travels, and in their games it all comes working out like beer from a barrel." [26] Educated at home, pampered by indulgent parents, left pretty much to develop at will, neither Fanny nor Tom acquired a disciplined mind. Nor for that matter had their father, but in his case necessity forced him to write, while pride dictated he write as well as he could.

Pious ladies of the Evangelical persuasion came to call upon Hood. They found his humor immoral. They also felt a strong compulsion to convince the poet in person of the errors of his ways. One asked him "What good his 'Whims and Oddities' would do his soul?" After this visit Hood penned "My Tract," the prose pendant to the "Ode to Rae Wilson, Esq.," and equally savage in its indictment of Evangelical "piety." Though the tone is strained and the irony often silly ("And verily if they be the Righteous, I am content to be the Lefteous of the species"), Hood's sincere indignation at the "saints'" hypocrisy transcends many awkwardnesses. Good deeds, not words, designate the truly religious:

> I implore you to spend a few years, say twenty, in this self-scrutiny, which may be wholesomely varied by the exercise of a little active benevolence; not, however, in sending tracts instead of baby-linen to poor lying-in sisters, or in volunteering pork chops for distressed Jews, or in recommending a Solemn Fast to the Spitalfield weavers, or in coddling and

pampering a pulpit favourite, but in converting rags to raiment, and empty stomachs to full ones, and in helping the wretched and indigent to "keep their souls and bodies together!" [27]

Yet, exactly because his indignation was terribly sincere, Hood did not write effective satire. His pen lacked bite, his spirit vindictive savagery. He had difficulty presenting a logical argument without either getting off the subject or breaking his thought with a pun; his mind was too undisciplined, his temper too easy-going, to maintain the sustained indictment that satire requires. Nor could he get sufficiently outside his subject to view it with perspective. For effective satire fury alone does not suffice; intellectual conviction demands a reasoned refutation. Unable to conceive the other side's position, or why Evangelicals thought the way they did, Hood lacked the subtlety of presentation that renders especially telling satire such as Swift's *A Modest Proposal*.

Despite his children's assertion that he possessed a religious nature, what Hood himself believed is difficult to pin down. He came from a nonconformist background, and throughout life he persistently refused to value the rites of one denomination above another, as he persistently refused to let others impose their narrow creeds upon him. In letters he makes no mention of ever going to church; his few references to a Supreme Being seem decidedly perfunctory. Humanism characterizes his attitude toward life in this world; his tolerance he gave to those who were honest with themselves and left others alone.

On August 24, 1841, Theodore Hook, editor of the *New Monthly*, died after a long illness. Henry Colburn was forced to search for a new editor. As Hood's contributions to the magazine had recently been few, and as he had made none to the July and August numbers, Jane wondered if the *New Monthly*'s owner would think her husband eligible. But Colburn did. Eager to get a man of Hood's caliber but just as eager to get him cheap, he sent over his assistant, Frederic Shoberl, to sound him out. Hood had pride, however; he would take the editorship—but only if he received the same terms as had Hook. Not knowing Hook's salary, he queried Dilke, though to no avail. Colburn offered £200; Hood, thinking Hook's salary £300, held out for that amount. Casting a sad eye back on the near-destitution of past months that had forced acceptance of the Literary Fund's once-refused grant, a long-harassed Jane Hood wrote early in September to Mrs. Elliot, "All is settled." But her judgment was premature. Several weeks of anxiety elapsed before the final arrangements; not until September 17 could she announce in triumph, "This very evening it is settled that Hood is to be the editor at 300£ a year, independent of any articles he may write, which are to be paid for as usual." To the parched family fortunes the editorship came like sweet rain. Guaranteed financial stability for the first time in half a dozen years, Jane Hood could now breathe more easily at bill-paying time. The position once secured, Hood became laconic: "there was great competition for it, but I did not even apply, and was therefore selected." [28] On the contrary: he had wanted the job desperately —and he had gotten it.

"A Tete-a-Tete with the Editor" in the October issue cheerfully assures us that the shadowboxing between Hood and Colburn did have a successful issue. One of the first results of the poet's new alliance was the *Comic Annual for 1842*, a reprinting of his *New Monthly* contributions, among them "An Open Question" and "Miss Kilmansegg." During the two years he served as editor, taking advantage of the extra payment his own contributions brought, Hood produced for the *New Monthly* many poems, stories, and reviews. He knew prosperity as he had not known it before, and as he would not know it after. But though his financial position improved, his poetry suffered. Hood prosperous wrote on different subjects from those of Hood destitute; and he wrote less well. Adversity was needed to ignite his social conscience: relative affluence brought relative indifference. His *New Monthly* writings —mostly humorous and mostly in prose—rarely come to grips with controversial social and political issues. To an overworked Hood— he had to prepare for press each month a 150–page magazine— prose represented the easier medium. Finally, with a position that provided sufficient funds and commanded respect in the literary world, he felt he could lead a more active social life. Now in demand as a dinner guest, he enjoyed, despite protestations about the strain on his health, dining out, good company, and cheer. Dignitaries even began to ask him—always a sure sign of success —to lend his name to philanthropical causes.

At the end of the year the Hoods gave up the Camberwell cottage for more spacious lodgings on nearby Elm Tree Road, St. John's Wood, in the area then north of London near Regent's Park. Conscious they again had a home of which they might be proud, the Hoods invited friends and entertained modestly. His son Tom describes one intimate gathering:

> Though the boards did not groan, sides used to ache, and if the champagne did not flow in streams, the wit sparkled to make up for it. Quiet at large parties, at these little meetings my father gave full reign to his fun. . . . At these times, too, he would often set everyone laughing by his apt misquotations of Latin, none of which can be now remembered unfortunately, for he had a rare facility for twisting the classics.[29]

Sometime in 1841 Hood met Charles Dickens; the two men quickly became firm friends. In each, a refusal to tolerate cant, a sincere desire to remedy society's wrongs, and a straightforward heartiness made for mutual attraction. Both came from a lower middle-class background; both knew London inside out. Critics fond of pointing out Dickens's extensive experience of London slum life might note that Hood, city-born and bred, had often the opportunity in youth to explore the dark byways of the metropolis. His upbringing differed however in one essential way from Dickens's: while Dickens underwent a scarring apprenticeship to life in the blacking factory, Hood never had cause to question the values of his middle-class upbringing. No such traumatic experience—in choice of career, in love, or in life—ever shook his existence until late 1834. Though thirteen years Dickens's senior, Hood never showed the least urge to patronize the younger man, whose gifts, despite initial reserve, he soon recognized.[30] He also saw in Dickens a talent he himself possessed but slightly: a stable business sense. In years ahead he came to rely on his sound practical advice. While the two men, living apart, rarely met, surviving letters testify to easygoing confidence in each other's friendship.

Hood praised "Boz" liberally for his moral bias and for his belief in human goodness in the reviews of *Master Humphrey's Clock* and *Barnaby Rudge* he wrote for the *Athenaeum,* and in the reviews of the Christmas tales he wrote for *Hood's Magazine.* Dickens, for his part, was one of Hood's friends who served him best.

Hood inserted in the February, 1841, *New Monthly* "To C. Dickens, Esq.—On his Departure for America," doggerel lines wishing his friend well on his travels. Six months later, to welcome him back from America, a group of Dickens's friends organized a dinner. This July reunion dinner testified to the high regard and sincere friendship the young novelist inspired in many. Hood had claimed in his third Copyright Letter that the literary profession, as he knew it, fostered few jealousies and few professional rivalries; that so little ill will greeted Dickens's extraordinary success confirmed his view of the basic integrity of literary men. The dinner guests included John Forster, a reformed George Cruickshank, "Barry Cornwall," R. H. Barham, and the painters Charles and Thomas Landseer. Asked to take the chair, Hood begged off on grounds of health; Captain Marryat presided instead, William Jerdan serving as vice-chairman. Dickens, looking fit, accompanied by his wife and brother, displayed top form; he gave "a good warm-hearted speech, in which he hinted the great advantage of going to America for the pleasure of coming back again; and pleasantly described the embarrassing attentions of the Transatlantickers, who made his private house, and private cabin, particularly public." [31] After toasts were proposed to "Mrs. Boz, the Chairman and Vice," and to others of the assembled, Monckton Milnes toasted Hood's health "in terms my modesly might allow me to repeat to *you*," wrote the poet to Mrs. Elliot, "but my memory won't." [32] In a characteristic gesture of friendship Dickens sent Hood home in his own carriage. Jane had sat up for him. It was an evening long remembered.

The year 1842 saw the development of another warm friendship: that with the Reverend Joseph Hewlett. A jovial country parson with innumerable children (Hood once wrote him in awe, "I hardly know how to take your announcement of a 17th

Child . . ." [33]), Hewlett had long been a *New Monthly* regular. With parish duties in addition to his brood, one wonders how he found time to manage the monthly installment of his latest novel. Besides literary interests the two men, a year apart in age, had in common a genial outlook on life. Company of a jolly, sportive nature Hood always enjoyed, and Joseph Hewlett strikes one as a person of temperament and interests similar to those of Lieutenant Franck. But it was a mutual passion for the rod and tackle that cemented professional acquaintanceship into devoted friendship. Moreover, the ample warrens near Hewlett's parsonage at Wantage, Berkshire, kindled anew Hood's zest for rabbit hunting. During the good weather season of 1842 and 1843, after he had sent the *New Monthly* to press, Hood frequently went down to Berkshire by train for a long weekend of fishing and hunting. Except for the poem "A Black Job," the establishment of this friendship with the Reverend Mr. Hewlett virtually brought to an end his attacks on religious cant.

Hood published in the *Athenaeum* of June 11 and 18, 1842, his fourth and fifth letters on "Copyright and Copywrong." Written to aid the copyright bill again before Parliament, the two latest letters, like their predecessors, advocate more equitable copyright laws. The last change in them had taken place in 1814 when copyright was extended from the fourteen years of the Act of 1809 to twenty-eight; if the author was still alive, a second fourteen was added. And if at the end of this term the author was living, he received lifetime copyright protection. Although publishers' interests had defeated Talfourd's proposal in 1837, over the next few years the cause found new advocates. Taking up the copyright banner from Talfourd, now a judge and out of Commons, Thomas Babington Macaulay made two memorable speeches whose eloquence convinced the House to pass the bill that became the Copyright Act of 1842. It provided copyright protection for forty-two years, or for the author's lifetime, whichever was longer.[34] Though overshadowed by Talfourd at the beginning and by

Macaulay at the close, Hood through his "Copyright and Copywrong" letters and his correspondence with Talfourd over the
years helped to bring about this Act.

American and Belgian publishers deluged English bookshops
with reprints of English books. This practice angered Hood.
Dickens, he knew, had become the favorite of literary "pirates";
versions of his works, or quite different volumes altogether, went
under such transparent disguises as "Charles Dix" and "Bos." [35]
Merging self-interest into a desire to see permanent improvement
in publishing ethics, Hood hoped the new Copyright Act would
benefit the entire literary profession. Though he found English
publishers venial, American practices received his severest reprimand. No personal ill will did he bear Americans, he took care
to affirm in "Copyright and Copywrong," but comments in letters
reveal he rated them, as did Dickens, a boorish, uncultivated lot.
The only Yankee of importance in his fiction, repellent alike for
his breezy unconcern for others' opinions and for his unabashed
display of gumption, is the unnamed "yellow-faced man" of *Up
the Rhine*.

Dickens had informed Hood at the reunion dinner that his
"Copyright and Copywrong"—in which he stigmatized American
pirates as "Publicans and Sinners"—had been attacked in the
New World.[36] There Hood had told American publishers they
should simply refuse to republish English books. And he had
told them why:

> That America, in the absence of an International Copyright,
> can never possess a native literature has been foretold by the
> second-sighted on either side of the Atlantic. Indeed, accord-
> ing to Mr. Cornelius Mathews, in his speech at the public
> dinner given to Dickens at New York, the barren time is
> already come.... Such must be the inevitable result of the
> re-publication of English works on a scale that totally pre-
> cludes any native competition....[37]

In his opinion Mathews had but echoed other American writers,
among them, Cooper and Margaret Fuller. Lacking perspective or

knowledge or both, Hood was led to undervalue American literature. When he advocates that American publishers, in refraining from reprinting English works, act idealistically, according to patriotism and an altruistic wish to promote their own literature, he is altogether serious. The economic motivation of man he failed utterly to grasp. He imagined a patriotic American sitting in his study, mortified that English authors had written all the books "under a framed and glazed 'Declaration of Independence'" and that only the "paper and the covers [were]...of home manufacture." [38] While the image, needless to say, fails to convey entire conviction, "Copyright and Copywrong" does stress practical problems elsewhere, sufficiently to justify Edgar Allan Poe's comment: "The strong points of the question of copyright, generally, were never more forcibly, if ever more ludicrously, *put*." [39]

But Hood, having lived in the country and among the people, reserved his sharpest barbs for the Belgians. Two years of life in England had dimmed memories of pleasant hours. While Germany he had come to regard with a milder eye, Belgium was a different matter. When Hood damned the Belgians for pirating English books, he damned a people that he considered lived like parasites upon the creative work of others. With literary parasitism he could not charge Germany or America: Germans had a national literature and culture; Americans could at least read English. In consequence, more than those of other nations, Belgian piracies bore a greater stigma.

Traces of self-pity are evident as Hood sums up the sad lot of the present-day "Literary man":

So much for the distinctions bestowed on a Literary man during his life. [Hood had showed how few and empty they were.] Now for the honors paid to him at his death. We all know how he lives. He writes for bread, and gets it short weight;— for money, and gets the wrong change;—for the Present, and he is pirated;—for the Future, and his children are disinherited for his pains. At last, he sickens, as he well may, and can write no more. He makes his will, but, for any literary property, might as well die intestate. His eldest son is his heir, but the

[Publishers'] Row administers. And so he dies a beggar, with the world in his debt.[40]

Hood's interest in "high-flying, deep-diving, German Romanticism" [41] began early and lasted throughout his career. The years after his return from the Continent in 1840 mark the high point of this interest. Deep as his dislike for Rhinelanders ran, his respect for Germany's intellectual achievement, never quite obliterated during his stay abroad, continued and grew. The many references in his writings reveal a wide-ranging (but by no means thorough) acquaintance with German culture since *Werther*. Hood's most thought-provoking observation on German literature occurs in a tale he published in the *New Monthly*, "Diabolical Suggestions" (July, 1842), in which he expresses his horror at the perverse morality involved in the Devil's triumph throughout German romanticism. By "diabolical suggestions" Hood means, it would seem, self-induced hints from the darker forces within man that suggest apparently irrational acts rather than actual verbal promptings from Satan himself. Hood (or the story's first-person narrator) relates the adventures of a presumably fictitious friend, Horace, who, under the influence of a "diabolical suggestion," is gripped by the notion that if he loses a wager made with the Devil he must hand over to him body and soul. The passage in which he develops his theory of German romanticism, a long one, deserves quotation, for in it we have Hood's only extended exposition of his belief that "German Diablerie" could inspire great evil. And if we take as historical the narrator's admission that he did not read German romances in the original, we have additional evidence to support my contention that Hood read German literature only in translations. Horace speaks of the "source" of his misfortune:

"My mastery of the Teutonic language was the source of my misfortune. You are familiar, of course, with the German Romances?"

"Only in the translations."

"You know, then, the prominent part which is played by the Devil in their most popular stories. More prominent even than in Paradise Lost, where Satan figures, not in the ascendant, but as the rebellious antagonist of a still mightier Power, and the divine scheme of Human Redemption moves parallel with the diabolical plot for Human Perdition. In the German Romances, on the contrary, the Fiend possesses the earth, and reigns as absolutely as any Lord Paramount of the feudal ages. Nay, his sway extends beyond this world to the world to come, and he has power over life and death, not only the temporary, but the eternal. The legitimate Governor of the Universe has been deposed, and there is a frightful interregnum —Anarchy succeeds to Order—and the blind random decrees of Chance supersede the ordinances of a sciential Providence. Immortal souls are lost by the turn of a die or a card, or saved by some practical subterfuge or verbal evasion. Fraud and violence alone are triumphant. Justice is blind and Mercy is deaf—the innocent bosom receives the bullet that was moulded with unholy rites; and the maiden, whose studies never extended beyond her prayer book, is involved in the fate of the ambitious student who bartered his salvation for interdicted knowledge. In short, you seem to recognize that dreary fiction of the atheist—a World without a God. Such is the German Diablerie!" . . .

"After learning German, my first use of the acquisition was to go through all their Romances, and consequently a regular course of Diablerie—from the Arch Demon who inhabited Pandemonium, to the imp that lived in a bottle— from the scholar who bartered his soul, to the fellow who sold his own shadow. The consequence I might have foreseen. My head became stuffed with men in black and black dogs —with unholy compacts, and games of chance. I dreamt of Walpurgis Revels and the Wolf's Glen—Zamiel glared on me with his fiery eyes by night; and the smooth voice of Mephistopheles kept whispering in my ear by day. Wherever

my thoughts wandered, there was the foul Fiend straddling
across their path, like Bunyan's Apollyon—ready to play with
me for my immortal soul at cards or dice—to strike infernal
bargains, and to execute unholy contracts to be signed with
blood and sealed with sulphur. In a word, I was completely
be-Devilled." [42]

Earlier in the story, actually more a speculative essay than fiction, Hood took up Coleridge's dictum, "The wise only possess
ideas: the greater part of mankind are possessed by them," and
interpreted it to mean,

> *i.e.*, as a person is said to be *possessed* by an evil spirit or
> demon: a saying so true that we have only to look round us
> to discover hundreds of men and women, gentle and simple,
> in this state of mental thraldom; and in consequence, daily
> committing acts so mischievous to themselves or to others,
> as to seem the plausible results of Diabolical Suggestions.…
> An atrocious idea, wantonly entertained in the first instance,
> is pampered and indulged, till like a spoilt child it tyrannises
> over its parent; and vociferously overwhelming the still small
> voice of conscience and reason—perhaps stiller and smaller
> than usual, in the individual—compels him to submit to the
> growing imperiousness of its dictates.[43]

Though the German romantics whose novellas he devoured—
Chamisso's *Peter Schlemihl* and Hoffmann's *Klein Zaches genannt
Zinnober*, as well as Weber's opera *Der Freischütz* and the first
part of Goethe's *Faust*, he refers to explicitly—corroborated his
ideas, Hood had already adumbrated his theory of the "diabolical
suggestion" in his concept of the "incoherent fancy," a concept
sketched out twenty years earlier in his important essay, "A
Dream."

In "A Dream" he investigates the nature of his dreams and the
ways he felt them to differ from those in the *Confessions of an
English Opium-Eater*. "A large proportion of my dreams," he
noted, "have … an origin more or less remote in some actual

occurrence." [44] Hood does not tell us the dream origins of his
stories that end in a sudden anticlimax, e.g., those in *Up the
Rhine*, presumably because he would have lost the narrative's
dramatic illusion. Although an incident rooted in everyday reality
usually brought on his own dreams, they were not less fantastic
than those in his tales. Once, after a play of his had failed dismally,
he dreamt a fantastic dream vision. As Drury Lane blended into
Pandemonium, his own human agony engendered a vision—in
terrifying verisimilitude and precision of detail—of the fiends
of hell hooting down the play. He found he "could not disen-
tangle my own from my play's perdition. I was damned: but

DREAM.

whether spiritually or dramatically, the twilight intelligence of a
dream was not clear enough to determine." [45]

Since Hood felt powerfully alive to the danger of leaving his
readers believing in the reality of the supernatural, Horace in
"Diabolical Suggestions" is the only one of his heroes who actually
becomes damned through the effects of "German Diablerie."
Partly because his audience expected that he play the funnyman,
partly, too, because there was that in his nature—perhaps it is as
simple as English common sense mixed in with a certain prudish-
ness at the morality of playing with the Unknown—he held back
from probing realms of consciousness of which he was but dimly
aware. Though he adapted the devices and re-created the atmosphere of German romantic tales, he recoiled from letting the ulti-

mate implications of the supernatural stand and undercut its reality with an anticlimactic ending: the hitherto unquestioned reality of the story becomes a dream as the dreamer awakes at the close, rubs his eyes, and smiles that he could conceive such fantasies. Hood meant his readers, presumably, to do the same. While the grotesque element pervading much of his writing has hitherto been accounted for as a continuation of the English Gothic tradition, he hardly refers in the whole corpus of his works to such Gothic novelists as Mrs. Radcliffe.[46] Rather, Hood's *diablerie* derives from German romanticism, though he does give it his own twist, a twist marked by undercutting and characteristic restraint.

Undercutting of the reality established and restraint in the presentation of the supernatural characterize "The Desert-Born" of the 1837 *Comic Annual,* a poem in which the narrator awakes from a terrifying "nightmare." Was the horse's shriek real or was it "demon's mirth"? Hood refuses to say. In a verse extravaganza published in the June and October, 1841, *New Monthly,* "A Tale of a Trumpet," he combines a "diabolical suggestion" with a "moral." The poem's apparent theme concerns an old woman's deafness (the "Trumpet" of the title is an ear trumpet). When one day a peddler comes by and sells this long-frustrated would-be gossip such a trumpet, her greatly desired wish comes true, for now she can hear all the neighborhood chitchat. And a sordid series of tales it is. While thus far the incidents have remained within the confines of realism and credibility, the lines, "Meanwhile the Trumpet, *con amore,* / Transmitted each vile diabolical story," [47] arouse our suspicions. For with a trumpet which picks up every sound we enter once again into the *Märchen* world of German romanticism in its middle and late phases, when the *Märchen,* though maintaining its fantasy, blended into the realism of the approaching *Biedermeierzeit.* E. T. A. Hoffmann's fairy tale, *Der Goldne Topf,* is a characteristic example of this kind of *Märchen.* After Hood's grimalkin has stirred up the whole town, the outraged populace, determined to squelch the accumulating gossip, drag her away and toss her into the local pond. Going under for the last time, she recognizes, "foremost amid the stir," the peddler who had sold her the ear trumpet; in a sudden intuition she realizes, too late however to utter his name, that he is the Devil. Hood's "moral": such is the fate of busybodies who viciously circulate gossip with only imagined "Diabolical Trumpets." Unlike the tales in *Up the Rhine*, no dream ending occurs: the moral, explicitly stated, required that justice be done. But "German Diablerie" had provided him with a convenient twist.

Among Hood's longer poems are "The Knight and the Dragon" and "The Forge," ostensibly imitations, but actually humorous parodies of two Schiller ballads, "Der Kampf mit dem Drachen" and "Der Gang nach dem Eisenhammer." Hood explicitly called "The Knight and the Dragon," first published in *Up the Rhine*, a "new version" of Schiller's poem: "It may have less romance than the indigenous legends, but, perchance, all the more reality." [48] In this poem, a blend of the debunking and the playful, Hood, acutely aware of the ridiculous in life, responded strongly to the "reality" behind the "romance." Of the spate of travel books depicting the "beauties" of the Rhine that flooded England in the 1830's, two of the most vapid were Edward Bulwer's *Pilgrims of the Rhine* (1834) and Fenimore Cooper's *A Residence in France: with an Excursion up the Rhine* (1836). In bored reaction to the abundant verbiage of the latter travelogue, the *Athenaeum* reviewer of September 24, 1836, wondered "what can there remain to be said of 'musical Lurley' [Lorelei] or the 'castled crag of Drachenfels.'" Hood wondered too. In "The Knight and the Dragon" he eschewed both a grandiloquent depiction of Rhineland scenery and a romanticization of unromantic reality. Clearly one of his casual efforts, this mock-heroic ballad smiled irreverently at a poem wholly serious, and, in its jingling unconcern toward a highly moralistic treatment of the legendary and the supernatural, blithely rebuked Schiller for not keeping his feet on the ground.

Instead of the German poet's "Ritter, hoch zu Ross" in medieval Rhodes, Hood presents Sir Otto, a rapacious feudal robber baron, whose castle on the Drachenfels crest commands the Rhine.

In regard to plot, the chief similarity between the two poems—a superficial one indeed—is that both knights fight and kill a dragon, though each knight dispatches his monster in a quite different way. Heroically in Schiller:

> Und eh es ihnen Bissen sich
> Entwindet, rasch erheb ich mich,
> Erspähe mir des Feindes Blösse
> Und stosse tief ihm ins Gekröse,
> Nachborend bis ans Heft, den Stahl;
> Schwarzquellend springt des Blutes Strahl,
> Hin senkt es und begräbt im Falle
> Mich mit des Leibes Riesenballe,
> Dass schnell die Sinne mir vergehn.

Mock-heroically in Hood:

> Then the Knight softly goes
> On the tips of his toes
> To the greedy and slumbering savage,
> And with one hearty stroke
> Of his sword, and a poke,
> Kills the beast that had made such a ravage.[49]

Characteristic of Hood's parodies of situations German authors treated seriously is his ironic reversal of the opening stanzas of Schiller's ballad. There, crowds line the route to cheer the returning knight, successful in his slaying of the dragon. At the end of Hood's poem, however, after Sir Otto, equally successful, continues to pillage the countryside, the peasants cry out *against* him: "Would to the Lord, / That the Dragon had vanquish'd Sir Otto!" [50] It would have been altogether alien to Hood's intention to have captured either Schiller's moral tone or the high purpose of his pious knight. Since detailed parallels do not exist, an attempt to consider Hood's treatment as conscious satire would be tedious, yet one appreciates more fully the irony of his version after one comes to it fresh from a reading of the Schiller ballad.

The other Hood poem based upon Schiller, "The Forge," sub-

titled, significantly, "A Romance of the Iron Age," was first published in the July, 1843, number of the *New Monthly* and had its
origin in Schiller's "Der Gang nach dem Eisenhammer." The
poem's subtitle, like that of "Miss Kilmansegg," indicates Hood
thought "romance" unsuited for his own times, an "iron age" of
reality. As Edward Bulwer had recently translated many of Schiller's
ballads and poems for *Blackwood's Magazine* (September–
December, 1842; February–May, and August, 1843), Hood's poem
may well have drawn its inspiration more from his translation
"Fridolin; or the Message to the Forge" (November, 1842), than
from Schiller. Modeling his grotesque atmosphere explicitly on
the Walpurgis Night scene of *Faust I*, Hood added to it a plot
thread from Schiller's poem. He took, however, neither atmosphere nor plot seriously. As often in his borrowings, he changed
more than he appropriated; one incident in Schiller's poem led
him to imagine his entire narrative. Soon abandoning his source,
he slipped off into a kind of composition in which he felt uniquely
at home: the humorous extravaganza revolving around frequent
puns. Instead of "Ein frommer Knecht war Fridolin," Hood intro-
duces

> Young Fridolin; young Fridolin!
> So free from sauce, and sloth, and sin. . . .
> Of his duty so true a fulfiller—
> But here we need no farther go
> For whoever desires the Tale to know,
> May read it all in Schiller.[51]

The plot of "The Forge" runs roughly thus. In a long introduc-
tory section we come upon the "Stranger" staggering through the
supernatural apparatus of the German forest: Hood's fanciful re-
creation of the Wolf's Glen in Weber's *Der Freischütz*, spiced
with some of the grotesque humor of Faust's and Mephistopheles'
journey to the Blocksberg for Walpurgis Night. In Part II Hood,
inspired by Retzsch's engravings for "Der Gang nach dem Eisenhammer," depicts the ghastly blacksmiths: "Brutal monsters, with
bulky frames, / Beings Humanity scarcely claims, / But hybrids

rather of demon race, / Unbless'd by the holy rite of grace." [52]
Taking one brief incident from the Schiller poem—the heaving
of Robert into the forge's fire—Hood recounts with verve the
similar fate that befell his "Stranger."

Arriving at the forge, the "Stranger" (he is later revealed to be
Satan himself) nestles close to the fire; at a knowing wink from
their leader, the smiths hurl their unsuspecting and unoffending
guest into the flames. When he attempts to crawl out, they deal
him a death blow. Thus the "Stranger" meets his death as the
result of the smiths' malicious spite, and not, as did Robert in
Schiller's poem, as just retribution. The fire beginning to burn
"brimstone blue," the rejoicing of the smiths at the deed done
turns to terror for soon horrid shapes—beings adumbrated by Part
I's spectral atmosphere—"With forked tongues and venomous
stings, / On hagweed, broomsticks, and leathern wings, / Are
hovering round the Hut!" And Hood follows with his own comic-
fantastic Walpurgis Night:

> Sounds! that fill the air with noises,
> Strange and indescribable voices,
> From Hags, in a diabolical clatter—
> Cats that spit curses, and apes that chatter
> Scraps of cabalistical matter—
> Owls that screech, and dogs that yell—
> Skeleton hounds that will never be fatter—
> All the domestic tribes of Hell,
> Shrieking for flesh to tear and tatter
>
> .   .   .   .
>
> In and out, in and out,
> The gathering Goblins hover about,
> Ev'ry minute augmenting the rout;
> For like a spell
> The unearthly smell
> That fumes from the Furnace, chimney and mouth,
> Draws them in—an infernal Legion—
> From East, and West, and North, and South,

> Like carrion birds from ev'ry region,
> Till not a yard square
> Of the sickening air
> But has a Demon or two for its share,
> Breathing fury, woe, and despair,
> Never, never was such a sight!
> It beats the very Walpurgis Night,
> Displayed in the story of Doctor Faustus,
> For the scene to describe,
> Of the awful tribe,
> If we were *two* Göthe's, would quite exhaust us! [53]

Exhibiting great technical dexterity, the poem maintains, even increases its jocular tone and rollicking pace until the grisly end, when the avenging demons cut down one by one the murderous smiths. They all suffer horrible deaths and are afterwards—Hood's necessary "poetic justice"—thrown into their own oven. While "The Forge" illustrates Hood's unusual ability to imagine visually what he read in others, and from the slightest of incidents to conceive an entirely new rendering, the poem's distinction lies in the way he handled a serious theme with grotesque humor.[54] The first to observe Hood's "marked originality of manner" in poems like "The Forge," Poe thought it consisted of a "species of brilliant *grotesquerie*, uttered with a rushing *abandon* which wonderfully aided its effect...." [55]

Walter Savage Landor published in the December, 1842, *Blackwood's* his imaginary conversation, "Southey and Porson." Disliking Wordsworth the man, Landor attacked Wordsworth the poet. Edward Quillinan, the poet's son-in-law, and Crabb Robinson, his lifelong admirer, decided to retaliate. Without Wordsworth's knowledge, Quillinan wrote an "Imaginary Conversation, between Mr. Walter Savage Landor and the Editor of Blackwood's Magazine." He tried to get the conversation accepted in several periodicals, including the *New Monthly*, before he convinced the cantankerous Blackwood, who had published Landor's attack, to publish his own rejoinder in the April, 1843, number. Hood explained to Edward Moxon that he had refused to accept Quillinan's article because it "knocked down" Landor. Though tempted to participate in "a bit of pen & ink skrimmage," he decided not to, in part because of fear of Colburn's reaction, more because of his conviction that personal attacks, as well as political controversy, had no part in his editorial policy:

> However, I fear I must not meddle with the matter, by insertion of the article in the New Monthly—not that I should mind personally a bit of pen & ink skrimmage—in behalf of Wordsworth versus Landor—but it has been my aim as Editor of a Mag—to avoid all controversy with other Mags —and I know Colburn, if I were willing, would be very averse.... In the meantime I sincerely hope & trust that Landor's attack will do no more harm to Wordsworth or his fame than the assault on Wakly. My own notion of the probable result is, that the Poet will be asked again to the Duchess of Sutherland's or Windsor Castle, & that he will have another son (if there be one) made a Stamp Commissioner.[56]

The year 1842 ended on a note of cheer. At a long-delayed dinner party on December 6, the Hoods had as their guests friends old and new: the Dilkes and the Elliot brothers; Dickens and members of his entourage, including Forster and his "Mac," Daniel Maclise; Hewlett, Ainsworth, Barham, Procter, and Sir Charles and Lady Morgan. All enjoyed the evening. "I am very glad to hear that you think the party went off so well," a groggy Hood wrote Mrs. Dilke. "Of course next day we were rather snoozy gapey & indolent & like the wild Beasts after Barthemy Fair, very tame indeed." [57]

Hood worked under great strain. Though the chronicle of illness that constitutes so great a part of his letters becomes less oppressive in these years, he continued to labor under the burden of more than occasional sickness. Yet, content in many ways, he was less preoccupied with his maladies. He brooded less. But the chore of getting the *New Monthly* ready for press each month prostrated him. It left him irritable and nervous, a difficult man with whom to deal. After two years the strain began to tell. "I venture to say," he acknowledged to Hewlett on May 5, 1843,

> no man has gone thro a severer struggle for the last eight or nine years than myself—contending with wretched health, difficulties, dishonesty, & the treachery & misconduct of some who ought to have been friends & allies—but to my astonishment I find myself alive, whilst better lives, in the assurance phrase, have fallen in—& moreover contriving to rub on without losing ground. And I verily believe I have not been beaten, because I would not despond. . . .[58]

Hood reaffirmed his determination to keep up the fight: " 'Never say die' is a capital rule. I think if I had but given myself over,—the die would have been cast." [59] The familiar tone of harassment and weariness, absent from his letters for several years, reappears. Having brought hope and relative prosperity, the *New Monthly* years fast approached their end.

Hood's relations with Colburn steadily deteriorated during 1843. "Colburn's puffing propensities" lay at the root of the dispute. As the leading publisher of fashionable novels, he made every effort to get inserted in the newspapers paid or "stimulated" social gossip about them or their authors. In addition, obliging staff hacks, usually Frederic Shoberl or P. G. Patmore, took upon themselves to place—without consulting Hood—highly adulatory reviews in the *New Monthly*. Although the poet, like Carlyle, disliked this "puffing" practice intensely, believing that as editor it reflected upon his own integrity, his hands were tied. Difficulties also arose over contributions: those sent directly to Colburn's office risked interception by these subordinates, who passed sentence before Hood ever saw them. Though editor, he was decidedly not master in his own house.

"Copyright and Copywrong," with its harsh comments on the publishing trade, marked the first severe friction. "On the publication of my *last Copyright Letter*," wrote Hood to Dickens, Colburn "attempted to call me to account for writing in the Athm. I had all along told him I should write there & had done so, *till then* without an objection." [60] But it was the publication by Colburn in February, 1843, of *The Tuft-Hunter*, a three-volume novel purportedly by Lord William Lennox, that brought matters, long simmering, to a head.[61] Though the February *New Monthly* regarded the novel with admiration, a sardonic review, probably by Dilke, in the February 25 *Athenaeum* disclosed it to be a compendium of plagiarisms. With but slight change, Lennox— or his ghost writer—had taken over substantial passages from several Scott novels, including *The Antiquary* and *St. Ronan's Well*, from Henry Chorley's *The Lion*, and from Hood's own *Tylney Hall*. "You might have been perhaps severer upon it—" observed Hood, congratulating Dilke upon his exposure, "Lord L. is a fool, but the other [Shoberl, the presumed perpetrator of the fraud] is a thorough rogue, & double traitor,—the *system* deserves denouncing—however I have thundered a bit at the attempt to connect me with it—& am having my fun out of Colburn." [62] To *Punch* Hood sent off a sarcastic epigram.[63] But it was to his close friend Hewlett that he let off the exuberance of his outraged amusement:

> I must shortly give you a bit of literary gossip—such a mess with Lord W. Lennox's Novel—the Tuft Hunter! Plagiarisms of whole paragraphs from the Antiquary—St. Ronan's Well— Tylney Hall—12 pages from the "Lion" by Chorley—and plunderings besides I understand from H. Smith—James— Mrs. Hall—& Bulwer! To complete the thing *I* one of the copied was applied to, for a Preface, by Shoberl as a direct request from Lord L—who says he only suggested it—& the burthen of said Preface to be Copyright & Literary Piracy! ... I have been very angry and rather amused but as yet all is dark.... I never recollect such a Phenomenon during my literary experience! [64]

Henry Colburn was not amused. Though for some months no open break occurred, the incident further strained Hood's already

delicate relationship with him. Nervousness and failing health, a
strident mid-August letter to Franck reveals, were taking their toll.
"I have to write, till I am sick of the sight of pen, ink and
paper . . . ," said Hood, envying the new captain his life of ease.
He contrasted it with his own hard-pressed existence: "Why, for
one half the month I have hardly time to eat, drink, or sleep. . . ."
Furthermore, two years of forced haste to meet monthly dead-
lines had ruined his nerves.

> Seriously . . . you cannot imagine the hurry I live in, like
> most of my contemporaries, but aggravated in my case by
> frequent illness, which makes me get into arrears of busi-
> ness. . . . Sometimes at the end of the month, I sit up three
> nights successively, Jane insisting on sitting up with me, so
> that we see the sun rise now and then. . . .

"Then," Hood adds, "we are obliged to visit and be visited, which
we shun as much as we can, but must to some extent go through,
as I am a sort of public man." And having an important position, Hood learned, entailed "extra work." For the *Manchester
Athenaeum* he wrote a long letter on "the benefits of literature,"
and to commemorate the popular actor Edward Elton, who had
drowned leaving seven children destitute, he wrote, at Dickens's
earnest request, a "poetical address" which Mrs. Warner delivered
at the benefit performance at the Haymarket Theatre.[65] A weary
Hood had become a forty-four-year-old unsmiling "public man."
    The same day, August 14, that Hood wrote Franck, John Fowler,
either his legal representative or a go-between with Colburn, told
him the result of a meeting he had just had with the *New
Monthly*'s owner:

> Our interview was most unsatisfactory. He refuses to accede
> to the terms I have endeavoured to press upon him. He accepts
> your resignation of the Editorship . . . and intimates that he
> will enforce the alleged agreement for New Monthly articles
> by all means within his power. If not being Editor—you con-
> sent without legal obligation to contribute, he offers you 30

guineas a sheet for your Articles—himself to have the whole Copyright, and not to interfere with Contributions elsewhere (excepting Bentley's & Ainsworths Magazines). Also—he still offers to advance you on account of the forthcoming volume [Whimsicalities], 50£, but he declines to purchase your share of the Copyright.[66]

Hood had left Fowler no room to compromise. Except for the unavoidable publication of Whimsicalities, he severed all further

HUNGERFORD MARKET.

connection with Colburn and the New Monthly. It was a fateful step. Nervous and sick, Hood opted for the quick break. Once more he was on his own. A month later he was in Scotland, the break with Colburn accomplished, out of a well-paying job, two lawsuits with Baily coming up, and again open to offers from any quarter.

Before he left for Scotland, Hood asked Dickens for letters of recommendation to Professor Macvey Napier and to one of the many who had cried at Little Nell's death, Francis Jeffrey. "I may be able to write an occasional review in the Edinbro," a jobless Hood surmised; the *Athenaeum*'s pages closed to him "for certain reasons," [67] he hoped the Scottish quarterly would let him review *Martin Chuzzlewit*. "I long to have a talk with you on matters in general," he continues, obviously bewildered, to Dickens, "& but for the other trip should have taken a day at Broadstairs on purpose, for we have never yet had a regular gossip—or comparison of 'Notes.' " The meeting, unfortunately, did not take place. Dickens's sound business sense might have steadied the older man, impulsive and high-minded, but too apt to follow conscience in matters where conscience need not be followed. Believing that Hood had resigned the editorship at a bad time, the novelist did not scruple to tell his friend his opinion. Though he thought the terms of Hood's contract with Colburn despicable, he cautioned the poet not to make an irrevocable decision.[68] The whole was sound advice, but Hood, not to be headed, rashly followed his own bent.

Chapter 4

Poet of the Poor

Scotland came as a relief and a rest. Hood's three-week visit marked the first time since he had assumed responsibility for the *New Monthly* two years before that he had gotten away for an extended holiday. An "excellent" passage by steamer brought him, accompanied by young Tom, to Dundee on the morning of September 15. Upon leaving London he had felt "very much out of sorts," but the sea air had, as so often before, revived his spirits. "My father was received with open arms by the Scotch," wrote his son later, and "having a little Scotch blood in him, [he] was not slow in meeting their advances." [1] When he could overcome his shyness in strange company, the poet conquered everyone with his quiet warmth. While he had not kept up with the friends he had made during his youthful stay at Dundee, still he made every effort to look them up. But he had poor luck: one was away, another died during his visit.

Dundee itself he found "much altered." A small fishing port thirty years ago, it had since grown, "owing to the march of manufacture," into an industrial town. "To the east a remarkably fine crop of tall chimneys had sprung up in lieu of one,—all factories. But," added the author of "I remember, I remember," "I suspect they have been going [up] too fast." Dundee provided Hood with the change of air he greatly needed, and at the home of his Scottish aunt and uncle the cares of London seemed far away. "I have banished all thoughts of bookery," he wrote his wife, "and mean to take my swing of idleness, not always the root of all evil." [2] After a pleasant week, father and son left for Edinburgh.

Arriving in the Scottish capital during the Long Vacation, Hood had the ill luck to miss seeing several of its absent literary celebrities: "Wilson thirty miles off, Napier gone too." But he did go out to Craigcrook to meet Francis Jeffrey; and he saw the publisher

Blackwood as well as William Chambers, brother of the Robert he knew. Another day he spent in animated conversation with D. M. Moir, *Blackwood's* "Delta." Besides his visits, Hood engaged in extensive sightseeing; "I am delighted with the city," he wrote Jane, "—it exceeds my expectations." [3] After a week to ten-days' stay, strength and confidence restored, he took his return passage.

The beginning of October found Hood once again in London, once again without definite plans. Desirous of securing the editorship of an established journal, he made enquiries of Cunningham and Mortimer, publishers of *Ainsworth's Magazine*. Three parties had assured him Ainsworth was no longer editor. On October 19, to his surprise, Ainsworth himself wrote him saying that, though still editor, he would welcome him as contributor; he offered "16 guineas per sheet—the highest terms the Magazine can afford, and higher than are given to any other contributor." [4] Hood apologized for his error, but refused the offer. "At any rate the terms won't do," he confided to Dickens, "& I do not like the aspect of things. ... My *notion* is to see *Mortimer* tomorrow & know the rights of it—to decline the thing—& reopen an old arrangement with Bentley." [5] Supposing the editorship of *Bentley's Miscellany* open, Hood wrote on October 21 to Bentley. By the twenty-fifth Bentley had informed him, Hood told Dickens, not only that it was not, but that he had "not the remotest idea of making any alteration...." [6] To Bentley's formal note Hood replied stiffly that had he known the editorship was filled, he would not have offered his services. "Under this impression, and having paid off Colburn, I took the opportunity of offering my cooperation,—the loss of which," he reminded Bentley, "you were once pleased to consider as a grievance." [7] Bentley no doubt remembered the occasion three years before when Hood had not kept a contract for contributions.

While simultaneously negotiating on two fronts, Hood toyed with the idea of starting his own magazine. Independence of any kind always tempted him. His own journal and a completely free editorial hand—such a prospect enchanted the poet, cramped for two years by Henry Colburn's dishonest ethics. Nor did it exclude other projects. One was for a separate edition of "The Elm Tree," William Harvey doing the illustrations; another was for an edition of his German poems. Nothing came of either project; but by early November his plans—a frenzied paragraph to Dr. Elliot reveals them—had at last coalesced: "first, my two volumes from the 'New Monthly' [*Whimsicalities*] to prepare for the press, with tedious waitings on Colburn . . . & finally negotiations about to close for a new periodical! 'Hood's Magazine.' to come out 1st January!!!" [8]

Despite his rupture with Colburn and the consequent ill-feelings, aggravated with the passing of each month, Hood prepared for press two volumes of his *New Monthly* contributions written while editor. With most of the illustrations by the well-known comic artist John Leech, they were published in December, 1843, (the volumes carry an 1844 imprint) by Colburn as *Whimsicalities, a Periodical Gathering*. *Whimsicalities*, the preface indicates, has didactic purpose. Hood disclaims, however, any attempt at profundity: "As usual, the Reader will vainly look in my pages for any startling theological revelations, profound political views, philological disquisitions, or scientific discoveries." But he will do what he has always done: "instruct." For each article he feels obliged to tell the reader precisely what didactic purpose he has in mind:

> My humble aim has been chiefly to amuse: but the liberal Utilitarian will, perhaps, discern some small attempts to instruct at the same time. He will, maybe, detect in "The Defaulter," a warning against rash and uncharitable judgments; in the "Black Job," a "take care of your pockets, from the Pseudo-Philanthropists"; in "Mr. Withering's Cure," a hint on Domestic Economy; in the "Omnibus," a lesson on Prudery; and in the "News from China," a satire on maternal over-indulgence, and the neglect of moral culture in the young. . . . [9]

The "some small attempts to instruct," rarely obvious upon a first reading, remind us that Hood often is, when apparently most "comic," in fact most "serious."

Among *Whimsicalities'* "moral" poems, "A Black Job" stands out. In it Hood satirizes both the excesses of Evangelical fervor and the willing credulity of those who give unquestioningly to utopian schemes. When "A knot of very charitable men / Set up a Philanthropical Society" to aid the Negro, Hood asks why:

> And what might be their aim?
>   To rescue Afric's sable sons from fetters—
> To save their bodies from the burning shame
>   Of branding with hot letters—
> Their shoulders from the cowhide's bloody strokes,
>   Their necks from iron yokes?
> To end or mitigate the ills of slavery,
>   The Planter's avarice, the Driver's knavery?

If not "To end or mitigate the ills of slavery," what then? Education?

> To school the heathen Negroes and enlighten 'em,
>   To polish up and brighten 'em,
> And make them worthy of eternal bliss?

Obviously not. A "Philanthropical Society" would never lower itself to such a practical "aim."

> Why, no—the simple end and aim was this—
> Reading a well-known proverb much amiss—
>   To wash and whiten 'em!

The whiter the Negroes were scrubbed, the "pseudo-Philanthropists" assumed, the more pure and blessed they would become in God's eyes. Purposely making their project absurd, Hood mocks their misguided charity. A more active interest in the Negro's physical welfare on earth, he implies, might well replace such an impractical aim. No efforts, of course, prevail to lighten their black skins, "Satan's livery." But the Society's Chairman, "the philanthropic man," insists that "Because Humanity declares we must!" the task must go on:

> "We've scrubb'd the negroes till we've nearly killed 'em,
> And finding that we cannot wash them white,
> But still their nigritude offends the sight,
> *We mean to gild 'em!*" [10]

Hood attacked not only the fatuous "aim" of the "pseudo-Philanthropists" but also their assumption of racial superiority when he had them propose "To benefit the race of man, / And in particular that dark variety, / Which some suppose inferior...." [11] His own egalitarian belief he stated in "The Workhouse Clock": "For surely ... men are all akin, / Whether of fair or sable skin, / According to Nature's scheme...." [12] Though few contemporaries held this view, Hood always had. Another poem, "Pompey's Ghost," a "pathetic ballad," questions—in the lines "You think because I'm black I am / The Devil, but I ain't!"—common acceptance of a stereotype. The motto from Cowper pinpoints the "moral": "Skins may differ, but affection / Dwells in white and black the same." [13] Color, Hood realizes, is arbitrary.

The Evangelical and Quaker campaign to abolish slavery in British possessions, he admitted, had done much good. But having attained its goal in 1833, Evangelical moral fervor in years after sought new outlets, and found them in schemes less laudatory: [14] schemes that to outsiders like Hood often appeared ridiculous. His prose introduction to "The Doves and the Crows" indicates that he was well aware that "Victory had brought with it a very embarrassing result. The Abolition, in annihilating Slavery," he writes,

> had also abolished the Abolitionists; and a vast stock of sensibility and sympathy, and zeal and humanity, which had heretofore found a vent in another hemisphere, was left quite a drug upon hand.

Identifying the abolition movement more with the Quakers than with other sects, Hood asks: "What will the Quakers do next?" And replies:

> The most obvious answer was, that they ought to continue their patronage to the Emancipated; but the manner in which it should be done, was more difficult to indicate.

That Hood was unimpressed by either Evangelical "patronage" or "the manner in which it should be done" both poems, "The Doves [Quakers] and the Crows [Negroes]" and "A Black Job," amply, if humorously, demonstrate. But he realized that the interest in reform abroad was, in effect, a refusal to look at the need

A REVERSE IN BUSINESS.

for reform at home. "How the 'Sable sons of Africa,'" he ponders, "became so signally the favourites, the pets, the 'curled darlings,' of the sedate, sober, silent, serious, sad-coloured sect [the Quakers], overlooking the Factory Children, and other white objects of sympathy, is a moral mystery. . . ." [15] This "moral mystery" Hood never pretended to understand. Though he in no way denies that Negroes should receive help, he argues in, for example, the essay "The Black and White Question" and in the poem "The Sweep's Complaint" that problems at home demand first attention.

"You know [Edwin] Landseer's Doggish picture of 'Laying Down the Law,' " Hood wrote Hewlett, "well, I have written some dogrel verses to go with the print...." [16] Addressing Landseer as "Thou great Pictorial Aesop," he asks him, "What is the moral of this painted fable?" And he answers his own question: the right of the poor to due process of the law. This, the poem "Laying Down the Law" demonstrates, "lay" beyond their resources. In this poem Hood has animals, as in *Le Roman de Renart*, protest against society and triumph over the "system." Belonging to a line of humorous moralists that uses animals to criticize society, a line that runs from Aesop to Boccaccio, from La Fontaine to James Thurber, Hood too felt no constraint about explicitly stating his "moral": "As human suitors have had cause to weep— / For what is Law, unless poor Dogs can get it / Dog-cheap?" [17]

"The Elm Tree," subtitled "A Dream in the Woods," is one of Hood's few late romantic poems. Written in imitation of Keats's style, it deals too, in its serious preoccupation with death, with a subject about which Keats had profound understanding. Though on the surface a poem about the cutting down of a tree, it is actually more: an allegory of Life and Death, and of Death's eventual victory. The opening stanza's mysterious sound echoes throughout the poem. It is a sound that "from a Tree ... came to me," the "me" being the poem's "I," its persona—or Hood himself. Not a forest sound, however, it is rather "As if beneath the dewy grass / The dead began to groan." It is omnipresent:

> But still the sound was in my ear,
> A sad and solemn sound,
> That sometimes murmur'd overhead,
> And sometimes underground—
> 'Twas in a shady Avenue
> Where lofty Elms abound. [18]

This "sad and solemn sound," hovering about the tree and yet not of it, anticipates the coming of Death.

In Part II another sound interrupts the wailings of the dead: the "Woodman's" axe-blows crashing through the forest. As they

banish "bird and beast" from around the elm, in poetry tradition-
ally the tree of sorrow, silence makes more audible the "sad and
solemn sound." The ancient "Woodman," a primeval figure, is
but a deputy for Death, perhaps even for Him who determines
when Death shall strike, God. His "sturdy arm and steady aim" fell
the elm. This particular tree, "yonder blasted Elm that stands /
So like a man of sin," is like he "Who, frantic, flings his arms
abroad / To feel the Worm within," a man, in short, very much
like the death-haunted Hood himself. The "Elm" (it is capitalized
throughout the poem), which had "thrice the human span . . .
stood erect as man," must be, "like mortal Man himself, / Struck
down by the hand of God." At the close of Part II there is only
silence. "The Echo sleeps." [19] Death has conquered.

And yet, Part III reveals, not wholly. Death itself, a "grisly
Phantom," comes nigh. A note of social protest enters the poem.
Death seeks high prey, but "haughty Peer and mighty King . . .
Shall lodge . . . well" within an "oaken cell." The poor man, how-
ever, "he who never knew a home," shall find in the elm his last
and only refuge:

> "The tatter'd, lean, dejected wretch,
>   Who begs from door to door,
> And dies within the cressy ditch,
>   Or on the barren moor,
> The friendly Elm shall lodge and clothe
>   That houseless man and poor!"

In Part I the poet, "As one who walks afraid," had looked "Beyond
the green arcade," and seen the sky, a "glimpse of Heav'n." [20]
But the houseless pauper of Part II is given no such promise of
redemption.

Death vanishes, and the skies, overcast at his arrival, clear. Nature rejoices, bursts into life. Only "on my sadden'd spirit still /
The Shadow leaves a shade." For Hood realizes that Death has
come, not to fell elm or oak, but rather to fell "conscious, moving,
breathing trunks / That throb with living blood"—in short, human
beings. The "I" of the poem, obviously Hood, has a "secret, vague,
prophetic gloom":

> As though by certain mark
> I knew the fore-appointed Tree,
> Within whose rugged bark
> This warm and living frame shall find
> Its narrow house and dark.[21]

Though possibly a death wish, it is more likely that when Hood espies the "mystic Tree" that will contain his mortal remains, he indicates an acceptance of his own death as near. Death had always been an axial theme of his poetry and the inseparable companion of his life, but never before had he faced it with such direct honesty.

On December 16, 1843, occurred an event of capital importance in the career of Thomas Hood. When *Punch*'s Christmas issue came out on that day, it contained two poems by him. One was "The Pauper's Christmas Carol." The other was "The Song of the Shirt."

Hood's first acquaintance with *Punch* went back to 1841 when, to his mild annoyance, he found his name listed without his permission among the contributors to the first number: "MR. T. HOOD, Professor of Punmanship, Begs to acquaint the dull and witless, that he has established a class for the acquirement of an elegant and ready style of punning." Vouching for the Professor's abilities, the magazine claimed that the "very worst hands are improved in six short and mirthful lessons." [22] The next year, 1842, Hood's old friends and printers of the *Comic Annuals*, Bradbury and Evans, acquired a two-thirds share in the magazine and at the end of the year took over full control. Given Hood's comic talent and the magazine's modest success, he was soon asked to become a contributor. "You will be glad to hear that I have made an arrangement with Bradbury to contribute to *Punch*," he wrote Dickens, "but that is a secret I cannot keep from you." His first contribution to a magazine whose type of humor so well accorded with his own was a caustic epigram on *Punch*'s then favorite butt of ridicule, Lord William Lennox, and over the next few months he scribbled off a dozen or two conundrums. In the same letter to Dickens he observed, "It will be light occasional work for odd times." [23] And so it was—for a while.

Hood's first serious contribution to *Punch*, "A Drop of Gin," appeared on November 18, 1843. To depict the grotesque victims of drink, the "magnified monsters," he recalled the diabolical blacksmiths, the "brutal monsters" in Retzsch's engravings for Schiller's "Der Gang nach dem Eisenhammer":

> Gin! Gin! a drop of Gin!
> What magnified monsters circle therein!
>   Ragged, and stained with filth and mud,
>   Some plague spotted, and some with blood!
> Shapes of misery, shame, and sin!
>   Figures that make us loathe and tremble,
>   Creatures scarce human that more resemble
> Broods of diabolical kin,
> Ghosts of vampyre, demon and Jin!

Once lured into the "Palace of Gin," the weary wretches, past earthly salvation, soon go under:

> Gin! Gin! a drop of Gin!
> Oh! then its tremendous temptations begin,
>   To take, alas!
>   To the fatal glass;—
> And happy the wretch that does not win
>   To change the black hue
>   Of his ruin to "blue"—
> While angels sorrow, and demons grin—
>   And lose the rheumatic
>   Chill of his attic
> By plunging into the Palace of Gin! [24]

As in Zola's *L'Assommoir*, the "Gin Palace"—Walter Jerrold surmises that it was Hood who popularized this expression [25]—exercises a magnetic attraction on those who have abandoned hope; once man has succumbed to gin's "tremendous temptations," no reprieve is possible. Yet Hood recognizes he must not judge: "we are neither Barebones nor Prynne"; or condemn: "Let Anger be mute, / And sweet Mercy dilute, / With a drop of pity, the drop of Gin!" Zola did not explicitly ask for pity, but Hood did: what can man do when, penniless, without food and deep in debt, "darkly, Adversity's days set in," when "time elopes / With all golden hopes"? [26] Only the misery of life forces man to gin.

With this poem Hood became a dedicated man. The concern for the poor and their welfare manifest in "A Drop of Gin" represents no radical change of direction, but had been, on the contrary, a major concern of his work after 1835. That Hood had before affirmed humanitarian views and that he had affirmed them with force is a point, however, that needs insisting upon, for recent critics of Hood, among them Professors Cuyler, Whitley, and Reid, insist otherwise. Thus Cornelius M. Cuyler, writing of Hood's interest in social problems, asserts: "the change came only at the end of 1843." [27] Thus Alvin Whitley: "Although Hood's present reputation is based almost entirely on his humanitarian verse, the major portion of his career was unconcerned with social or political problems, and only a pre-disposed eye could find evidence of them in any earlier work." [28] And thus also J. C. Reid: writing of Hood's "new social vein," he states: "he had done little more than glancingly refer to social matters in such poems as 'The Assistant Drapers' Petition' before 1843." [29]

This is simply not the case. As the "change" was not precipitate, no "pre-disposed eye" is needed. In late 1843, however, Hood's feelings did grow in intensity and they did cause a shift of emphasis in his poetry. He had long played moralist to society; he was—if such a being exists—a comic *homme engagé*. But once he realized in late 1843 that people did take him seriously when he wrote seriously, he felt more secure in throwing off his comic mantle. In the last year and a half of his life he wrote other poems that, without humor and without puns, show his desire to teach freed from the shackles, if such they were, of comic poetry.

"A Drop of Gin" marks this turning point: it begins a series of eight poems whose seriousness is unquestionable. With its publication, Hood's commitment to expose contemporary injustice and to help remedy it by his verse never faltered. These eight poems are, in order of publication, "A Drop of Gin," "The Pauper's Christmas Carol," "The Song of the Shirt," "The Lady's Dream," "The Workhouse Clock," "The Bridge of Sighs," "The Lay of the Labourer," and "Suggestions by Steam." "A Drop of Gin," in essence a sincere plea though containing several puns, serves as transition from the boisterous "Miss Kilmansegg" to the punless "Bridge of Sighs."

Punch's Christmas number, besides "The Song of the Shirt," contains the often-overlooked "Pauper's Christmas Carol." A workhouse pauper finds incongruous only one day of "famous cheer" in "Two-and-fifty weeks of toil":

> Full of drink and full of meat,
> On our *Saviour's* natal day,
> *Charity's* perennial treat;
> Thus I heard a Pauper say:—
> "Ought not I to dance and sing
> Thus supplied with famous cheer?
>
> . . . .
>
> "After labour's long turmoil,
> Sorry fare and frequent fast,
> Two-and-fifty weeks of toil,
> Pudding-time is come at last!
> But are raisins high or low,
> Flour and suet cheap or dear?
>
> . . . .
>
> "Fed upon the coarsest fare
> Three hundred days and sixty-four
> But for *one* on viands rare,
> Just as if I wasn't poor!
> Ought not I to bless my stars,
> Warden, clerk, and overseer?" [30]

Each stanza ends with the ironic refrain: Heigho! / I hardly know— / Christmas comes but once a year." The pauper's wistful sadness does not cloak his—and Hood's—deep bitterness. Nor does the poem exist in a sentimental vacuum. In a factual article, "Christmas-Day in the Workhouses" (December 26, 1842), *The Times* reported the total number of inmates in each of the London workhouses and whether the number of "in-door" and "out-door" poor had increased or decreased since the year previous. This article, or one similar, Hood may well have recalled when he wrote his poem. For each workhouse the article reported, without ironic intention, of what consisted the annual "Christmas-day fare": portions, severely rationed by the authorities, of the "old English cheer" of—I take one sample fare—"roast beef [6 oz.], plum-pudding [1 pd.], and porter [1 pt.]...." Such once-a-year regalement led Hood, with ironic intention, to have his pauper wonder: "But shall I ever dine again? / Or see another feast appear?" [31]

"I send the Song of the Shirt—Will it be too grave for Punch?" Hood queried Mark Lemon, the magazine's bright young editor; "if not there may be some more of it." [32] He accompanied the manuscript with a note that left it to Lemon's discretion whether to put it in the journal or in the "waste-paper basket." [33] Though the "London Charivari" protested—was not *Punch* intended to be comic?—Lemon put it in the journal, gave it a page to itself, and surrounded it with an incongruous comic border. Years later he recalled that Hood, not thinking highly of the poem, had told him that he had already sent it off to three other journals and that all three had rejected it. But not Jane Hood: "Now mind, Hood, mark my words, this will tell wonderfully. It is one of the best things you ever did!" [34] And it was.

The opening stanzas—showing a poverty-stricken seamstress at her work in a shabby, almost bare room—establish the scene:

> With fingers weary and worn,
> With eyelids heavy and red,
> A woman sat, in unwomanly rags,
> Plying her needle and thread—
> Stitch! stitch! stitch!

In poverty, hunger, and dirt,
And still with a voice of dolorous pitch
She sang the "Song of the Shirt."

. . . . . .

"Work—work—work
Till the brain begins to swim;
Work—work—work
Till the eyes are heavy and dim!
Seam, and gusset, and band,
Band, and gusset, and seam,
Till over the buttons I fall asleep,
And sew them on in a dream!

"Oh, Men, with Sisters dear!
Oh, Men, with Mothers and Wives!
It is not linen you're wearing out,
But human creatures' lives!
Stitch—stitch—stitch,
In poverty, hunger and dirt,
Sewing at once, with a double thread,
A Shroud as well as a Shirt."

Death, the seamstress sighs, will come as a relief to such a life of inhuman misery. Hood inserts his *moralitas* in the fifth stanza: "Oh, God! that bread should be so dear, / And flesh and blood so cheap!" [35]

Stanza eight closes with the poem's one pun:

While underneath the eaves
The brooding swallows cling
As if to show me their sunny backs
And twit me with the spring.

While some critics have thought in bad taste a pun on "twit" in this intensely serious poem, I find that "twit," its laughter both irreverent and terribly cruel, accentuates the girl's bleak fate. Echoes of Wordsworth and of Hood's own lament of lost innocence, "I remember, I remember," haunt her desire to escape her fate for "only one short hour" and wander at will in the countryside:

> "Oh! but to breathe the breath
> Of the cowslip and primrose sweet—
> With the sky above my head,
> And the grass beneath my feet,
> For only one short hour
> To feel as I used to feel,
> Before I knew the woes of want
> And the walk that costs a meal!"

But "No blessed leisure for Love or Hope" is permitted her, not even tears: they would hinder her from sewing. Hood closes with the wish that "the Rich" will hear her "Song of the Shirt." [36]

Throughout the Hungry Forties *The Times* fought one bitter campaign after another against intolerable working conditions and against the New Poor Law. It carried frequent accounts of the abject circumstances under which London seamstresses struggled for existence. Many of Hood's poems are close to his age and many have a journalistic origin—none more so than "The Song of the Shirt." [37]

The Times's police report of October 26, 1843, records the case of a poor widow, "a wretched-looking woman named Biddell, with a squalid, half-starved infant at her breast." She had contracted to sew trousers together for a slopseller named Henry Moses at 7*d.* the pair; out of this wage she had to supply her own needles and thread. To obtain "dry bread" for herself and her two young children, she pawned several articles of the material entrusted to her; unable to redeem the security she had given, she had been hauled into court. Forced to sew trousers together all day every day, she claimed overwork and near starvation as excuse for not fulfilling her contract. Moses's foreman maintained that, if "honest and industrious," she could earn a "good living." When pressed by the magistrate to state what he considered a "good living," he replied about "7*s.* a week." [38] The prisoner agreed, but "only if she were to work by night as well as by day." The magistrate, observing that "the affair was one of very common occurrence in that part of the metropolis," was hesitant to sentence Biddell to the House of Correction; he sent her instead to the workhouse. In a second case on the same day a "smartly-dressed" woman demanded the arrest of a girl for pawning some shirts; the woman "said that her contract for the shirts was 1½d. each, and she gave them out to be done for 1¼d." The magistrate, though he ordered the return of the shirts, refused a warrant.

The next day, October 27, *The Times* responded to these cases with a long leader and a supporting factual article, "The White Slaves of London," both of which expressed outrage at such conditions. According to the leader, for Biddell to earn "her cruelly miserable pittance" of 7s. she would have to work 96 hours a week, "16 hours every week-day, or nearly 14 hours every day, including Sunday." Savage against the rich who "are scandalously neglect[ing] their duty" and against slopsellers and middlewomen, it concluded that a London seamstress was from "every moral point of view, as much a slave as any negro who ever toiled under as cruel taskmasters in the West Indies."

On October 31 *The Times* published a "justification" of his work contracts from Henry Moses himself. In the same issue it published another letter, dated October 28, from "An American." He had read *The Times*'s reports, wondered how true they were, and decided to find out for himself. When a ragged woman, "decent but infirm," accosted him and besought him to buy a spray of flowers, he asked her if he might see where she lived. She agreed, took him to her home, and

> ushered me into a mean and miserable apartment, about 10 feet square, which contained no other furniture than a crazy chair, without bottom, and one or two cooking utensils. By the light of a farthing candle I discovered two poor children, shivering with cold (for there was no fire in the grate), with scarce a whole, and certainly not a warm, garment on their backs. . . . In one corner of the room lay a parcel of shavings

on the floor, covered by an old and battered baize, and this she said was their only bed.

Though common to many of the cases reported in *The Times*, details in this letter closely parallel those in Hood's poem: the letter's "crazy chair, without bottom" corresponds to the "broken chair" of the "Song"; the "scarce a whole, and certainly not a warm, garment on their backs" to "rags"; the "only bed" a "parcel of shavings on the floor" to "a bed of straw." [39] Hood undoubtedly saw this letter and the reports of the Biddell case in *The Times*. He may even have seen "Famine and Fashion" in the November 4th *Punch* and the sarcastic poem subjoined to the article, "Moses and Co." Every writer on Hood has assumed these cases provided the immediate inspiration for the composition of "The Song of the Shirt."

But the sad plight of London seamstresses had engaged Hood years before he read of the Biddell case. In "Miss Kilmansegg" he deplored the lot of women who "sit all day to hem and sew, / As females must—and not a few— / To fill their insides with stitches!" [40] And in "The Defaulter" (*New Monthly*, January, 1843), he abruptly reproached a generic character, "Female Sensibility," for her misdirected sentiments. In details and in vocabulary—"stitches," "seam," and "gusset"—he clearly anticipates "The Song of the Shirt." "My dear young lady," Hood begins,

I can appreciate your motives and do honour to your feelings. But before you go round with your book among relations, acquaintance, and strangers, soliciting pounds, shillings, and pence, from people of broad, middling, and narrow incomes, just do me the favour to look into yonder garret, exposed to us by the magic of the Devil on Two Sticks, and consider that respectable young woman, engaged at past midnight, by the light of a solitary rushlight, in making shirts at three-halfpence a piece, and shifts for nothing. Look at her hollow eyes, her withered cheeks, and emaciated frame, for it is a part of the infernal bargain that she is to lose her own health and find her own needles and thread. Reckon, if you can, the thousands of weary stitches it will require to sew, not gussets, and seams, but body and soul together: and perhaps, after all her hard sewing, having to sue a shabby employer for the amount of her pitiful earnings. Estimate, if you may, the terrible wear and tear of head and heart, of liver and lungs. Appraise, on oath, the value of youth wasted, spirits outworn, prospects blasted, natural affections withered in the bud, and all blissful hopes annihilated, except those beyond the grave.[41]

From this prose paragraph emerged Hood's hymn to injured Woman. While the Biddell case may well have decided him to prepare the "Song" for publication, the existence of this hitherto ignored prose "synopsis"—as close in its details to the "Song" as the three cases reported in *The Times*—a year before the publication of the poem strongly suggests that Hood may have conceived the poem before January, 1843. (It also makes more credible his telling Lemon that three journals had already rejected it.) [42] Not at all the kind of poem that would suit the *New Monthly*'s pages, Hood may have put a draft of the "Song" aside, then decided to capitalize on it when he saw the furor caused by the Biddell case. He came in time to consider it the key poem of his career.

The poem made history. In *The Age of Paradox* John Dodds cites it as "perhaps of all poems in the decade the one to make the deepest impact on the largest number of people." [43] As it stands, the "Song" has a unity that none of *The Times*'s cases has: of place—the bare room; of time—any and all time; of action—the woman speaks in and of her misery. Hood's seamstress, like Arnold's Wragg, is a symbol for nameless, uncounted thousands. In time the poem became, as Richard Garnett noted, one of the "genuine *Volkslieder*" that had their birth in the nineteenth century's squalid industrialism.[44] Reprinted in many newspapers— *The Times, The Examiner,* and *The Sun* among them—it was soon hawked about the streets on ballad sheets; ladies wove Hood's lines onto "moral" pocket handkerchiefs; translations appeared in French, German, Italian, eventually in Russian. "But what delighted, and yet touched, my father most deeply," remembered his daughter Fanny, "was that the poor creatures, to whose sorrows and sufferings he had given such eloquent voice, seemed to adopt its words as their own, by singing them about the streets to a rude air of their own adaptation." [45] As the "Song," published anonymously, "ran through the land like wild-fire," several persons had the audacity to claim they had written it. Hood was obliged to send a note to *The Sun* to acknowledge his authorship publicly, though Dickens, for one, had guessed it right away. Throughout the nineteenth century the "Song," its didactic value unquestioned, ranked as the most popular of Hood's poems. People alive today remember learning it by heart as youngsters either at home or in school.[46]

While "The Song of the Shirt" carried his name from one end of England to the other, preparations for the first number of *Hood's Magazine* had moved forward rapidly. In December, 1843, Hood looked upon the establishment of a magazine bearing his name and under his editorship as the apex of his career, the deserved reward of a lifetime's labor. The situation portended well: seemingly solid financial backing; sufficient written material by him for a good start; as editor, he would have a free hand and need not truckle to publisher "puffing"; lastly, his health held out admirably. Christmas Day, 1843, indeed provided occasion for rejoicing. Soon afterwards Hood changed residences, moving within the same neighborhood to New Finchley Road; in honor of his erstwhile patron and dedicatee, he christened his new and last home "Devonshire Lodge."

Edward Gill Flight had first approached Hood in mid-October about editing a new magazine; he offered to provide financial backing. Rebuffed in his search for the editorship of an established journal, Hood proved receptive. *Hood's Magazine and Comic Miscellany*, a December letter to Hewlett announced, will be in "quantity . . . 7 sheets—2/6 price—& in each number we propose to give a very good plate or *a work of art.*" "Series or Continuations" he decided to avoid, for he realized he lacked the means to publish them afterwards in volume form; moreover, "There has grown up a strong prejudice from the badness of so many of them." [47] He later relaxed—inevitably—his ban against serials, notably in favor of his own novel *Our Family.* Free to choose the kind of articles he wished to publish, Hood opted for variety and quality: "We do not lay any stress on the signature," he wrote Charles Mackay, "if the stuff be good." [48]

The magazine's "Prospectus," written in December, reaffirmed his long-held editorial principles. The *Comic Miscellany* of the title implied he would provide "harmless 'Mirth for the Million,' and light thoughts, to a public sorely oppressed . . . by hard times, heavy taxes, and those 'eating cares' which attend on the securing of food for the day, as well as a provision for the future." [49] Hood promised, as he always did, not to raise a "maiden blush"; nor would he take a stand on the Tractarian controversy. Political subjects he thought to avoid entirely, though "his notorious aversion to party spirit" did not impede his protesting against social wrongs, as would demonstrate "The Bridge of Sighs" and "The Lay of the Labourer."

During the hectic week that preceded the publication of the first number of *Hood's Magazine* on January 1, the poet grew convinced that a trade combination had formed against him: "I expect to see ½ the trade arrayed against me, Colburn & all." [50] He found the supposed antagonism "*flattering* in one sense—as they fear us. They will neither hang up a board nor put the book in a window—nor take one they can help." [51] Whether Hood had cause for his fear, or whether his sensitivity to persecution, imagined or real, was aroused unnecessarily, remains difficult to say. He did, after all, have good reason to suspect that a trade combination wanted to strangle the new venture at birth: his long-time advocacy of improved copyright laws, his active part in the formation of the stillborn "Association for the Protection of Litterature," and his recent rupture with Colburn—all had put him in bad standing with Publisher's Row. Relations with his former publisher had now deteriorated completely; Colburn shabbily refused to accept letters for Hood addressed to Great Marlborough Street, *New Monthly* headquarters, and endorsed them "not known to Mr. Colburn." [52] Prompt reception of his mail being crucial, such pettifogging tactics naturally outraged Hood. He found "this ... so dirty a trick" that he responded with a dozen savage "Lines on being 'Unknown to Mr. Colburn.'" [53] Thoroughly angered, Hood threatened, "And if he gives me any more cause I'll 'Rae Wilson' him." [54]

Trade combination against him or not, the success of the first number of *Hood's Magazine* surpassed its editor's fondest hopes. Upon receiving his copy, R. H. Barham wrote immediately to Hood's good friend Hewlett: "I like his first number much. The Haunted House is capital." [55] Other friends sent him their sincere congratulations; *Hood's Magazine*, during the short span its editor actually performed his functions, became a noteworthy periodical. "Its merit as a magazine of fiction," comments Walter Graham, "perhaps exceeded its value as a 'comic miscellany.'" [56] Contributors included "Barry Cornwall," Mrs. Norton, Bulwer, Hewlett, Monckton Milnes, "Delta," Robert Browning, and Charles Dickens. Mrs. S. C. Hall offered to send "occasional sketches," "the payment to be 'the pleasure she will feel in assisting, however humbly, in the success of his periodical: as a tribute of veneration to the author of the Song of the Shirt.'" [57] Not only did the magazine sell 1,500 copies—an almost unprecedented sale, Blackwood assured him, for a first number—but it represented a distinct personal triumph for Hood himself. He had written over half of it: forty-six pages of poetry and prose and a further ten of reviews. Of the number's contents the first and most often praised item is "The Haunted House."

In his last years, Hood had become less and less able to make comic capital of the spectre of Death. *"Tout ce qui touche à la mort est d'une gaieté folle,"* once wrote Champfleury, and for most of his adult life Thomas Hood would have agreed. But by the time he came to write "The Elm Tree" and "The Haunted House" his understanding of death had deepened; now, with Keats, "Darkling" he listened, "half in love with easeful Death...." Similar in atmosphere to "The Elm Tree," "The Haunted House" resembles it too in its chief defect: lack of movement. Nothing quite happens. The pace of Hood's poems tends to run to extremes: very swift—"The Desert-Born," "Miss Kilmansegg"; or very slow—"The Elm Tree," "The Haunted House." Neither extreme wholly succeeds. In both latter poems an atmosphere of gloom, desolation, and death prevails; both poems focus on one central object—an elm tree, a haunted house; both poems, weak in plot, abound in carefully chosen details. Subtitled "A Romance," "The Haunted House" is meant to be considered, the poet implies, as a "dream." The familiar pattern repeats itself once more: through a dream Hood masks his unease before the supernatural, here before the reality of death itself. Purposely, the opening stanzas are ambiguous:

> Some dreams we have are nothing but dreams,
> Unnatural, and full of contradictions;
> Yet others of our most romantic schemes
> Are something more than fictions.
>
> It might be only on enchanted ground;
> It might be merely by a thought's expansion;
> But, in the spirit or the flesh, I found
> An old deserted Mansion.[58]

In Part I we stand in the garden, as deserted as the house, and confront the scene of desolation. In Hood's "wasteland"—Victorian literature has many such—nature is not stunted, as in Browning's "Childe Roland to the Dark Tower Came"; [59] rather, it has grown rank and defeated man's efforts to impose his will upon it:

> With shatter'd panes the grassy court was starr'd;
> The time-worn coping-stone had tumbled after;

And thro' the ragged roof the sky shone, barr'd
With naked beam and rafter.

. . . .

The flow'r grew wild and rankly as the reed,
Roses with thistles struggled for espial,
And vagrant plants of parasitic breed
Had overgrown the Dial.

. . . .

But Echo never mock'd the human tongue;
Some weighty crime, that Heaven could not pardon,
A secret curse on that old Building hung,
And its deserted Garden.

. . . .

For over all there hung a cloud of fear,
A sense of mystery that spirit daunted,
And said, as plain as whisper in the ear,
The place is Haunted! [60]

This last stanza, nine times repeated with minor variations, unifies
the poem's atmosphere; it forces the reader to wonder what mystery the house contains. As Hood shifts the focus from one image
of decay to the next, the succession of static descriptions heightens
the atmosphere of death-in-life. No detail is so insignificant, W. H.
Hudson claims, that Hood "cannot wring from it some fresh and
horrible suggestion of doom, and ruin, and utter devastation." [61]
While valid, this observation misses the point: details, however
masterly, should have a purpose beyond themselves. In other Victorian poems the hero challenges the wasteland—Childe Roland; or
is conquered by it—Arthur in Tennyson's *Idylls of the King*; but
in Hood's "deserted Garden" no one rises to confront the unnamed horror.

In Part II we enter the house itself, or do we? "Howbeit, the
door I push'd," writes Hood, "—or so I dream'd." [62] Climbing the
stairs, we see a "BLOODY HAND" on banner, curtain, and case-
ment window. But the heavy suspense and the carefully wrought

images of interior decay lead to no climax; the poem ends with its mystery unresolved. We are left asking the question: "What happened?" Indeed Hood even asks it for us: "What shrieking Spirit in that bloody room / Its mortal frame had violently quitted?" The house is under a "secret curse" because a murder has been committed, but we never learn whose or why. The admittedly impressive accumulation of detail serves no purpose: Hood did not know what to do with it. Having already implied that his poem was a "dream," he could not, as so often before, further shatter the dramatic illusion by letting the reader wake up at the close. Nor could he make it credible. It is a characteristic of romanticism in its decline not to believe in the reality of the world created; Hood could establish and sustain an atmosphere quite skilfully, but he could not make the world he created meaningful.

Another contribution to the January number, "A Dream by the Fire," deserves recognition as one of Hood's more unusual prose tales. In it he again shows his reluctance to face the supernatural squarely as well as his wish, through undercutting, to make it palatable to his readers. The human warmth of the opening scene—a crackling fireplace in an inn, old cronies singing songs, ale and beef—recalls a jovial Lamb atmosphere. An unnamed stranger, the story's first-person narrator, finds in a corner "my bosom friend, the friend of my soul, my other self, old Mann —or old humanity as we used to call him . . . for he had a large heart and a liberal hand, loved everybody in the world but himself, and deserved to be as largely loved in return." Not only is "Mann" or "old humanity" a generic character, to some extent symbolic, but the story itself is allegorical, though, as we discover, inconsistently so. Mann may even represent, Hood hints, the stranger's "other self." After the two friends drink themselves into a stupor, they drop off to sleep. Some time passes before the stranger awakes to find the lamps out, the fire extinguished. "I never felt so cold and dreary in my life," he exclaims; not seeing his friend, he calls out. Mann replies "as from somewhere under the floor." As the stranger creeps toward a "glimmer of light," he discovers he is in the inn's cellar. He comes upon Mann at last, almost naked; lying in a gigantic coffin, he is picking at the black earth which envelopes him, "as if he had been buried alive and was trying to break out. ... What a mystery it was! As if I and Mann had actually passed, by death, from the upper world, its light, its warmth, and human society, to the dark chambers of the grave! And was it really so?" [63] The tale proceeds eerily. The thought that death may have come upon him unawares forces the stranger to recognize the blessings of the earth now that they are his to enjoy no longer. His companion too preoccupied in his task to concern himself with another, he begins to comprehend man's essential solitude. A haggard, wasted creature approaches—Mann's wife, but without word or glance from her husband, she passes on. "There was no time *there*, then, even for love! My soul sank within me. What an eternity was before me; dead even to hope!" Two other forms straggle forth—a girl and a boy, Mann's children, dragging the burden, like Bunyan's Christian, of their sins: "In years and size so young, in face so carefully old, like pain-ridden dwarfs! ... But the father looked not at his children; the children glanced not at their father." [64] Why, the stranger asks himself, has such an awful destiny been meted out upon "Mann" and his family; in sickness patient, in poverty munificent, he seemed to have led an exemplary life on earth.

The sense of his own worthlessness gnaws at the stranger's conscience. "No self-deceit," he realizes, exists "in that pitch-black prison, the Condemned Cell of the Soul." Pricked by remorse, he exchanges places with Mann; when he sees his own wife and children approaching, he is forced to contemplate "those dear young faces, so prematurely old, hunger-pinched, and puckered with cares—precociously informed of the woes of the world—children, without childhood." Unable to bear the sight he shrieks, "I am, I am in ———" [65] He awakes; the fire roars still. It has been a bad dream.

Mann is Everyman. His companion, the "stranger," represents he who can partake in the lot of Everyman. But the implications of reality Hood undercuts in two ways: first, for the greater part of the story the stranger observes Mann, does not partake in his agony; second, the story is, as was probably "The Haunted House," but a dream. The idea of spirits flitting past a sinner in agony Hood got from Dickens's "A Christmas Carol" (which he reviewed and warmly commended in this same January number), where the Christmas spirits cower a fearful Scrooge. The haggard women and children of Hood's story show a remarkable parallel to the last vision which the Ghost of Christmas Present shows an unrepentant Scrooge—two ragged, wolfish children glaring from beneath his mantle. "They are Man's," calls the Spirit. "And they cling to me, appealing from their fathers. This boy is Ignorance. This girl is Want. Beware them both, and all of their degree, but most of all beware this boy, for on his brow I see that written which is Doom, unless the writing be erased." When Scrooge inquires if they have no "refuge or resource," the Ghost echoes his words ironically: "Are there no prisons? . . . Are there no workhouses?" [66]

"A Christmas Carol" Edgar Johnson considers "unavowed allegory." [67] So, too, we may consider Hood's less successful, imitative story: an allegory of man's fate. No one—even those whom we think the best among us—escapes final tribulation. An indifferent Divine Being, Hood implies in this tale, rewards everyone equally miserably; a good life on earth has no bearing on the afterlife. Though critics have considered psychologically unsound Scrooge's rapid about-face from unrelenting, flintlike indifference toward humankind to generosity, not for psychological reasons did Hood choose to give Mann and the stranger neither redemption nor understanding. A dream ending, adumbrated in the title, would leave his readers feeling more comfortable; for this reason he kept the allegory unfocused, the point blurred. Because that which might provoke a strong reaction in his readers—or in himself— was alien to his temper, Hood steadfastly shied away from coming to terms with the great moral issues. In his dream-visions and in his supernatural tales he preferred to dissolve the reality created: he wished his readers to believe that all had been airy fabric. Only in some of his social and humanitarian writings did he let stand, increasingly as the years went by, the ultimate implications of his position.

Hood's Magazine surmounted the obstacles that faced most fledgling journals. "The Mag is going on well—capital notices," the editor wrote Hewlett in mid-January; "the difficulty is to get them to customers in Glasgow & c.—the people want them but the trade are wilfully *backward* in forwarding them." [68] Confident in "our resources of every kind," a relaxed Hood exuded to Bradbury: "We have almost all the public press at our back, & such notices as Booksellers cannot buy!" [69] The trade combination he thought he could beat, and he felt pride in the real success of his magazine.

When Hood learned at the end of January that Edward Flight had haggled with the printers, Bradbury and Evans, over payment for the first number, the first crack in the structure on which he had based his future hopes appeared. He had not previously entertained qualms about the probity of Flight and his brother, apparently a silent partner, T. Flight, but his remaining faith in their integrity soon vanished. Thus began for Hood three months of constant anxiety. More than once he prepared to throw up his hands and abandon hope, but each time, through a series of fortuitous circumstances, the magazine did come out. Convinced that his break with fate had come at last, he suffered greatly in the realization that his hopes and dreams were crumbling about him, vanishing in the wake of the Flights' chicanery.

Hood soon discovered that the Flights had paid neither contributors nor stationers. When he asked them why, they pleaded bankruptcy one day—and denied they had the next; in any event, they refused further support for the magazine. If hauled into court, they would, Hood claimed, attempt this ingenious solution: "T. Flight is to walk off with the assets," he wrote Hewlett, "& E. Flight is to take the debts. But I hardly think the Creditors will stand a dissolution of partnership just before the break, & after they had told Ward they should fail." [70] According to Jane Hood, the Flights had "engaged in the speculation without sufficient means to carry it on—having been tempted by the goodness of the speculation, and hoping to scramble through it." [71] They even denied they had promised to pay her husband anything for the editorship. "In short," concluded a weary Hood, engulfed by a sea of troubles, "a regular shuffle." [72]

He found it necessary to rid himself of the pair. *Hood's Magazine*, "having been well advertised, ... does not now want much to carry it on; so there will be no difficulty in getting another partner." [73] Although the poet feared the disagreeable rupture with the Flights might make his beloved "Mag" lose ground, it continued to prosper despite all problems. "The thing promises capitally," he confided to Hewlett,

> contributors are flowing in & from various indications I am making a stir. So you had better send your paper *here* at once— for I have no doubt of going on, & am preparing a number; with a new name, for a fresh start. My name never stood higher than it does now; I mean to have better terms & a share in the property.... For my own sake, as he has compromised me with the public I shall explain the whole thing in a New Prospectus & appeal to the support of the press.[74]

Voluntarily or under pressure the Flights left. When Dickens recommended to him Andrew Spottiswoode, the Queen's printer, as backer, Hood insisted upon assurances of his reliability. Time pressed. On March 24 he wrote a new friend, Frederick Oldfield Ward, "I have come to the conclusion that a number for 1 April cannot be brought out.... As there *must* be a break in the publication,—there *must* be a sort of new announcement for a fresh start, which might include a full explanation—Showing that in spite of a new title—the spirit of the work would be kept up by the same Editor & contributors." [75] Ward, who had volunteered to work as the magazine's unpaid subeditor and who in this capacity performed valiant service, calmed Hood's nerves by convincing him that the magazine could continue and that, despite the Flights' threats of legal retaliation, it could keep the same title. No time remained, Hood declared, to prepare a new issue, but Ward accomplished the impossible: he engaged Spottiswoode and the magazine had an April number. Hood told Dickens that when Ward asked Flight how he reconciled his actions with his conscience, Flight audaciously replied, "Conscience ... Sir, I have lived too long in the world to be *a slave to my conscience!*" "Was not this capital?" demanded a stunned Hood.[76]

The poet had a conscience, however. The rupture with the Flights and the month-to-month uncertainty of the magazine's publication greatly heightened his mental anxiety. Moreover, an attack of influenza in March confined him to bed. Thus began Hood's final illness, a complication and aggravation of the half-dozen maladies he had suffered from for years; only intermittently in the less than fourteen months that remained to him did he summon up the energy to rise from his sickbed. April brought another relapse—and recovery: "my three doctors between them could not discover any really unsound place in my lungs," he wrote Mark Lemon. "My breath is now lengthening my cough all but gone—& my chief complaint is weakness—but that is gigantic. But I am notorious for rallying at the worst—so I hope in a day or two to be on my legs." [77]

"I am going to dine today with three M. P.'s," wrote Hood to Hewlett in March, "—a sign of the times." [78] Largely because of the overwhelming success of "The Song of the Shirt," he had begun to receive a new kind of attention. Sir John Bowring, a friend from *London* days, recalled that "the anti-Corn Law league was desirous of making him their poet-laureate by engaging him in their service, and I invited Cobden, Bright, and some others of the leaders of that formidable body to meet Hood at my table, but his death put an end to any such arrangement." [79] The meeting was arranged, Jane Hood thought, "to engage him to write songs for the League." [80] But since it took place in March, 1844, more than a full year before Hood's death, other factors determined his refusal. Most likely, as the "Prospectus" for *Hood's Magazine* had again professed neutrality, he did not want to compromise publicly his lifelong disavowal of partisan politics. He may also have felt he could do more by writing other poems in the vein of "The Song of the Shirt," poems which, while free of political bias, could strongly condemn society's injustice. Moreover, when Bowring made his offer, cares and ill health burdened Hood; he could have done little to aid publicly a cause whose goals he had long applauded privately.

BLIND TO HIS OWN INTEREST.

As Hood's physical condition worsened in May, he was compelled to hand over care of the magazine to Ward. "Disease of the heart, my Esculapians say," joked Hood to D. M. Moir, even in the face of death making light of his maladies, "aggravated by old marsh fever, [is] ... producing a state similar to the ancient Sea Scurvy." [81] Both Elliots attended him constantly during three crucial weeks. That Dr. William Elliot, living ten miles off in Stratford, came daily to see him, Jane deemed "an extraordinary act of friendship." [82] She found her husband more seriously ill than at any time in the past, and the long strain began to tell on her nerves. A slight recovery in the middle of May prompted Hood to consider with optimism the prospects of getting out the June number of *Hood's Magazine*.[83] But on the twenty-first he suffered a relapse, brought on by the impossibility of getting a publisher, and despaired. Hood's physical health was always intimately tied in to his mental happiness: "Last night he fretted dreadfully," wrote Jane on the twenty-second to Elliot, "and, at one this morning, was seized so suddenly with short breathing, and fullness of the chest, I thought he could not live." [84]

Once again Ward came to the rescue and accomplished another miracle: he got H. Renshaw on the shortest notice to publish the June number. "The Echo," the magazine's answers-to-correspondents column, announced the gallant fight Hood was waging against the mortal disease that sapped him. If he hoped to live, the poet slowly realized, he must do what he had never before done: take a complete rest. Resigned to become editor only in name, he gave over effective direction of his magazine to Ward. He had done his best and he could do no more.

Chapter 5

The Cheerful Philosopher

Hood's Magazine, despite financial difficulties and its editor's illness, kept on: circulation rose steadily, while contributions remained at a high level. To the February, April, and May, 1844, numbers Hood somehow found time to contribute several poems, and in the May issue he even began a novel.

"The Lady's Dream" (February) tells of a lady of affluence who, tossing fitfully on her "couch so warm and soft," like Miss Kilmansegg, cannot fall asleep. When she does, she dreams an "awful dream" of the human misery that she, sheltered since early childhood from "life," has never tried to alleviate. The neglected poor now return to plague her:

> "And oh! those maidens young,
>   Who wrought in that dreary room,
> With figures drooping and spectres thin,
>   And cheeks without a bloom;—
> And the Voice that cried, 'For the pomp of pride,
>   We haste to an early tomb!'
>
>   . . . . . .
>
> "And still the coffins came,
>   With their sorrowful trains and slow;
> Coffin after coffin still,
>   A sad and sickening show;
> From grief exempt, I never had dreamt
>   Of such a World of Woe!
>
>   . . . . . .
>
> "For the blind and the cripple were there,
>   And the babe that pined for bread,
> And the houseless man, and the widow poor
>   Who begged—to bury the dead;

> The naked, alas, that I might have clad,
> The famish'd I might have fed!" [1]

From suffering seamstresses the vision extends to encompass all of suffering humanity As the lady undergoes pangs of conscience, worse than the tortures of hell, she realizes that she has been thoughtless, that she has " 'walk'd through life / Too heedless where I trod. . . .' " She has indeed, and to underscore her frivolity Hood recalled the coquette of Pope's "The Rape of the Lock" and entitled the accompanying engraving, showing skeletal sylphs hovering about a lady, "The Modern Belinda." A sentimental poem, "The Lady's Dream" is overpunctuated with the exclamation marks characteristic of his poetry and other poetry of the period. Though neither the lady nor her plight much arouses his sympathy, he ends the poem, as he does "The Song of the Shirt," with the "moral" made explicit: "And yet, oh yet, than many a Dame / Would dream the Lady's Dream!" [2]

While the March issue contains from Hood's pen only the witty review of R. H. Horne's *A New Spirit of the Age*, April opens with his fine humanitarian poem, "The Workhouse Clock." It is an excellent example of what Sainte-Beuve, as early as 1839, called *"la littérature industrielle."* In this poem Hood excoriates the debasing effects which the New Poor Law and the workhouses had upon the *Lumpenproletariat*. The masses streaming through the London slums, the collective counterpart of the types Henry Mayhew described individually in *London Labour and the London Poor*, constitute the "poor slaves of Civilization's galley."

> Who does not see them sally
> From mill, and garret, and room,
> In lane, and court and alley,
> From homes in poverty's lowest valley,
> Furnished with shuttle and loom—
> Poor slaves of Civilization's galley—
> And in the road and footways rally,
> As if for the Day of Doom?

Some, of hardly human form,
Stunted, crooked, and crippled by toil;
Dingy with smoke and dust and oil,
And smirch'd besides with vicious soil,
Clustering, mustering, all in a swarm.
Father, mother, and careful child,
Looking as if it had never smiled—
The Sempstress, lean, and weary, and wan,
With only the ghosts of garments on—
The Weaver, her sallow neighbour,
The grim and sooty Artisan;
Every soul—child, woman, or man,
Who lives—or dies—by labour.[3]

Hood, sympathetic, watches this "very torrent of Man" "gushing, rushing, crushing along": man dehumanized by an industrial existence. But the poem leaves his indignation unfocused; for, while a proper admonition, "Christian Charity, hang your head" suggests no remedy that will aid the ragged individuals going blindly along life's way. The poem, subtitled "An Allegory," ends on the pious hope that parish officials will show more awareness of the "outdoor" poor's misery, thus exchanging the "artificial dial" of the workhouse clock for the one "That stands in the light of Nature's sun, / And takes its time from Heaven." [4]

Under F. O. Ward's energetic direction, *Hood's Magazine* maintained its high standards. Hood had pretty much written the first number himself, but in months to come authors of distinction, wishing to aid a dying colleague, responded generously to Ward's requests for aid. Richard Monckton Milnes canvassed indefatigably for contributions, himself giving two poems to the April number, while "Barry Cornwall" sent in his poem "The Flax Spinners." Charles Mackay, who like Hood fought hard for social reform, contributed to almost every issue, as did, under the pseudonym "Suum Cuique," Hood's friend, Hewlett. For the May number Dickens took time out from a busy schedule and preparations for his Italian journey to pen a "Threatening Letter to Thomas Hood, from an

Ancient Gentleman. By Favour of Charles Dickens." Hood thanked him early in April, "I cannot say how delighted I was to learn from my friend Ward that you had promised me a little 'bit o' writin' to help me to launch afloat again." [5] Immediately following Dickens's "Letter" came Hood's own contribution for May, "The Bridge of Sighs."

"I have all but done a poem on 'the Bridge of Sighs,'" wrote Hood to Ward in April, "ie Waterloo, and its Suicides." [6] Venice's *Ponte dei Sospiri* led to fearful prisons; those condemned to them, sighing as they crossed the bridge, abandoned all hope. Around Waterloo Bridge, its modern rival in despair, centered London's squalor; Sam Weller in *Pickwick* describes its arches as "fine sleeping places." [7] Suicides favored it. Nancy in *Oliver Twist*, good despite her sins, contemplates the Thames's "dark water": "How many times do you read of such as I who spring into the tide, and leave no living thing, to care for, or bewail them. It may be years hence, or it may be only months, but I shall come to that at last." [8] Hood, taking one innocent victim, nameless, once again condemned society's injustice through Woman. Hers is the age-old plight of innumerable helpless women: of Gretchen in *Faust*, of the unnamed suicide in James Thomson's "City of Dreadful Night," of Mimi in *La Bohème*, of "l'Inconnue de la Seine" in Max Frisch's *Die Chinesische Mauer*.

A poor seamstress is brought up drowned from the Thames:

> One more Unfortunate,
> Weary of breath,
> Rashly importunate,
> Gone to her death!
>
> Take her up tenderly,
> Lift her with care;
> Fashion'd so slenderly,
> Young, and so fair!

This last stanza, five times repeated with variations, unifies the poem—and prepares the "moral." Society, having forced her to choose death, has no right to judge her act. The crime lies rather in society itself for permitting such misery to exist; its inhumanity forced her to do what she did:

> Make no deep scrutiny
> Into her mutiny
> Rash and undutiful:
> Past all dishonour,
> Death has left on her
> Only the beautiful.[9]

As the trimeter and tetrameter lines of "The Workhouse Clock" had sped the poor through London's alleys, so the dactylic dimeters of "The Bridge of Sighs," varied with occasional trochees, provide the headlong pace suitable—Poe's phrase is apt— to the theme's "wild insanity." [10] Without home and estranged from all humankind, she gladdens before death:

> Where the lamps quiver,
> So far in the river,
> With many a light
> From window and casement,
> From garret to basement,
> She stood, with amazement,
> Houseless by night.
>
> The bleak wind of March
> Made her tremble and shiver;
> But not the dark arch,
> Or the black flowing river:
> Mad from life's history,
> Glad to death's mystery,
> Swift to be hurl'd—
> Any where, any where
> Out of the world! [11]

Alvin Whitley has pointed out that, like "The Song of the Shirt," "The Bridge of Sighs" drew its inspiration from *The Times*'s reports of an actual case.[12] On March 25, Mary Furley, forty years of age, "was indicted" of "the wilful murder of her infant child" and of "attempted suicide." Recently released from the Bethnal-Green workhouse, she had tried to support herself by making shirts at the rate of 1¾d. per piece. On her way to buy bands she discovered that her purse "had been lost or stolen from her pocket." Upset—screaming "she would prefer a watery grave to going back to the workhouse"—she hurled her youngest child and herself into the Regent's Canal. Although she was soon rescued, the child was dead. Throughout her trial, at which she was undefended, she maintained that "death would have been a happy release to her...." The magistrate, a Mr. Justice Maule, insisted upon the death penalty. In two leaders *The Times*, protesting that the "New Poor Law [had] brought this creature to the verge of madness," affirmed that neither legally nor morally was Mary Furley guilty. Its outcry was effective: the execution was postponed, and the sentence eventually commuted to transportation for seven years. In his "Threatening Letter" Dickens showed awareness of this case; taking the role of a crusty old reactionary, he chided Hood that

> only one judge [Maule] . . . knows how to do his duty now. He tried that revolutionary female the other day, who, though she was in full work (making shirts at three-halfpence a piece), had no pride in her country, and treasonably took it in her head, in the distraction of having been robbed of her easy earnings, to attempt to drown herself and her young child.[13]

Where Dickens ironized, Hood romanticized. Regent's Canal was metamorphosed into the grander Thames and the traditional Waterloo Bridge; Mary Furley, "middle-aged" and mother of ten, became young, beautiful—even childless (though Hood has her guilty of unidentified "stains" or "slips"). "Only the time of year, March," writes Whitley, "and the fact of her chivvied homelessness remain." The despairing existence of the seamstress in "The Song of the Shirt," Hood intends us to realize, finds its inevitable climax in the suicide of "The Bridge of Sighs." For all his generation the poem had immense appeal: "The Bridge of Sighs,"

Thackeray wrote, "was his Corunna, his Heights of Abraham,—sickly, weak, wounded, he fell in the full blaze and fame of that great victory." [14] Rhetorical exaggeration yet essential truth, Thackeray's praise attests to the poem's remarkable effect upon the conscience of the age.

Three other stanzas—either a fragmentary second part or a discarded version—adhere faithfully to the original facts.

Weary with troubles
That Death must deliver
Once more life bubbles
Away in the river—

. . . . . .

The moon in the river shone
And the stars some six or seven—
Poor child of sin, to throw it therein
Seemed sending it to Heaven.

. . . . . .

Cover her, cover her,
Throw the earth over her—
Victim of murder inhumanly done;
With gravel and sod—
Hide—hide her from God,
And the light of the sun! [15]

Although in the second stanza the victim is unquestionably the girl's illegitimate child, in the third it is ambiguous. If the child, "perhaps," as Whitley suggests, "the legal murder of a morally blameless murderess"; but if it is the girl who is the "Victim of murder inhumanly done," it becomes a murder which a guilt-ridden society refuses to face, a murder which, by its very fact, condemns it. Hood's indictment against his society has become more severe, morally unanswerable.[16]

Upon several occasions in the ten years since he had completed his first novel, *Tylney Hall*, Hood had expressed his intention to write another. Once in charge of his own magazine, he found the needed incentive. Serialized from May, 1844, to February, 1845 (illness prevented the June installment), *Our Family: A Domestic Novel*, though scarcely half complete, represents a decided improvement over *Tylney Hall*. The plot is uncomplicated: a poor country doctor, openhearted and generous to excess, becomes through his ill-advised but well-meant actions the victim of a series of minor disasters that portend ruin for himself and his family. Though the novel breaks off just when the family fortunes reach their lowest ebb, we may suppose that Hood planned a happy ending with justice triumphant and confidence in the doctor restored. Told retrospectively from the point of view of the doctor's then newly born twins, the novel through its frequent references to "our family," "my father," and "my mother" exudes an atmosphere of warmth. At times the children's reverence for a father besieged by hardships makes the story read like a fictional *Memorials*.

As in *Tylney Hall*, minor characters command attention for their idiosyncrasies. *Our Family* houses even more eccentrics: Kezia, the goodhearted, gullible maid of all duties; Mrs. Prideaux, the twins' ominously evil nurse; Jenkins Rumbold, their egregious godfather—it is he, Laurence Brander supposes, who will have "a change of heart like Scrooge to rescue the family"; [17] lastly, "Catechism" Jack, an idiot boy whose only intelligent speech is to repeat the catechism at the most inopportune moments. He is portrayed with only slightly less skill than "Unlucky" Joe in *Tylney Hall*. When Hood describes an "eccentric," he heightens his individuality by endowing him with idiosyncrasies, but he does not stress them, as Dickens often did, to the extent that the character becomes a grotesque—a practice for which he once reproached Dickens.[18]

In his physician Hood enshrined the composite virtues of the Elliot brothers. High-minded, of "Dickensian affability," the doctor dominates the scene with his integrity and sunny disposition, though his Hood-like lack of awareness of the deceit surrounding him greatly facilitates his fall. The extent of his goodness challenges credulity: when a fly falls into the inkstand, he fishes it out and sentimentalizes—"Poor creature—poor harmless, helpless creature!" By refusing to sell opium to the poor, a common medical practice then, he does his reputation irreparable harm. His insistence on the necessity of vaccination for his own children draws a protest even from his wife. Similar regard for medical progress, coupled with ignorance of local custom and unwillingness to comply with local prejudice, dooms Lydgate to defeat in his attempt to bring medical reform to Middlemarch.

From his assistant, a former practitioner, the doctor hears a somber estimate of the poor:

> I know them well: when the poor once catch a prejudice in their heads, it's as obstinate as ringworm. I lost my own practice by it when I was a doctor on my own account. My patients were mostly provincials of the lower and middle class, but all brutally ignorant, and of course superstitious, and devout believers in witchcraft.[19]

Hood depicts both the parish poor and the workhouse inmates unsympathetically in this novel, but he does pointedly juxtapose their plight with the vanity of the squirearchy. On his way to the squire's manor the doctor peeps into the cottage of a poor family who have just lost their only child.

> On the bed—if bed it might be called, for it was a mere heap of straw, matting, rushes, and rags, covered by a tattered rug —sat the mother, rocking herself to and fro, over the dead child, wasted to a skeleton, that was lying stark across her lap. Beside her sat her husband, staring steadfastly, stupid with grief, at the flame of the rushlight, his hollow cheeks showing yellow, even by the candle light, from recent jaundice. . . . My father saw no more, for the light that had been flickering suddenly went out, and added Darkness to Sorrow and Silence.[20]

When the doctor arrives at "Great House," he discovers that the lady of the manor has sent for him only to cure her pet Brazilian monkey. Hood has contrasted, though unsubtly, the sincere grief of the virtuous poor with the exaggerated hysteria of the idle rich.

Perhaps it is unfair to question the sincerity of Hood's fellow-feeling with the poor or to consider the extent to which this fellow-feeling extended to personal involvement. In *Our Family*, however, he draws no character from the poor with sympathy. Even the grief-stricken couple, to whom the returning doctor anonymously gives the fee he has so casually earned at "Great House," viciously turn against him. Except for the servant Kezia, the other characters are invariably miserly, ingrate, even sadistic. The doctor, moving in a world in which he receives insults and abuses from all sides, unfailingly turns the other cheek. In all probability Hood planned to show the other side of human nature, but as it stands, *Our Family*, though sympathetic to the poor as a class, presents an uncommonly harsh picture of them as individuals.

June, 1844, brought the Hood household to its severest crisis: Jane and Thomas came close to separation. The strain of his three-month illness, aggravated by constant anxiety over the magazine's fate, almost wrecked his nineteen-year marriage. Jane herself during this period was frequently unwell. Although Hood's nervous temperament must have severely taxed his wife's nerves, she does not, for her part, appear blameless. "I am writing, but not in good cue," he told Ward in a letter marked "private,"

for my mind is sadly distressed by causes hinted to you. My wife was out all day yesterday, & encouraged I suspect by some of her family has taken up a position of defiance that must lead to our severance—Nothing less than that she will not account for what she has received, nor come to me for Cash in future. I cannot even learn what she took up from Renshaw —nor any thing what became of it. Of course such a position, for my own sake & my childrens I must not suffer—& unless she gives way my mind is made up. But it is very fatal to me in working as you may suppose. This for your own bosom. Of course she must have no money without my order.

In a postscript, Hood, weary beyond despair, adds: "I almost give up hopes of recovery with such trouble before me. My shortness of breath seems coming on again. I have been on the eve of writing to Dr Elliot to say his care of me is in vain." [21] This sad document indicates the ravages which strain and ill-health had effected on his sensitive, basically kind nature. Though we do not know how, Thomas and Jane soon became reconciled again, and in the short months left no further shadow came over their lives.

Early in July Hood went to stay at Vanbrugh House at Blackheath, then just outside London, where he remained until September. Restless when inactive, he wrote there, despite doctors' orders forbidding mental excitement, further chapters of *Our Family*. In "The Echo" for July he thanked those who had wished him well during his illness and observed: "Indeed, for the future, as at present, the serious and incurable nature of my complaints will require my whole stock of that cheerful philosophy which it has been my aim to recommend, heretofore, by my pen and personal practice." [22] For four months (June through September) control of the magazine passed almost entirely to Ward; while Hood helped select articles and occasionally read proof, he edited, in most other respects, "by proxy."

Hood's relationship with Ward, the magazine's assistant, at times acting, editor, is more complex than previous biographers have made out. Always a shadowy figure, he permits only a mixed judgment: during the last year he was Hood's right-hand man, without whose indefatigable energy the magazine would surely have failed; yet Hood soon became strongly irritated by what he considered to be Ward's "political" and "immoral" articles and by his editing methods. Their friendship was closest in the first months.

Hood thought Ward's article "The Polka" (August, 1844)

condoned immorality; he disliked, too, the undercover advocacy of Fourierism. In a private letter he remonstrated with him:

> Your argument . . . in the article . . . certainly reads like a recommendation to carry the costume & capers of the public Ballet into private life. If I understand your sliding scale of Modesty, the most delicate may dance in the shortest petticoats, & the purest of all in fig-leaves. . . .
>
> As to Coleridge's village, doubly remarkable for the simplicity & purity of the inhabitants & for men & women bathing higgle de piggledy together—did the great Samuel Taylor mean to applaud? or wonder? or simply to mystify with pure nonsense? At any rate, you must show me that the purity prevailed in consequence not in spite of such wet socialism. . . .[23]

The risqué sentences that offended Hood in "The Polka"—the dance then sweeping the land despite stiff opposition from Young England—are, presumably, the following: "We approve of a moderate display of the 'bounteous-waving' bosom—God's most beautiful creation. We think that whatever is lovely is pure—if looked at with pure eyes. Indulgent nature has drawn no line along the neck—saying, thus far thou shalt go and no further." Hood's shocked reaction reveals something of his delicate sensibilities, and we are again reminded how carefully he always tried to avoid raising a "maiden blush."

A month before, Ward had inserted in the July number "The Premier," a eulogy of Peel disguised as an impartial study of the office of prime minister. Although he promised for the following number a study of "The Leader of the Opposition," the August "Echo"—written by an angry, non-political (at least publicly) Hood—announced it "unavoidably deferred." Both "The Premier" and "The Polka" led the poet to reprimand his acting editor. As Ward had objected to his calling him "a chick in Authorship & inexperienced," Hood apologized, said he felt no "editorial jealousy," and affirmed he had not "needlessly interfered" with Ward's management.

Thus I presumed as "Editor in Chief" to protest against a
series of political articles to which you had somewhat rashly
pledged yourself—telling me that you did not care for my
prospectus—wherein I had elaborately disclaimed such subjects. I also ventured to resist a proposed alteration of the
very title of the Magazine by dropping the "Comic Miscellany," a descriptive addition deliberately adopted & expressly
intended to indicate what had been a popular feature of
Hood's periodicals. And lastly I took the liberty of objecting
to certain passages in the Polka but with so little success that
not even two words of it were given up to me. . . .[24]

He reiterated his sensitivity "on certain points such as my literary
character & abstinence from politics. . . ." Though sympathetic to
Peel and his program, he disliked Ward's political *engagement*
for it controverted his lifelong public dissociation from party
politics and his equally long-standing refusal to countenance or
condemn political figures. Hood was not equivocating: he sincerely
believed in the worth of a detached position.

Thus Hood's side. Ward, too, acted in accordance with principle, and, he thought, in the best interests of both parties. In an
August 4 letter to Dr. Robert Elliot he claimed that he had inserted "The Polka" because the "mag [is] declining in sale for
want of a fillip," and that because of his article is "this month
improving in sale" (Hood later denied this). Having continually
to deal with an ailing, often cranky editor tried the reform-minded
Ward's patience. The following carries some truth: "Hood's carrying on the mag alone is a perfect delusion. I young, strong, and
active scarcely get it out each month. Hood alone—will be late the
very first month. Spotiswoode [*sic*] will instantly throw it up. . . .
Hood's disease makes him fretful, nervous, suspicious to the last
degree." Each stood in a difficult position: the older man stuck
to the principles, expressed in the "Prospectus," of a quarter-
century's authorship; the younger, interested in "modern" trends
in society and politics, wished to escape these editorial shackles.

While Hood rested at Vanbrugh House, his friends made efforts to secure him a government pension. No doubt the idea of a pension first arose during his physical collapse in the spring. It seems F. O. Ward applied to Monckton Milnes, who in turn interested Bulwer;[25] while the chief intermediary between Hood's party and the Prime Minister, Sir Robert Peel, was Sir Robert's close friend, a man long known for his support of the arts, Sir Francis Egerton. The patience which Hood's friends showed throughout the long and difficult negotiations testifies once again to the kind of friendship he inspired. Though to facilitate their efforts his friends told Peel he knew nothing of the negotiations, Hood was of course in on them from the start.[26]

To present his plight before the Prime Minister, Hood's friends, or perhaps Ward alone, drew up the "Case of Mr. Thomas Hood." This document was based on a remarkable letter Hood wrote to Ward in mid-July, a letter in which he reaffirmed the basic tenets of his literary credo. They had changed very little over the years.

On politics: "I have not given up to party even a *party*ciple of what was meant for mankind, womankind or children. It is true that I may be said to have favoured liberal principles, but then, they were so liberal as to be Catholic—common to old, young, or new England."

Morality: "I have not devoted any comic power I may possess to lays of indecency or ribaldry. 'I stooped to truth,' as Pope *stoop*edly says, 'and moralised my song.'"

Religion: "I have never written against religion, anything against pseudo Saints and Pharisees notwithstanding; some of my serious views were expressed in an Ode to Rae Wilson in the *Athenaeum*."

Poverty: "Personally I am not very sensitive on the score of poverty, since it has been the lot of many whose names I most do venerate. The reproach clings not to them, but to the country they helped to glorify."

Humanity: "And yet after all, much as I have suffered from it, I do not repent my good opinion of my fellows. There is a faith in human goodness, to renounce which altogether is, in its kind, an impiety. It is a total loss when a man writes over his heart 'No trust.'"[27]

The "Case of Mr. Thomas Hood" posed paradoxes: to rest
Hood needed money; yet to earn money he had to write; and to
write in his present state would bring on quick death: "So that
he is driven to this frightful alternative; to neglect the warnings of
physicians—or the claims of his family; to sacrifice his life by
exertion—or his income by repose;—to choose between Death and
Destitution." Adjoined to the "Case" was a "Medical Certificate
of the Disease of Mr. Thomas Hood," which Dr. William Elliot
drew up and signed on July 23 and which another doctor co-signed
two days later. Predicting a life for his patient of at best a few
years, Elliot concluded, "In my opinion, he will never recover to
the enjoyment of even his former indifferent strength. . . ." [28] One
already hears the death knell.

Peel sympathized with the request that Egerton had forwarded
him. "Mr. Hood's works," he replied on August 23, 1844,

> —at least the humorous ones—are very familiar to me. If I
> can secure for him out of the general scramble one hundred
> per ann. for life I will do so. In the mean while I enclose
> the sum of £150 which may be applied to the relief of his
> immediate necessities of which I sincerely lament to hear.
> He may receive this sum without the slightest scruple. It
> comes from a very limited fund called the Royal Bounty, and
> the acceptance of it will not impose any personal obligation,
> or any such restraint as a sensitive and independent mind
> might discover in private bounty. [29]

The entire correspondence between Peel and Egerton and later
between Peel and Hood reveals both the good-heartedness of
Peel, and, incidentally, the kind of business to which a prime
minister was subject in times before huge bureaucracies. After
several more interchanges of letters, Peel, out of the three or four
hundred pounds at his disposal, allocated £100 for Hood's pension. "I wish it were more," he told Egerton, "but small as it is it
has this recommendation—It is a public acknowledgment of
literary Eminence." In view of Hood's precarious health he offered to settle the pension on "any near female relative."

The pension's smallness piqued Hood. Believing his literary skills deserved greater recompense, he half determined to refuse so piddling a sum. "Seriously it seems to me the reverse of liberal," he wrote Ward, "—& assigns me a place so much beneath that which the public has bestowed on me, I feel exceedingly tempted to decline." [30] To his friend he cited authors of less renown whom he believed had received more. Ward agreed: he wished to ask Bulwer to press a claim for £350.[31] But either wiser heads prevailed or Hood had sober second reconsiderations, for he soon wrote to both Egerton and Peel, thanking them sincerely. Peel replied in flattering terms, claimed there was "little which you have written and acknowledged which I have not read . . . ," and expressed a desire to make Hood's personal acquaintance. Another letter of the same day, November 16, announced to him that the Queen had formally approved a Civil List pension of £100, effective last June, on Mrs. Hood. Flattered by Peel's "handsome judgment & liberal praise," Hood thanked him and accepted. The long and complicated negotiations had ended.[32]

Hood returned to London in September and to the best of his limited energies threw himself back into the tasks of editor, now, as he found "sad arrears to get through," made even more trying. Illness often prostrated him; though he did not give up, the arrears remained. On October 1 he explained to the secretaries of the *Manchester Athenaeum*—who had invited him to come to a soirée over which Disraeli would preside—that his deteriorating health precluded even the shortest trips. "I am sorry to say," Jane Hood wrote Franck, "he is never well now—unable to walk the shortest distance without suffering, and feeling every change of weather." [33] "My life now," Hood informed D. M. Moir, "is made up of alternations of effort & exhaustion." [34]

Over the summer Moir, Milnes, Samuel Phillips, and G. P. R. James had sent contributions for the magazine, as had Robert Browning, who offered several poems, "The Laboratory (Ancien Régime)," "Garden-Fancies," and "The Boy and the Angel." For the November *Hood's Magazine* Edward Bulwer sent from his sickbed a dramatic sketch, "The Death of Clytemnestra."

Like many of those who contributed, Bulwer did so gratis in consideration for Hood; even those who did not know him personally offered help. "Pray accept my most heartfelt thanks," Hood wrote Bulwer in gratitude,

> for this, & the great interest you have otherwise taken in my behalf [Bulwer's influence in getting Hood his pension]. I can accept Kindnesses from literary men, as from relations, which I could not take from others. . . . It is not well perhaps for me to work so much—but besides the necessity for exertion, from long habit, my mind refuses to be passive, & seems the more restless from my inability to exert much bodily activity. I sleep little & my head instead of a shady chamber, is like a hall, with a lamp burning in it all night. And so it will be to the end. I must "die in harness," like a Hero—or a horse.[35]

The agricultural depression of 1844, which had caused widespread unrest among unemployed farm laborers, led Hood to write "The Lay of the Labourer" for the November *Hood's Magazine*: it pleads in prose for fair play in regard to agricultural workers and in poetry for their right to a job. Not to find employment, he thought, like Carlyle, R. L. Stevenson, and modern labor psychologists, a more pitiable plight than even the least remunerative work. Entering a rural tavern patronized by the poor, the narrator —as Hood signed "The Lay" we may assume the sentiments expressed in it are his—evinces discomfort listening to their talk:

> The topics, such as poor men discuss amongst themselves:—the dearness of bread, the shortness of work, the long hours of labour, the lowness of wages . . . but accompanied by such particular revelations, such minute details, and frank disclosures, as should only have come from persons talking in their sleep.[36]

For the narrator it is indeed a nightmarish "revelation" to hear of "Fathers, with more children than shillings per week—mothers

travailing literally in the straw—infants starving before the parents'
eyes, with cold, and famishing for food." Successful at last in fully
identifying himself with the poor, Hood wrote proudly in "The
Lay": "As my works testify, I am of the working class myself. . . ." [37]
One of the company stands up and sings a "lay." He only wants
work:

> Ay, only give me work,
>   And then you need not fear
> That I shall snare his Worship's hare
>   Or kill his Grace's deer;
> Break into his lordship's house,
>   To steal the plate so rich;
> Or leave the yeoman that had a purse
>   To welter in a ditch.
>
> Wherever Nature needs,
>   Wherever Labour calls,
> No job I'll shirk of the hardest work,
>   To shun the workhouse walls;
> Where savage laws begrudge
>   The pauper babe its breath,
> And doom a wife to a widow's life,
>   Before her partner's death.

The farmer bard disclaims all intention of arson:

> To a flaming barn or farm
>   My fancies never roam;
> The fire I yearn to kindle and burn
>   Is on the hearth of Home;
> Where children huddle and crouch
>   Through dark long wintry days,
> Where starving children huddle and crouch,
>   To see the cheerful rays,
> A-glowing on the haggard cheek,
>   And not in the haggard's blaze! [38]

Individuals, as always, aroused in Hood greater compassion than
abstract causes. "The Lay of the Labourer," like "The Song of the

Shirt" and "The Bridge of Sighs," had its origin in an actual case: that of Gifford White. White, aged eighteen and unemployed, had sent a letter "to the Farmers" of Bluntisham, Huntingdonshire, threatening that if he and his fellow laborers were not given opportunity to work, they would "set fire to the whole of this place...." [39] For his threat alone he was sentenced to transportation for life. Hood, while insisting he did not mean "to palliate Incendiarism," argued the sentence too severe.[40] He sent a marked copy of "The Lay" to Sir James Graham, the Home Secretary, even though he believed—and contemporaries agreed—that Graham was "a cold, hard man, bigoted to the New Poor Law"; Graham indeed acknowledged receipt only in a curt note.[41] Hoping that *The Times* would "take up the subject," Hood sent another copy to the editors.[42] Like "The Song of the Shirt," "The Lay" enjoyed instantaneous popularity: newspapers commented enthusiastically on the article; some even reprinted the poem in entirety; the "capital notice" in the *Anti-Corn Law League* especially pleased Hood.[43]

Why did the plight of Gifford White, whom he had never seen, so affect him? For White did more than symbolize to Hood the condition of the "famishing wretches, pleading vainly for work": [44] his spectre came to obsess him:

> Nevertheless, amidst the dismal chorus [of the "Starving Unemployed"], one complaining voice rings distinctly on my inward ear; one melancholy figure flits prominently before my mind's eye ... the Eidolon of a real person, a living breathing man, with a known name.... For months past, that indistinct Figure ... amidst trials of my own, in the intervals of acute pain, perchance even in my delirium ... has recurred to me, more or less vividly.... [45]

Always keeping a report of the White case by him, Hood spoke to his friends "of the *actual* 'haunting' of the spirit of that unhappy living victim of a panic." "I feel convinced," wrote his son in the *Memorials*, "that the Phantom spoken of (those, who choose, may attribute it to the state of my father's health) was as really impressed on the brain as if it had been actually transmitted by the retina of the eye." [46]

Illness had brought the "Phantom" of Gifford White before his eyes. Like many invalids, Hood at heart relished the syndromes of his disease: they were the most fertile source of his genius. "Of all the know-nothing persons in this world," once admonished the poet—who admitted to infinite experience—"commend us to the man who has 'never known a day's illness.' He is a moral dunce: one who has lost the greatest lesson in life; who has skipped the finest lecture in that great school of humanity, the Sick Chamber." [47] Poe wrote—and he was right—that "the genius of Hood is the result of vivid Fancy, impelled, or controlled,—certainly tinctured, at all points, by hypochondriasis." [48] Disease of course, Thomas Mann to the contrary, did not heighten Hood's creative powers, but it did give them direction. A body diseased often leads to a mind diseased: from earliest youth death was omnipresent in his mind. His febrile imagination, nurturing gruesome visions of disease and death, transmogrified them into his poetry without his becoming aware that what he accepted as normal in life, others found abnormal. Only once in his published writings—in "The Lay of the Labourer"—does a glimmer of self-awareness come. "It may be," Hood writes there of Gifford White, "that some peculiar condition of the body inducing a morbid state of mind— some extreme excitability of the nerves, and through them of the moral sensibility, concurred to induce so deep an impression, to make so warm a sympathy attach itself to a mere Phantom, the representative of an obscure individual, an utter stranger." [49]

After mid-November Hood rarely left his bed for more than one or two hours—and then only to repose in an easy chair. Though even in bed he continued to work, he knew "alas, that too many things must go undone." [50] His frustration at enforced passivity caused his smothered resentment of F. O. Ward to flare up into anger. Ward wanted, first of all, to take the whole credit for securing him his pension and to publish his correspondence with Peel. But Hood was especially pained at his alloting him an ever-decreasing share in the magazine's management: "I am to be pensioned off," he wrote Elliot in November,

> —& virtually give up the Mag—for 8 pages a month would not allow even the carrying on the novel—which I presume Ward is then to assume. This may seem harsh, but his conceit is so insatiable & his conduct is so very strange that it is not reconcilable with any straightforward principle....

The aging invalid, in despair, fought off visions of replacement by Ward—"young, strong, and active." Though he did retain control of *Our Family*, his distrust of Ward's political designs increased: "But he surely did not consider *me* when he formed a scheme for turning the Mag. into a political one & told me in answer to my protest that he did not care for my prospectus...." The upshot of the crisis was his decision "*never to accept any service or help from him again.*" [51] But it was a decision the bedridden Hood had soon to rescind: he knew at heart he could not do without Ward's aid, given generously and without salary.

"The Lay of the Labourer" exhausted Hood. "Mrs. Peck's Pudding," his "Christmas story" opening the December *Hood's Magazine*, evinces unfocused sentiment and flabby prose. "I have pumped out a sheet already of Christmas fun...," [52] Hood wrote Elliot, and the metaphor is appropriate: both pumper and that "pumped out" give clear sign of declining creativity. In the story a poor widow delegates her children to forage for the ingredients of her traditional Christmas pudding; too poor this year to buy them herself, frustrated by misguided offers of help, she represents human helplessness before a complex world.

"I have kept up my spirits," Hood wrote Hewlett in mid-December, "and done my drawings for next number." [53] But by the end of the month, divining "the actual presence of a certain and near death," he knew, recalled his daughter, "this was the last Christmas we were all to share in this world." [54] On December

30 he informed his old friend William Jerdan that "my life is not worth a year's purchase: my health & body are so shattered. . . ." [55] The end approached.

To the January *Hood's Magazine*, besides a laudatory review of Dickens's "The Chimes" and additional chapters of *Our Family*, Hood contributed the short lyric, "Suggestions by Steam":

> When Woman is in rags and poor,
>   And sorrow, cold, and hunger tease her,
> If man would only listen more
>   To that small voice that crieth—"Ease her!"
>
> Without the guidance of a friend,
>   Though legal sharks and screws attack her,
> If man would only more attend
>   To that small voice that crieth—"Back her!"
>
> So oft it would not be his fate
>   To witness some despairing dropper
> In Thames's tide, and run too late
>   To that small voice that crieth—"Stop her!" [56]

In its plea to man's conscience to show mercy to Woman the poem recalls "The Bridge of Sighs," while expressions such as "sharks and screws" (i.e. swindlers and extortionists) reflect Hood's apt use of slang, his interest in music-hall and street songs, and the unusual apprenticeship in poetry he underwent writing jingles and sketches for popular comedians. In the January "Echo" he describes amusingly the sittings for the bust which Edward Davis made of him—a bust which his children deemed a "fine and remarkable resemblance." [57]

Hood's health collapsed totally at the end of January; his body functioned only with great difficulty. On February 4 Ward, with whom he had somehow become reconciled, wrote a frenzied letter to Bulwer:

. . . he is dying—violent hemorrhage, extreme emaciation and rapidly increasing dropsy, leave no longer any hope, any doubt of the event. . . . His genius remains as active and unclouded as ever. In the midst of all his sufferings he still longs to write, if we would let him. He sits plotting his novel, and last night told me how he intended to carry the story on.

In his estimate of his friend he rose to eloquence:

> Greater poems than any he has written die with him—appeals on behalf of humanity that would have deeply stirred the times and set his name among the more illustrious of the age.[58]

Though Hood had strained his creative powers to their uttermost, he was gainsaid satisfaction with a job well done. A writer for the *Eclectic Review*, who knew him, remembered that he "lamented greatly" his inability to do more, "for he seemed to view himself as having a work—a great work to do, and earnestly did he desire to accomplish it. This was to have made a complete series of poems, illustrating every form of social misery, and earnestly advocating its removal." [59] Though he had already done much, Hood felt he had hedged in his commitment to full charity. In February, 1845, he wrote Peel:

> I would have written one more paper—a forewarning one— against an evil, or the danger of it, arising from a literary move- ment in which I have had some share, a one-sided humanity, opposite to that Catholic Shaksperian sympathy, which felt with King as well as Peasant, and duly estimated the mortal temptations of both stations. Certain classes at the poles of Society are already too far asunder; it should be the duty of our writers to draw them nearer by kindly attraction, not to aggravate the existing repulsion, and place a wider moral gulf between Rich and Poor, with Hate on the one side and Fear on the other.[60]

But in the end, though his sense of duty gave him qualms that he had not spoken out forcefully until too late, he had achieved not only understanding but full emotional empathy with the plight of the English poor. Rarely had anyone less deserved an uneasy conscience.

Although Hood had long known that death was near, his sense of humor never abandoned him, nor his sense of perspective—as the following lines reveal:

> I'm sick of gruel, and the dietetics,
> I'm sick of pills, and sicker of emetics,
> I'm sick of pulses' tardiness or quickness,
> I'm sick of blood, its thinness or its thickness,
> In short, within a word, I'm sick of sickness.[61]

The oft-quoted stanzas, "Farewell, Life! My senses swim," [62] which appeared in the February *Hood's Magazine*, were his poetic adieu, sentimental yet moving in their hope of an afterlife. Ward saw in them "Vague forebodings, restless alternation of despair and feverish hope—the Death flickerings of his genius." [63] They were his last creative effort.

While Hood's slow dying limited, soon forbade his writing for his cherished "Mag," others kept up the high standard of contributions. Several tales—among them his own "Results of German Study: The Two Miners" (February)—reflect the enormous popularity of ghastly horror stories set in exotic regions, Bohemia, the Harz, Norway, Spain, while others capitalize on the new vogue of mystery attached to the great metropolis, a vogue instigated by Balzac and especially by Eugène Sue's *Les Mystères de Paris*. The March number contains, besides a long leading article by Ward, Landor's Imaginary Conversation, "Dante and Beatrice," two contributions by Milnes, and Browning's "The Tomb of St. Praxed's" (the original title)—the poem Elizabeth Barrett considered his finest contribution to *Hood's Magazine*. April, rich in poetry, led off with Browning's "The Flight of the Duchess," included Landor's "To Major-General W. Napier," his "Prayer of the Bees for Alciphron," Keats's song, "Hush, hush, tread softly; hush, hush, my dear," and G. H. Lewes's ironic essay "A Word to Young Authors on Their True Position."

After January Hood lived on in great pain, often unconscious, but whenever able, cheerful with his family, cordial to his friends. One friend wrote:

A short while ago we sat for hours by his bed-side in general and cheerful conversation. . . . Then he spoke of the certain and unavoidable event about to take place with perfect un-reserve, unruffled calmness . . . and upon the one great subject of a death-bed hope, he declared himself, as throughout life, opposed to canters and hypocrites,—a class he had always detested and written against; while he set the highest price upon sincere Christianity. . . .[64]

The March "Echo" announced that during February "his physical strength had completely given way." [65] On February 7 he made his will, leaving, except for a few books reserved as keepsakes for friends, "all . . . that I possess . . . to my dear wife, to be used for her benefit and that of our dear children. . . ." [66] On March 12 the poet wrote his uncle and aunt in Scotland, "I little thought to have been alive at this date . . . but only bodily—for my mind has been calm and resigned. . . ." [67] And three days later his last letter to Hewlett: "Still alive—but enormously swollen with dropsy & cannot last long." [68]

To friends and acquaintances Hood wrote farewell notes, ac-companying each with an engraving of his bust. In one letter to a G. B. Webb, dated March 19, the last letter of his that has come to my attention, he unconsciously portrays himself in his relation-ship to his thousands of unknown readers; his easy cheer in death's presence reveals his lack of self-pity. Someone else might have dashed off a few hasty lines, unthinking. Hood did more. "Sir," he began,

> I have much pleasure in acceding to your wish, though I did not write the lines on Mr. Bish, having at the time to fry some other fish.
>
> As I am about going I know not where, if you want another Autograph, you must apply to my Heir.
>
> I am Sir
> Yours most obediently
> Thos: Hood [69]

The announcement in the March *Hood's Magazine* that death was overtaking its editor brought a touching response from his public: old friends, acquaintances, even strangers came by to visit. They offered their best wishes, verses, even money; neighbors called to help; "Game, wine, and fruit were sent to tempt the failing appetite, and evidences of thoughtful kindness came even from strange and unknown hands." [70] Deeply moved by these many instances of generosity, Hood, at last reconciled to the world's ways, exclaimed during his final spring on earth:

> It's a beautiful world, and since I have been lying here, I have thought about it more and more; it is not so bad, even humanly speaking, as people would make it out. I have had some very happy days while I lived in it, and I *could* have wished to stay a little longer. [71]

The April "Echo" had announced abandonment of hope, but not until May 1 was it given up entirely. On that day he had a few moments of lucidity and uttered to his wife, perhaps in sad memory of their near separation a year ago, "Remember, Jane, I forgive all, *all* as I hope to be forgiven." "Dying, dying," were his last words. Soon afterwards he lapsed into a deep coma that lasted through May 2, and on the third, at half past five in the afternoon, death came.

THE MISSING VESSEL

Epilogue

Samuel Phillips conjectured that Hood might "have a becoming resting place in Westminster Abbey," [1] but when the family learned that the privilege of burial in the Poets' Corner cost £200 in fees, the plan was abandoned. Financial considerations, supported by Milnes's recommendation, dictated he be buried in the new cemetery at Kensal Green. The burial took place on May 10, a beautiful spring day, in the presence of his immediate family and of his faithful friends—Ward, Milnes, and the two Elliots among them.

Since both the £150 from the Royal Bounty and the first year's pension of £100 were exhausted, Hood's financial position had greatly deteriorated in the last year. The shift in proprietorship of *Hood's Magazine* from the insolvent Flights to the more reliable Spottiswoode and Renshaw undoubtedly lost him money, while his year-long illness, an expense in itself, prevented him from writing as much as usual and from giving the magazine his full effort. During the last three months he could write nothing. He died in debt and Jane, to pay expenses, including those of the funeral, had mortgaged her pension—so thought R. H. Barham—for more than one year. [2] Already in January, 1845, she had written to Peel—without her husband's knowledge—in the hope he might again help pay their debts. [3] Once again the Prime Minister responded with characteristic generosity, sending her £100. Late in April, while Hood hovered on the brink of death, Jane secretly asked the Council of the Royal Literary Fund if she could apply for a grant in her own name. "It would add to poor Hood's sufferings," a sympathetic Samuel Phillips explained to W. H. Ainsworth on May 1, "if he were aware that charity had been extended to him. He is proud and foolish in this respect, and has already refused handsome gifts proffered by noblemen...." [4] After Jane had made

194

Devonshire Lodge
New Finchley Road
St John's Wood
19 March.
1845.

Sir

I have much pleasure in
acceding to your wish, though I
did not write the lines on Mr.
Bish, having at the time to
fry some other fish.

As I am about going I
know not where, if you want
another Autograph, you must
apply to my Heir.

I am Sir
Yours most obed.t
Tho.s Hood

G. B. Webb Esq.re

a formal appeal on May 19, a committee of Barham, David Salomons, and the engraver, William Harvey, met a few days later and awarded her and the children a final grant of £75.[5]

Proposals were soon afoot for a subscription. Phillips, in a second letter to Ainsworth of May 6, "proposed to form a committee of noblemen and gentlemen for the purpose of procuring subscriptions on behalf of the poor widow.... Hood was a great favourite, and I have no doubt the public will be glad to shew their sense of his talent and genius."[6] A Hood Memorial Fund was established, with Thomas Reseigh in charge and with Ward, Milnes, and Phillips as active participants; Cowden Clarke, Harvey—even Thomas Carlyle—lent their names. By August the Fund had realized the amount of £1,386 15s. 6d., "representing sums from all sorts and conditions of men and women ... from the half-crown sent by 'A Few Journeymen Tailors' to the fifty pounds contributed by Sir Robert Peel."[7] Ward asked Dickens his opinion whether the subscription should be continued; Dickens replied on August 14 that "all that can be done has been done in the matter of Mrs. Hood's Subscription." He based his decision on practical, not literary, grounds. "My estimate of the great genius of poor Hood is as high as it is possible for man to form, and always has been, consequently I set her case on very lofty grounds indeed."[8] Accepting Dickens's logic, the Committee closed the Fund.

But the money raised by the subscription somehow did not suffice; in her last years Jane often experienced dire poverty. In September, 1845, she asked Peel if he could arrange a scholarship for Tom at Charterhouse, but the Prime Minister had to reply that he had already committed his single presentation.[9] Hood's constant illness and the long struggle to make ends meet had taken their toll, but in her quiet way Jane had been happy with both her husband and her life. She did not complain at misfortune. During the last six months of Hood's life, hardly stirring from the house, she tended him with care; his death affected her deeply. Worn out and frequently ill, she survived him by only a year and a half, dying on December 4, 1846. Upon her death the pension settled on her by Peel ceased, but the intervention of Lord John Russell led to its renewal for £50 upon the orphans.

The Hood children fared better. Neither Fanny nor Tom suffered from poverty in adulthood, though neither, perhaps, realized the literary potential each undoubtedly had. In any event their childhood precocity came to little: maturity found them pleasant companions but indifferent writers. Sister and brother collaborated on the two-volume *Memorials* (1860) and on the still standard ten-volume *Works* (1869–1873). Neither possessed much talent for editorial work: in the *Memorials*, besides the expected Victorian reticence, they transcribed Hood's letters carelessly and gave no indication of omissions. His published writings fared worse: the whole Arthur Symons rightly deemed a hodgepodge, a "posthumous cruelty" to Hood.

Money was scraped up for Tom to go to Oxford, where he matriculated in 1853 at Pembroke College with hopes of entering the Church. Returning to London several years later without a degree, he wrote for various journals, worked for a time in the War Office, then in 1865 became editor of *Fun Magazine*, *Punch's* chief rival. In the 1860's he churned out several three-volume novels, popular then, forgotten now, of which the best is perhaps *Captain Master's Children*. 1867 saw the first *Tom Hood's Comic Annual*, and each year until his death he put out a new volume. His *Rules of Rhyme*, first published in 1869, rapidly went through many editions. Though his humorous writings and his sketching powers show that, in some slight measure, he possessed his father's gifts, "Tom"—as he was christened and always known—[10] early earned his chief reputation, that of *bon vivant*. "Of late years," wrote S. C. Hall in 1883,

> he avoided his friends, who saw little of him for some time before his death. But he lacked early guidance; at college he was altogether without restraint, and being remarkably handsome of person, with qualities that made way "in society," he was, no doubt, courted by the many who liked him, and it is

little wonder if for a time he went astray; contracting habits that certainly shortened his life—a life full of promise.[11]

Deliberately obscure, Hall leaves the puzzle of the younger Hood's life unresolved. Twice married, Tom died in 1874, a year under forty. Frances Freeling Hood married the Reverend John Somerville Broderip in 1849. Shy and retiring by nature, she was well-suited for life as a clergyman's wife in the quiet Somersetshire parish of Cossington. During her maturity she wrote in rapid succession many volumes for children, fables and fairy tales which her brother illustrated. Brother and sister kept close, revered almost to the point of worship their deceased parents, and led lives seemingly untroubled by their society's problems. From the little we know of them, both failed to interest themselves in the social and humanitarian causes for which their father had long and valiantly fought, though both, in editing his letters and works, honored them and him. Dying relatively young in 1878, Fanny left behind three daughters. In 1922 the two surviving daughters bequeathed to the Bristol Public Library the greater part of their rich collection of her father's literary remains. Today there are no direct descendants of Thomas Hood.

Upon the instigation of Eliza Cook, the poetess, a committee was formed in 1852 to raise funds for a funeral monument in Hood's memory.[12] The project, sponsored by the Whittington Club, advanced rapidly. Hood's old friends, De Quincey, Mary Russell Mitford, "Barry Cornwall," and Charles Mackay lent their names, as did Macready, Lady Morgan, Macaulay, and even Longfellow, who had not forgotten his meeting with the poet in 1842.[13] One of Thackeray's last acts before setting out for America was to write Milnes, "give £1 for me to Hood's Tomb, please." [14] While many gave generously, Hood's children recorded with especial pride the contributions from the nameless poor: "trifling sums from Manchester, Preston, Bideford, and Bristol—from a few poor needlewomen—from seven dressmakers—from twelve poor men." [15] Charles Dickens, asked for a donation, refused in the belief he best served his friend's memory otherwise. The proceeds from an entertainment suggested by George Grossmith, "An Evening with Hood," and other public performances swelled the subscription, so that by the beginning of 1853 the committee had raised a sum sufficient to commission the sculptor, Matthew Noble, for a monument. The unveiling took place on July 18, 1854, at which time Monckton Milnes, before many of Hood's friends and admirers, gave an oration commemorating his services to literature. Coupling Hood's name with Dickens's, he praised both as "great benefactors of our species, not only on account of the amusement which they give us, but because they are great moral teachers." [16]

Tom Hood thought the monument had "not its peer in England, whether for the universal subscriptions which raised it, or for the chaste and unique novelty of its design," but modern taste will probably judge the design otherwise.[17] Bas reliefs decorate three sides; each illustrates a scene from "The Dream of Eugene Aram," "The Song of the Shirt," and "The Bridge of Sighs." A replica of the bust Edward Davis made of Hood crowns the monument; underneath it is engraved, at the poet's wish, the words he thought best fit to commemorate his life: "He sang the Song of the Shirt."

Notes

Note to Preface

1. Donald J. Gray, "The Uses of Victorian Laughter," *Victorian Studies*, X, 2 (Dec., 1966), 146–47.

Notes to Introduction

1. R. W. King, *The Translator of Dante: The Life, Work and Friendships of Henry Francis Cary* (London, 1925), p. 146.
2. *The Victorian Temper* (New York, 1964), p. 10.
3. *The Works of Thomas Hood*, edited by His Son and Daughter [Tom Hood and F. F. Broderip] (London, 1869–73), VI, 412. Hereinafter cited as *Works*.
4. *Essays by Divers Hands*, ed. Harold Nicholson (London, 1947), n.s. XXIII, viii–ix.
5. *Robert Browning* (London, 1952), p. 3.
6. *Works*, VI, 386–87.
7. *Memorials of Thomas Hood*, edited by His Son and Daughter (London, 1860), II, 13. Hereinafter cited as *Memorials*.
8. In his unpublished dissertation (Johns Hopkins, 1943), "Thomas Hood: An Illustration of the Transition from the Romantic to the Victorian Era," p. 267.
9. *The Poetical Works of Thomas Hood* (New York, 1873), p. xxxi.
10. *Memorials*, I, 5.
11. *Ibid.*, p. 3.
12. Perhaps Hood made a second trip to Scotland. See the unpublished letter to George Rollo (*ca*. Sept., 1819) in the Manuscript Division, New York Public Library.
13. *A Second Gallery of Literary Portraits* (New York, 1850), pp. 106, 104–5.
14. *Sonnets of This Century* (London, 1887), p. lv.
15. *The Listener*, Aug. 29, 1963, p. 320.
16. Reid, *Thomas Hood* (London, 1963), p. 241; Brander, *Thomas Hood* (London, 1963), p. 16.

17. *Works*, V, 38–40. Other poems by Hood in the *Odes and Addresses* having to do with social and humanitarian causes include the "Ode to Richard Martin, Esq." and the "Ode to H. Bodkin, Esq."

18. *Ibid.*, pp. 64–66. Hood modeled his washerwoman's "Remonstrance" upon Swift's "Mrs. Frances Harris's Petition."

19. *Ibid.*, X, 32.

20. In *Pen and Pencil* (New York, 1858), pp. 132, 134. As was then the custom, Jane Hood usually referred to her husband as "Hood."

21. *New Monthly Magazine*, XVI, lxii (Feb., 1826), 232. The British Museum possesses the only copy known to survive. "The Progress of Cant" and a caricature of Edward Irving, then at the height of his fame, caused defenders of Evangelical Christianity, among them Rae Wilson, to attack Hood for irreligion. It was the beginning of a lifelong persecution. See the *Eclectic Review*, n.s., XIX (March, 1846), 288.

22. Alvin Whitley charts the course of Hood's dramatic career in "Thomas Hood as a Dramatist," *University of Texas Studies in English*, XXX (1951), 184–201.

23. *The Letters of Charles Lamb*, ed. E. V. Lucas (London, 1935), III, 419–20.

24. *Poems of Thomas Hood* (London, 1897), I, lix.

25. On this, as on later occasions, the Duke of Devonshire helped Hood pay his debts. In gratitude the poet dedicated to him both the 1831 *Comic Annual* and *Tylney Hall*.

26. Hood's letter to Tilt and Tilt's reply are in the Cameron collection.

27. *Letters of Thomas Hood from the Dilke Papers in the British Museum*, ed. Leslie A. Marchand (New Brunswick, 1945), pp. 15–17, 22–23, 19–20.

28. *Ibid.*, pp. 24, 26.

29. *Memorials*, I, 50.

Notes to Chapter 1: *Life Along the Rhine*

1. *Memorials*, I, 52.

2. In later years Hood became convinced that he had caught a touch of malaria when passing through Holland in 1835. See *Memorials*, II, 203–4, and also the "Medical Certificate of the Disease of Mr. Thomas Hood" in the British Museum.

In his unpublished dissertation, "Thomas Hood" (Harvard, 1950), Alvin Whitley prints in an appendix (pp. 291–439) complete and accurate texts of sixty-three unpublished or partly published Hood letters. Regarding quoted material that is in both the *Memorials* and in Whitley's dissertation, I quote from the texts in the dissertation in preference to the frequently garbled and incomplete texts in the *Memorials*; I give, however, page numbers for both.

3. *Memorials*, I, 65.

4. C. P. Brand, *Italy and the English Romantics* (Cambridge, 1957), pp. 23–24, 45.

5. Geneviève Bianquis, *La Vie quotidienne en Allemagne à l'époque romantique* (Paris, 1958), p. 86. My translation.

6. *Memorials*, I, 69.

7. *Works*, VII, 156.

8. *Memorials*, I, 70.

9. In his letters Hood usually wrote "de" or "De" Franck; I have kept the German form.

10. *Memorials*, I, 106.

11. See chap. 5, n. 28.

12. Memorials, I, 103.

13. *Athenaeum*, Oct. 17, 1840, p. 829; *Memorials*, II, 249.

14. *Works*, V, 107. On Hood's artistic talent cf. also the *London and Westminster Review*, XXIX, i (April, 1838), 141–44.

15. *Notes and Queries*, 8th Series, VII (Feb. 2, 1895), 84. William Tegg was the son of the publisher Thomas Tegg, whom Hood is thought to have caricatured in *Tylney Hall* as "Thomas Twigg." Cf. also Charles MacFarlane ("... like the rest of us, he [Hood] had no head for business, no system, no management, and he spent the money as fast as he got it"), *Reminiscences of a Literary Life* (London, 1917), p. 106; and the *London and Westminster Review*, XXIX, p. 140.

16. One of them, Hood's "Answer to Pauper," signed by "Overseer," first appeared in the *Athenaeum* of February 18, 1832; he wrote it in answer to a poem, written by Bryan Waller Procter, "Reply to a Pastoral Poet," that had appeared in the same journal three weeks before. Hood's poem does not disguise its irony:

> "What right have such as you to dun
>   For sun or moonbeams, warm or bright?
> Before you talk about the sun,
>   Pay for window-light!
> Talk of passions—amorous fancies;
>   While your betters' flames miscarry—
> If *you* love your Dolls and Nancys,
>   Don't we make you marry?"

"Overseer" concludes "If such as you don't like this world, / We'll pass you to the next" (*Works*, VI, 229). Cf. also Hood's "Sonnet to

Lord Wharncliffe, on his Game-Bill" and the "Poems, by a Poor Gentleman" in the *Comic Annuals* of 1832 and 1834, respectively.

17. *Works*, I, 136–37.

18. *Ibid.*, p. 226. Cf. Blake's two poems, "The Chimney Sweeper," in *Songs of Innocence* and *Songs of Experience*, and Lamb's essay, "The Praise of Chimney-sweepers," in *Essays of Elia*.

19. *Ibid.*, II, 167–68.

20. *Ibid.*, pp. 169, 172.

21. *Ibid.*, p. 171; "black beadles" is probably a pun on "black beetles." Hood may be echoing Isabella in *Measure for Measure*, III, i, 79–81: "And the poor beetle, that we tread upon, / In corporal suffer- ance finds a pang as great / As when a giant dies."

22. *Ibid.*, III, 87.

23. Henry Chorley in the *London and Westminster Review*, XXIX, 1 (April, 1838), 140.

24. *Works*, II, 238.

25. *The Poetical Works of Thomas Hood* (London, 1873), p. xxiii.

26. Marchand, p. 33.

27. *Ibid.*, pp. 34–35.

28. *Memorials*, I, 155.

29. *Ibid.*, p. 156.

30. *Works*, VII, 158. Schopenhauer quotes Hood in his essay. See *Studies in Pessimism: A Series of Essays*, sel. and trans. Thomas Bailey Saunders (London, 1913), p. 132.

31. *Memorials*, I, 179–80. In 1842 Hood turned Jane's adventure into a macabre tale, "The Tower of Lahneck" (*Works*, VIII, 156–68).

32. *Memorials*, I, 191–92.

33. Hood collection, Bristol Public Library. Published passages of this letter in *Memorials*, I, 204–9.

34. Cf. an excised passage of Hood's letter to John Wright of April 20, 1837 (Hood collection, UCLA), where the poet is at pains to refute his friend's impression that excessive drinking had brought on his illness: "For I am really contrary to your supposition very moderate in what I drink. . . ." The now temperate Hood claimed not to have touched spirits since his return from Berlin. Perhaps M. H. Spielmann sounded the right note when he wrote, "And did not Thomas Hood suggest, when he was told that by his love of wine he was shortening his days, that anyhow he was lengthening his nights?" (*The History of "Punch"* [New York, 1895], p. 289).

35. *Works*, VII, 251. The letters often served as trial runs for scenes in *Up the Rhine*. When Hood relates an incident on his Berlin march

both in a letter and in the novel and the tellings show no great variants. I occasionally quote from the novel. For these quotations a footnote is always supplied.

36. *Ibid.*, p. 250.
37. *Ibid.*, p. 255.
38. *Memorials*, I, 231.
39. *Ibid.*, p. 225.
40. *Works*, VI, 336–37.
41. In the announcement for the *Comic Annual* published in the *Athenaeum* (Oct. 1, 1836), Hood's language, though puns weaken its force, was even more outspoken:

> You ask me for an announcement of THE COMIC for 1837 ... I have been meditating a Manifesto.
>
> Politics are undeniably the standing orders of the time; but possibly the *standing orders* may now signify those classes who keep on their legs in the presence of the privileged or *sitting orders*. ...
>
> It becomes a serious question, then—ought not THE COMIC to have its barrel adapted as a political organ. ...
>
> The *Comic Annual* itself shall answer the question; and you will have a hint of my designs, when I tell you that they will comprise cuts at such popular and unpopular subjects as follows:—The Collision—The Peers and their Treatment of Bills—Church Revenue—Corn Question—Poor Laws—Spain, its War and its Loan—Registration—Imprisonment for Debt—The Papal Bull—Municipal Reform—The Jew Bill —Railroads—Dissenters' Unions—Civil War—and Agricultural Pressure. ...

Only "The Jew Bill" and "Agricultural Pressure," however, called forth poems—"The Blue Boar" and "Agricultural Distress"; but other subjects, "Railroads" and "Civil War," he returned to in "The Corresponding Club" and "Sketch on the Road: The Railway" of the 1839 *Comic Annual*. Hood also affirmed the apoliticality of his stance: "As to the writing I shall keep my own counsel, whether it will incline to right or left, or be bolt upright" (*Works*, VI, 331, 333–34).

When he came to write the preface to the 1837 *Comic*, Hood realized "that the present Volume will seem not quite to square with the Circular: you will expect a little more political pepper and spice than will be found in the seasoning" (*Works*, VI, 335). Absence from home necessitating a delay in getting news, Hood claimed, was the main reason he changed his mind. Still, two other motives suggest themselves: a wish not to offend any portion of his reading public which might resent a serious message; and, in addition, his habitual inability to face problems directly as long as an equivocal way out served.

In both the *Athenaeum* version and the original MS (in the Pierpont Morgan Library) entitled "Protocol" is written "Hamburg, 28th August, 1836." Though the date seems logical, I cannot explain "Hamburg." In none of Hood's letters that I have seen is there reference to a trip to Hamburg. At this time, to my knowledge, the Dilkes had arrived and the Hoods were busy taking them out to see the review of the Prussian army.

42. *Bookman* (London), LXIV (Sept., 1923), 277.

43. *Works*, VI, 335.

44. *Ibid.*, p. 338.

45. *Ibid.*, pp. 350–52. Marchand publishes a first draft of this poem in *Letters of Thomas Hood*, pp. 95–96.

46. Vol. I, no. I, p. 8. Quoted from *Works*, VI, 276.

47. *Works*, VI, 276.

48. *Ibid.*, III, 48.

49. *Ibid.*, VI, 365.

50. *Ibid.*; *London and Westminster Review*, XXIX, 1 (April, 1838), 127–28.

51. *Works*, VI, 361.

52. *English Literature, 1815–1832*, p. 152.

53. *Works*, III, 93.

54. *Memorials*, I, 251.

55. Five years later Hood wrote two additional letters on the copyright laws, once again before Parliament. They were also first published in the *Athenaeum* (June 11 and 18, 1842). See chap. iii.

56. *Works*, VI, 381–82.

57. *Ibid.*, p. 388.

58. *Ibid.*, pp. 388–89.

59. *Ibid.*, p. 392.

60. *Ibid.*, p. 404.

61. *Memorials*, II, 13.

62. *Works*, VI, 412–13.

63. ALS, Columbia University Library. Transcription from Alvin Whitley, "Thomas Hood," p. 351. This letter, eighteen pages in typescript transcription (pp. 344–62), is crucial for an understanding of Hood's state of mind at this time.

64. *Memorials*, I, 248.

65. *Ibid.*, p. 267.

66. Whitley, "Thomas Hood," p. 353 (*Memorials*, I, 277).

67. Whitley, "Thomas Hood," pp. 356–57, 353 (*Memorials*, I, 279, 277).

68. *Memorials*, I, 268. Transcription from the MS letter in the Hood collection, UCLA.

69. *Ibid.*, p. 272.

70. Whitley, "Thomas Hood," pp. 355, 362 (*Memorials*, I, 278, 284).

Notes to Chapter 2: *Ostend*

1. Whitley, "Thomas Hood," p. 360 (*Memorials*, I, 282).

2. Charles M. Doughty, *Travels in Arabia Deserta*, introduction by T. E. Lawrence (New York, 1953), p. xvi.

3. Whitley, "Thomas Hood," pp. 351–52.

4. *Memorials*, I, 302.

5. *Ibid.*, p. 275.

6. *Works*, VI, 344.

7. In his *Notes Abroad and Rhapsodies at Home* (1837). Quoted from Alfred Ainger, *Poems of Thomas Hood* (London, 1897), I, lv.

8. *Works*, VI, 414. Prefatory letter "To the Editor of the *Athenaeum*."

9. *Ibid.*, p. 301. Any person present at a meeting, assembly, or concourse of people—so the bill ran—for any " 'pastime of public indecorum, inconvenience, or nuisance, or for public debating upon or discussing any subject, or for public lecture, address or speech . . . shall forfeit for the first offense any sum not less than 5*s.*, nor more than 10*s.* . . .' " (*ibid.*, p. 298). Hood caricatured Agnew "with his bill" in a humorous woodcut (*ibid.*, IV, 205).

10. Ainger, I, liv, gives the fullest account of this incident.

11. *Works*, VI, 296–97.

12. Quoted from "Note to American Edition" in *ibid.*, p. 279.

13. *Ibid.*, pp. 280–81. The OED defines a "spencer" as a "short double-breasted overcoat without tails worn by men in the latter part of the 18th century and the beginning of the 19th."

14. Ainger, I, liv. He notes: "In one pleasing passage, indeed, Mr. Wilson had indicated Hood, with delicate allusion to his Christian name, as that journal's 'favourite Tom-fool.' "

15. *Ibid.*, pp. lv, lvii.

16. *Memorials*, I, 108.

17. *Works*, VI, 273. *Comic Annual*, 1833.

18. *Works*, II, 170.

19. *Ibid.*, VI, 336. Preface to the 1837 *Comic Annual*.

20. Cuyler, "Thomas Hood," p. 279.

21. *Works*, VI, 416–17.

22. *Ibid.*, p. 422.

23. *Memorials*, I, 290. Though in "Miss Kilmansegg" Hood was also to fulminate against "the Evil Spirit of Party," elsewhere he gives indication of views distinctly "liberal." To Dilke he confessed that his characterization of Richard Orchard in *Up the Rhine* "is vastly unlike the character of that pig-headed, purblind, bigotted being, an English agricultural country gentleman; a species identified with Corn Laws, No Popery, 'Bible, Crown, and Constitution,' and all other creeds and opinions that are sown by narrow instead of *broad* cast" (*Memorials*, II, 42). To Franck he sounded a similar note: "As for England, *we* Liberals must beat sooner or later; the money and commerce interests will beat the landed, who have too long had it their own way; and then no more corn-laws!" (*ibid.*, p. 9). In this letter though he spells "Liberal" with a large "L," from the context and from remarks elsewhere I do not think he meant strict allegiance to the party of Grey and Russell. Moreover, in the 1830's, political programs that verged toward the "liberal" or the "conservative" were less rigidly delimited to the Liberal or Tory parties than they became a few decades later.

Hood took in an 1838 letter to Dilke his most extreme stand: "But I'm a low-lived, ungenteel, villainous, blackguard Radical. There is a deep stigma on the Have-nots trying to take from the Have-some-things, but what ought to be the stigma on the have-every-things trying to take from the Have-nothings? Chorley has proclaimed me a 'Liberal' [in the *London and Westminster Review* (April, 1838), p. 125]; I don't mind being called at once a Moderate Republican" (Jerrold, p. 392). But if a "Moderate Republican," one who without reservation supported England's monarchy. One, too, an undated fragment shows, somewhat contemptuous of Parliament: "and finally the donkeys *on* the Commons are as sagacious as some members *in* them" (*Memorials*, II, 329). The most revealing clue to his apparently shifting political philosophy comes in a November, 1844, letter to Sir Robert Peel: he states there that his "favourite theory of Government is, 'An Angel from Heaven, and a Despotism' " (*ibid.*, p. 240).

Hood's seeming inconstancy resolves itself into constancy when we note that he was always on the side of the oppressed, the poor; consequently, favoring measures that would rectify society's injustices, he supported whichever party or policy seemed more "liberal." An "Independent" more than anything else, Hood looked to a national party that, in its benevolent desire to foster England's welfare, would rise above questions of self-interest. In politics he could not compromise his idealism. I find no evidence he ever voted in a General Election.

24. *The Age of Paradox* (New York, 1952), p. 23.

25. Cf. Bertram L. Hughes's unpublished dissertation (Cornell, 1936), "The Social Protests in Early Victorian Poetry," p. 16.

26. *Works*, VI, 414.

27. *The Making of Victorian England* (Cambridge, Mass., 1962), p. 128.

28. Hood collection, Bristol Public Library.

29. Morgan Library. Transcription from Whitley, "Thomas Hood," p. 364. That the "dammd Torch business" continued to rankle in his mind may be inferred from his mentioning it in a letter to Peel seven years later (*Memorials*, II, 246).

30. *Memorials*, II, 23.

31. *Works*, VII, 267.

32. *Ibid.*

33. *Ibid.*, I, 452.

34. *Memorials*, I, 288.

35. *Ibid.*, II, 23. The *"Radical* review" was the *London and Westminster Review* and the reviewer Henry Chorley [C.H.]; Hood's work was indeed regarded "favourably."

36. *Ibid.*, I, 292.

37. *Ibid.*, p. 293.

38. *Ibid.*

39. Hood collection, Bristol Public Library.

40. *Memorials*, II, 7.

41. *Ibid.*, p. 16.

42. *Ibid.*, I, 305–6.

43. *Ibid.*, p. 309.

44. *Ibid.*, p. 301.

45. *Ibid.*

46. *Ibid.*, II, 25.

47. Hood published two other fishing articles, based on hints in Franck's letters, in the *New Sporting Magazine*, February, 1840 ("The Lahn") and April and July, 1840 ("Fishing in Germany," Parts I and II).

48. *Memorials*, I, 332.

49. *Ibid.*, p. 321.

50. *Ibid.*, pp. 318–19.

51. *Ibid.*, p. 44.

52. *Ibid.*, p. 331.

53. *Ibid.*, p. 335.

54. Tom Hood, when editing his father's works, claimed that "unexpected circumstances [illness probably] brought the issue of the 'Hood's Own' numbers to a stand-still" (*Works*, III, 6).

55. *Works*, VII, 328.

56. *Memorials*, I, 335.

57. *Hood's Magazine*, III (June, 1845), 609–10. The writer is probably F. O. Ward. Another contemporary remembered a revealing comment by the poet: " 'Ah!' said Mr. Hood, bitterly, 'they laugh at my fun, but turn aside from my moral' " (*Eclectic Review*, March, 1846, p. 289). And Hood himself defined his serious purpose as early as 1827, in the preface to *National Tales*: "But because I have jested elsewhere, it does not follow that I am incompetent for gravity. . . . A life of mere laughter is like music without its bass . . ." (*Works*, V, 321).

58. "Radical" in Hood's case means not a clearly-defined program of action, but rather a highly idealistic point of view regarding possible improvement in man's condition. Hood never stated exactly where he stood on social reform. He left no formal writings on social subjects and he wrote no extended critiques in his letters. As evidence of his social and political attitudes we have only his humorous articles and usually humorous poems.

59. *Works*, III, 146–48.

60. Hood had written for the 1831 *Comic Annual* "The Parish Revolution" (*Works*, I, 89–101). While a "revolution" takes place, there is no presentation of protests. A comparison of the two articles, the first seemingly a trial run for the second, indicates a definite heightening in his awareness of social ills.

61. *Works*, III, 149–51.

62. *Ibid.*, p. 161.

63. *Ibid.*, VII, 294–98.

64. Auden thinks highly of Hood's humorous poetry. He reproaches Sir Arthur Quiller-Couch for "his unconscious assumption" in *The Oxford Book of Victorian Verse* that "comic or light verse is not quite poetry. . . . Consequently, when he has to represent Thomas Hood, he takes it for granted that he must select from Hood's 'serious' poems, and these, unfortunately, are his weakest productions. When Hood (whom *I*, by the way, consider a major poet) tries to write a 'serious' poem, at best he produces an imitation of Keats, but when he is writing as a comic poet, he is like nobody but himself and serious in the true sense of the word" (*19th Century British Minor Poets*, ed., with an introduction, by W. H. Auden [New York, 1966], p. 17).

65. *Works*, III, 186–91.

66. *Ibid.*, VII, 301.

67. *Memorials*, I, 336. In five installments, six if we include a related article, "The Portrait," they run to about seventy pages in the

collected edition. Walter Jerrold republished them in 1930 under the title, somewhat misleading, *Thomas Hood and Charles Lamb: The Story of a Friendship.*

68. *Works*, II, 360.

69. *Ibid.*, p. 358.

70. No. 48, *The Works of Samuel Johnson, LL.D.* (London, 1825), II, 233.

71. Marchand, p. 52.

72. Morgan Library. Letter to Miss Hannah Lawrance.

73. *Memorials*, II, 48.

74. *Ibid.*, p. 34.

75. *Ibid.*, I, 320.

76. Whitley, p. 359 (*Memorials*, I, 281); Hood collection, Bristol Public Library; *Works*, VIII, 279.

77. *Memorials*, II, 34.

78. Hood collection, Bristol Public Library.

79. *Ibid.* A different letter.

80. *Works*, VII, 1.

81. *Essays in English Literature, 1780–1860, Second Series* (New York, 1895), p. 111.

82. Four other travel books, often mentioned in Hood's letters, influenced the development of *Up the Rhine*: Mrs. Frances Trollope, *Belgium and Western Germany* (1834); Aloys Schreiber, *Die Engländer in Baden* (1834), long excerpts of which Hood read in the *Athenaeum's* translations; Frederick von Raumer, *England in 1835* (3 vols.; 1836); and Prince Pückler-Muskau's then-famed *Briefe eines Verstorbenen*, Volumes III and IV of which Mrs. Sarah Austin translated in 1832 as *Letters from a Tour in Germany, Holland, and England.*

83. Of particular interest in Hood's assessment of the German scene is his shrewd analysis of anti-Semitism, his awareness perhaps heightened by his own feeling of isolation from German society. I quote a short passage:

> Yes—Heine abused Prussia, and he was a Jew. So did Börne, and he was a Jew too, born at Frankfort—the *free* city of Frankfort, whose inhabitants, in the nineteenth century, still amuse themselves occasionally, on Christian high days and holidays, with breaking the windows of their Hebrew townsmen. What wonder if the galled victims of such a pastime feel, think, speak, and write as citizens of the world! As Sterne does with his Captive, let us take a single Jew. Imagine him locked up in his dark chamber, pelted with curses and

solider missiles, and trembling for his property and his very life, because he will not abandon his ancient faith, or eat pork sausages. Fancy the jingling of the shattered glass—the crashing of the window frames—the guttural howlings of the brutal rabble—and then picture a Prussian censor breaking into the room, with a flag, in each hand, one inscribed Vaterland, the other Bruderschaft—and giving the quaking wretch a double knock over the head to remind him that he is a German and a Frankforter! (*Works*, VII, 185)

Hood supported the then unsuccessful movement to repeal the civil disabilities placed on the Jews. In "The Blue Boar" (*Works*, VI, 340–49) he makes the "boar"—an Evangelical dullard, piglike in his obstinacy and in his acts—defend Sunday "blue" laws and other repressive measures against religious and personal freedom. In his aggressive intolerance the "boar" manages to look completely ridiculous, and the poem ends with the "moral" made explicit. The House of Lords withstood Jewish emancipation until 1858. At this time a "blue boar" was also, according to Eric Partridge's *Dictionary of Slang and Unconventional English*, a vulgar expression for a "venereal chancre."

84. *Works*, VII, 158.

85. Hood collection, Yale.

86. Hood collection, Bristol Public Library.

87. For such an agreement the only evidence is MacFarland's untrustworthy account: "Some arrangements were made with his creditors, by means of his brother-in-law, Reynolds, . . . and by some other friends . . ." (*Reminiscences of a Literary Life*, p. 107). This account suggests that Hood found backers who guaranteed his financial integrity and that he negotiated an agreement through J. H. Reynolds. In his letters, however, he never mentions either the creditors or the debts that had forced him into exile. In the spring of 1840 (and until his death five years later) he did not have the money to pay off his creditors.

88. *Memorials*, II, 236.

89. Peter F. Morgan, "John Hamilton Reynolds and Thomas Hood," *Keats-Shelley Journal* (hereinafter referred to as *K-SJ*), XI (Winter, 1962), 94.

90. Hood collection, Bristol Public Library; *Memorials*, II, 83.

91. Hood collection, Bristol Public Library.

92. Hood collection, UCLA.

93. Jerrold reprints (pp. 408–12) Hood's October 17 letter "To the Editor of the Athenaeum." Earlier the poet had written to Serjeant Talfourd, who had renewed the struggle in Parliament for a just copy-

right law, offering to draw up a formal petition detailing his charges against Baily. The original MS of the "Petition of Thomas Hood, Esq." is in the Cameron collection. Talfourd published an expanded, generalized version in his *Three Speeches Delivered in the House of Commons in Favour of a Measure for the Extension of Copyright* (London, 1840); it is reprinted in Hood's *Works*, VIII, 105-7. The poet reviewed Talfourd's *Speeches* favorably in the *Athenaeum* of February 8, 1840 (reprinted in *ibid.*, pp. 103-5).

The suit against Baily dragged on, a constant source to Hood of bitterness and frustration. When he finally won it in 1844, the victory was pyrrhic. But in 1840 he needed but its successful conclusion "to clear up my mental weather" (*Memorials*, II, 82).

94. Hood collection, Bristol Public Library.

95. Bodleian Library. His letters to Bentley are in Whitley, "Thomas Hood," pp. 369-74.

96. Hood collection, Bristol Public Library.

97. Whitley, "Thomas Hood," p. 370.

98. *Memorials*, II, 80.

99. *Ibid.*, p. 81.

Notes to Chapter 3: *The* New Monthly *Years*

1. *English Literary Periodicals* (New York, 1930), p. 286.

2. *Works*, VII, 333, 337, 335, 338. First published, *New Monthly*, August, 1840. "To adopt the blue" refers to Sunday blue laws; Nero was the zoo's lion. Hood had often before deplored the limitations in regard to amusements and Sunday pastimes imposed by Parliament on the working classes. Cf. his observation in the "Literary Reminiscences," (1838):

There is something painful and humiliating to humanity in the abjectness of mind, that too often accompanies the sordid condition of the working classes; whereas it is soothing and consolatory to find the mind of the poor man rising superior to his estate, and compensating by intellectual enjoyment for the physical pains and privation that belong to his humble lot. Whatever raises him above the level of the ox in the garner, or the horse in the mill, ought to be acceptable to the pride, if not to the charity, of the fellow creature that calls him brother; for instance, music and dancing, but against which innocent unbendings some of our magistracy persist in setting their faces, as if resolved that a low neighborhood should enjoy no dance but St. Vitus's, and no fiddle but the Scotch. (*ibid.*, II, 198)

3. *Victorian Prelude: A History of English Manners, 1700–1830* (New York, 1941), p. 186.

4. Hood so rendered, in an 1839 letter to Dilke, homage to Dickens's *"morale,"* his "true-heartedness," his "manly assertion of Truth *as* Truth" (*Memorials,* II, 41).

5. *Works,* I, 298.

6. *Ibid.,* VIII, 312.

7. *The Dickens World* (London, 1960), p. 124.

8. *Ibid.,* p. 75.

9. *Works,* I, 412–13.

10. Arthur Symons, *The Romantic Movement in English Poetry* (London, 1909), p. 332.

11. In his unpublished dissertation "Thomas Hood: a Critical Study," (University of London, 1937), p. 168.

12. *Works,* VII, 369.

13. *Ibid.,* pp. 372, 373.

14. *Ibid.,* pp. 380, 381, 382.

15. *Ibid.,* pp. 407, 408, 406.

16. *Ibid.,* pp. 416, 418.

17. *Ibid.,* pp. 439, 452, 454.

18. "Recollections of Thomas Hood," *British Quarterly Review,* XLVI (Oct., 1867), 342.

19. *The Romantic Movement in English Poetry,* p. 332.

20. *Memorials,* II, 82.

21. K. J. Fielding, "The Misfortunes of Hood: 1841," *N&Q,* CXCVIII, 12 (Dec., 1953), 535. Cf. also William G. Lane, "A Chord in Melancholy: Hood's Last Years," *K-SJ,* XII (Winter, 1964), 54–58.

22. Fielding, p. 535.

23. *Ibid.,* pp. 535–36.

24. *Memorials,* II, 97.

25. *Ibid.,* pp. 94–95.

26. *Ibid.,* pp. 99–100.

27. *Works,* X, 352–54. Hood's sister, Jessie, had been "excited by a circle of Canters like yourself, into a religious frenzy, and is at this moment in a private mad-house" (Jerrold, *Thomas Hood,* p. 408—a passage omitted in the version of "My Tract" given in *Memorials,* II, 113–20). The narrow Evangelical views of another sister, Elizabeth Hood, strained brotherly tolerance; he said of her, "she was so pious that every time she sat down she hatched out a prayer-book" (Jerrold, p. 393). In condemning the dangers of religious excess, then, Hood knew whereof he spoke. Once he even proclaimed: "Give me rather declared infidels than such professing Christians!" (undated fragment, *Memorials,* II, 329).

28. *Memorials*, II, 122, 123, 127. Although the precise terms of Hood's contract with Colburn are not known, he indicated at the time of signing complete satisfaction. Hook's salary, however, according to R. H. Dalton Barham, had been £400. *The Life and Remains of Theodore Edward Hook* (London, 1850), I, 267.

29. *Memorials*, II, 124–25.

30. But in sharp contrast to the enthusiasm with which he greeted Dickens's novels in the 1840's stands Hood's first reaction, excised by his children from the *Memorials*: "I was amused by Boz—" he wrote Wright in 1837 of *Pickwick*,

> but there is no great power in it.—Sam Weller is the best. It is all a sort of Tom and Jerryism,—but a grade above in gentility—tho still vulgar. There could never be a greater proof of the want of perception in theatrical people than the attempt to dramatize it—There isn't an atom of plot—very little story—and no passion. Yates' apology that it was very difficult as a subject & had therefore only a few hours devoted to getting it up was perfect! Some of the designs are clever—for instance the dinner. I don't think the popularity of Boz will last or that he has a compass or range for anything else. (Hood collection, UCLA; published portions of the letter, *Memorials*, I, 265–70)

It is uncertain whether Hood based his first opinion on Yates's "entertainment" *Pickwick*, on the *Athenaeum* extracts, or on his first reading of the novel. In any event, further perusals led him to reverse his judgment completely.

31. *Memorials*, II, 136–37.

32. *Ibid.*, p. 137.

33. Brooke collection. Born in 1800, Hewlett died in 1847.

34. Cf. Sir Frank Mackinnon, "Notes on the History of English Copyright," Appendix II, Sir Paul Harvey, ed., *The Oxford Companion to English Literature*, 3rd ed. (Oxford, 1947).

35. When late in 1842 he came across an "American Notes" by "Buz," Hood wrote to Dickens: "It is hard for an individual author or Publisher to proceed agt. men of straw. There ought to be a Literary Association for the Suppression of Piracy—a fund subscribed by Authors Booksellers and friends to letters—out of which to proceed agt. the very first offender—similar to the provincial Associations for the persecution of Felons. Eh?" (Whitley, "Hood and Dickens: Some New Letters," *HLQ*, XIV, 4 [Aug., 1951], 399). From Hood's suggestion, and a previous one by G. P. R. James, an association came into being that held several meetings. It fell apart when the linchpin

to its success, the co-operation of the publishers, was not accorded. Thomas Hood cherished the idea of a literary association, and Dickens backed it enthusiastically. Cf. Whitley, *HLQ*, p. 399, n. 59, and Hood's letters to Dickens, pp. 399–404.

36. Hood had published in the *New Monthly* for August, 1842, Dickens's oft-reprinted plea for extension of international copyright to America. For Dickens's activities on behalf of copyright, better known than Hood's, besides the relevant pages of the Forster and Johnson biographies, see Hood's letter to Dickens in Whitley, *HLQ*, pp. 396–98, and notes 50–54.

37. *Works*, VIII, 274–75.

38. *Ibid.*, p. 275.

39. *The Complete Works of Edgar Allan Poe*, ed. James A. Harrison (New York, 1902), XII, 235.

40. *Works*, VIII, 282.

41. *Ibid.*, II, 288.

42. *Ibid.*, VIII, 215–17.

43. *Ibid.*, p. 206. Cf. Godwin's Caleb Williams who, suspecting his master Mr. Falkland of murder, asserts: "In fine, the idea having once occurred to my mind, it was fixed there for ever (*Caleb Williams*, with an introduction by George Sherburn [New York, 1960], p. 124). The theory of "diabolical suggestions" motivating man's actions would seem to be a common one in the psychology of the age.

44. *Works*, V, 138. Though published in 1826, "A Dream" was written before 1822.

45. *Ibid.*, p. 137. In "A Dream" Hood admitted having a vision of Dr. Faustus. The idea of a pact with the Devil haunted his phantasmagoric imagination during his entire life.

Many of Hood's poems were based in part on dreams, among them the well-known "Dream of Eugene Aram." Closely modeled in theme and structure upon Coleridge's "The Rime of the Ancient Mariner," it resembles it too in that both Aram and the mariner have an uncontrollable desire to confess. Though based on a historical case of the eighteenth century, "for the more imaginative part of the version," Hood states in the preface, "I must refer back to one of those unaccountable visions, which come upon us like frightful monsters thrown up by storms from the great black deeps of slumber." Recollecting in tranquillity the terror of his dream, Hood continues: "My mental anguish was indescribable;—the mighty agonies of souls tortured on the supernatural racks of sleep are not to be penned—and if in sketching those that belong to blood-guiltiness I have been at all successful, I owe it mainly to the uninvoked inspiration of that terrible dream." Aram suffers unremittingly from "that horrid, horrid dream [that]

/ Besets me now awake!" Like De Quincey, whom this passage recalls and who experienced himself the terrible visions he recorded in "The Pains of Opium," Hood feared too, as his undercutting of his dream visions testifies, the horror his nightmares brought him (*Works*, VI, 438, 456).

46. In "The Progress of Art" Hood makes a playful reference to Mrs. Radcliffe: "Not Radclyffe's brush did e'er design / Black Forests, half so black as mine" (*ibid.*, IV, 180). Neither's "Black Forest" seems very ominous.

47. *Ibid.*, VII, 359.

48. *Ibid.*, p. 136.

49. Stanza 21 of Schiller's ballad; Hood, *Works*, VII, 147. Bulwer translated the passage thus in the February, 1843, *Blackwood's*:

> No time to foil its fast'ning foes—
> Light, as it writhed, I sprang, and rose;
> The all-unguarded place explored,
> Up to the hilt I plunged the sword—
> Buried one instant in the blood—
> The next, upsprang the bubbling flood!
> The next, one Vastness spread the plain—
> Crush'd down—the victor with the slain;
> And all was dark . . . .

50. *Works*, VII, 149.

51. *Ibid.*, VIII, 296.

52. *Ibid.*, p. 298.

53. *Ibid.*, pp. 303–4.

54. In a letter to Dickens of September, 1843, Hood mentioned that he had "two other Poems, planned some time since, rather favorite subjects, and to be illustrated, like the German ones, Fridolin [Bulwer's title]—The Song of the Bell—The Fight with the Dragon &c." (Whitley, *HLQ*, p. 406 and n. 94). Hood hoped to get the poems published in volume form by Chapman & Hall, Dickens's publishers. I find no trace of Hood's adaptation of Schiller's "Das Lied von der Glocke"; probably he over-optimistically conceived finished a poem only "planned." Bulwer had published his rendering in the March, 1843, *Blackwood's* as "The Lay of the Bell," and the April number contained a bad imitation by Charles Mackay, "The Founding of the Bell."

55. Harrison, ed., XII, 216.

Few figures, whatever their eminence, were exempt as butts of Hood's humor. Not even Goethe constituted an exception. Although Hood admired the German poet, he did not hesitate to express disbelief when he thought him unconvincing. Moreover, he found, as eventually did Goethe, the excesses of romanticism cloying; aspects of it placed too great a strain on his credibility. In these moments he poked fun, clowned, mocked, yet ever in a gentle way. One example of his innocent fun with Goethe is his "doctrine of Instinctive Antipathies"—his ironic reversal of the controlling idea in Goethe's novel, *Elective Affinities* (*Die Wahlverwandtschaften*), that some persons have an innate attraction toward each other (*Works*, VIII, 439). Another is "Symptoms of Ossification," his good-natured spoof of *Die Leiden des Jungen Werthers*, where he burlesques the death scene of Goethe's sentimental hero:

> O'er Goethe how I used to weep,
> With turnip cheeks and nose of scarlet,
> When Werter put himself to sleep
> With pistols kiss'd and clean'd by Charlotte;
> Self-murder is an awful sin,
> No joke there is in bullets flying,
> But now at such a tale I grin—
> I fear my heart is ossifying!

(*Works*, II, 233); cf. also the similar passage in *Up the Rhine* (*ibid.*, VII, 79–80) and Thackeray's parody, "The Sorrows of Werther."

56. Hood collection, UCLA. Letter written between February 7 and mid-March. On Landor, cf. R. H. Super, *Walter Savage Landor: A Biography* (New York, 1954), pp. 341 ff.

57. Marchand, p. 82; Lane, "A Chord in Melancholy," pp. 51–52.

58. Brooke collection.

59. *Ibid*. A different letter, undated, though written about the same time.

60. Whitley, *HLQ*, p. 402.

61. Cf. Alvin Whitley, "Lord William Lennox and *The Tuft-Hunter*," *HLB*, VI (Winter, 1952), 125–33, the only full discussion of this amusing episode in literary immorality.

62. Marchand, p. 88.

63. *Punch*, IV, 115. Hood's "Epigram on 'The Tuft Hunter,' by Lord W. Lennox" ran:

> A Duke once declared—and most solemnly too—
> That whatever he liked with his own he would do;
> But the son of a duke has gone farther, and shown
> He will do what he likes with what isn't his own!

In months to come *Punch* ragged Lennox unmercifully.

64. Brooke collection. Published in part in Whitley, *HLB*, p. 127.

65. *Memorials*, II, 160–61, 153–57, 162.

66. Hood collection, Bristol Public Library.

67. Whitley, *HLQ*, p. 405. "There was great stress laid on the Athenaeums independence of booksellers," Hood wrote Samuel Phillips late in 1843, "none being in the proprietary—but the influence of publisher's *advert^{ts}* is very evident . . ." (ALS, Mass. Historical Society Library; Whitley, "Thomas Hood," p. 409). As Hood resigned the editorship of the *New Monthly* in part because of Colburn's deceitful tactics, then if his claim about the *Athenaeum* is true, he disliked both Dilke's boast of freedom from puffery and his flagrant malpractice. Colburn at least kept up no pretense. The slackening— or rupture—of Hood's long friendship with Dilke must have occurred soon after the *Tuft-Hunter* incident. Ethics, Alvin Whitley suggests, may have caused the break. Though Hood evinced indignation at the *Athenaeum*'s high-handed reviewing practices, his own works continued to find a favorable reception in its pages.

68. Whitley, *HLQ*, p. 406; Henry C. Shelley, *Literary By-Paths in Old England* (Boston, 1909), p. 359.

Notes to Chapter 4: *Poet of the Poor*

1. *Memorials*, II, 165.

2. *Ibid.*, p. 169.

3. *Ibid.*, p. 173.

4. Samuel M. Ellis, *William Harrison Ainsworth and His Friends* (London, 1911), II, 70.

5. Whitley, *HLQ*, p. 407. The terms offered Hood, 16 guineas a sheet, were half those offered by Colburn, but his offer of 30 guineas a sheet included the copyright. During the various negotiations Hood kept Dickens constantly informed. Every letter manifests a despairing want of confidence in himself.

6. *Ibid.*, p. 408. Hood quotes Bentley's reply.

7. ALS, Bodleian. Whitley, "Thomas Hood," p. 408.

8. Hood collection, Yale (a garbled version in *Memorials*, II, 178). In the letter "*Hood's Magazine*" is four times underlined. The letter also indicates Hood was at last to "come to issue with Baily." While I have not seen the legal records, P. F. Morgan, who apparently has, supplies the following information: "In Chancery Hood's amended Bill had been submitted 12 March 1844, to be answered 1 May. An order of the Court appeared 16 January 1845, and Hood's replication concerning 'the manifest insufficiencies of Baily's answer' twelve days later. Perhaps it was this case which Hood's

daughter says was unfinished at his death..." (Master's thesis, University of London, 1956), p. 410. Hood's correspondence, published and unpublished over the years 1840 to 1845, records various flurries of activity over the suits—two at least, one in Chancery, another in Common Pleas. J. H. Reynolds was Hood's advocate at the start, but a "Mr. Hook" soon took over the case—without remuneration. The Hood children praised his "skill and energy" (*Memorials*, II, 83). The suits tied up throughout this period profits from both *Hood's Own* and *Up the Rhine*. In addition to the expense to maintain them, his strength and peace of mind were taxed by what he called, in a letter to Hewlett, "the nervous uncertainties of the Case." Cf. also Rollins, *The Keats Circle*, II, 470–71; Lytton, *Life of Edward Bulwer*, II, 62–66; P. F. Morgan, "John Hamilton Reynolds and Thomas Hood," *K-SJ*, XI (Winter, 1962), 83–95; and William G. Lane, "A Chord in Melancholy: Hood's Last Years," *K-SJ*, XIII (Winter, 1964), 43–61. *The Times* of February 16, 1844, carried a report of a Hood-Baily trial. In his unpublished dissertation (University of London, 1937), R. E. Davies prints "The Order of Court" of "Tuesday the 16th day of January 1845..." (pp. 312–13; no source given).

The "Case of Mr. Thomas Hood" (British Museum), a brief summary of Hood's career prepared in July, 1844, in order to forward his claims for a pension, claims that "against Mr. Baily he has obtained a verdict at law." Presumably on the basis of this statement, Hood's most recent biographer, J. C. Reid, writes, "Hood's law-suit against Baily was eventually settled in his favour" (*Thomas Hood*, p. 240). But oversimplifying a complex legal situation, he takes into account neither the various suits nor the Order of Court of 1845.

More likely Hood obtained a "verdict at law" in Common Pleas but did not receive compensation in his lifetime in the court of Chancery. The "verdict at law" was indeed, as Hood put it to F. O. Ward, "my barren verdict and yet costly" (*Life of Edward Bulwer*, II, 64).

9. *Works*, IX, 34–35. *Whimsicalities* failed to make a profit; or so Colburn claimed. Hood, sceptical, later cautioned Hewlett, planning to publish a novel with Colburn, of his tactics: "It is not unlikely he may only offer *to share profits*... & of course there will be none to share,—any more than in my 'Whimsicalities'" (Brooke collection). Profits or no, Colburn republished the volumes in 1846.

10. *Works*, VIII, 322, 323, 325, 329. First published, *New Monthly*, March, 1843.

Hood's poem has a basis in fact: several societies did indeed exist to improve the Negro's welfare. The most important, called the "African Civilization Society," was headed by Sir Fowell Buxton, M.P. *The Times* in an editorial of November 26, 1842 (all quotations from this source), exposed the absurdity of Sir Fowell's plans. He "had at last, in 1840," it reported, "discovered the true remedy for slavery, which was to *civilize Africa* by introducing among the natives spades, pickaxes, ploughs, potatoes, and political economy, upon the newest European principles. For this purpose, nothing more (he said) would be necessary, than just to send a couple of steamers up the Niger, make treaties with the native chiefs, invent a general language for the use of the African continent, compile and put into circulation a universal dictionary, buy model farms, settle upon them a few Scotch farmers and liberated negroes . . ." etc. In 1840 a "great meeting" was held at the Evangelical bastion, Exeter Hall; present were the Consort, Prince Albert, Sir Robert Peel, Lord John Russell, Daniel O'Connell, and Archdeacon Samuel Wilberforce. The upshot of the meeting was that "Government steamers, and English crews, and 60,000£ of English money from the public Treasury, were devoted by the Queen's then advisers to the purposes of Sir Fowell Buxton and his new society." *The Times* expressed amazement that "any man in England, with any pretense to reason, could seriously and believingly swallow down such drivelling absurdity."

The expedition, as *The Times* foresaw, failed utterly. Though "the only result of all his exertions . . . [was] to make the evil much worse than when he began," Sir Fowell insisted upon making another attempt. *The Times* could not believe that "not merely conceited enthusiasts, but practical statesmen of all parties in the present day, are capable of acting upon subjects of the highest moral and social importance" with such "extreme shallowness of view." Nor could Hood. In "A Black Job" he mocks both the Society's Chairman, "the philanthropic man" obviously based upon Sir Fowell, and all such utopian schemes. "Looking back upon this whole transaction," *The Times*'s leader asserted—and Hood would have wholeheartedly agreed, —"the facts appear so marvellous, that we doubt if a more incredible narrative is to be found in the pages of *Gulliver* or *Munchausen*."

11. *Works*, VIII, 322.

12. *Ibid.*, IX, 200. First published, *Hood's Magazine*, April, 1844.

13. *Ibid.*, III, 215, 213. First published, *New Monthly*, Aug., 1840.

14. Noel Annan, *Leslie Stephen* (Cambridge, Mass., 1952), p. 11 and *passim*.

15. *Works*, VII, 321, 318. First published, *Comic Annual* for 1839. Hood also writes of the Negro in "Black, White, and Brown" (*ibid.*,

I, 57–63); and he twice reviewed books about them: John Briggs, *The History of Jim Crow* (*ibid.*, VIII, 90–93), and Reverend Pascoe Grenfell Hill, *Fifty Days on Board a Slaver* (*ibid.*, IX, 153–59). To Dr. Elliot he wrote on March 11, 1840: "They have made me an honorary Vice-President of the African Institute at Paris" (*Memorials*, II, 55) —a statement I have not been able to corroborate.

16. Brooke collection.

17. *Works*, VIII, 308, and 311—the poem's last line. First published, *New Monthly*, June, 1843.

18. *Ibid.*, pp. 177, 178. First published, *New Monthly*, Sept., 1842. At this time Hood lived on "Elm Tree Road."

19. *Ibid.*, pp. 184, 186, 187, 188.

20. *Ibid.*, pp. 190, 192, 181.

21. *Ibid.*, pp. 194, 191, 194.

22. *Punch*, I (July 17, 1841), 2.

23. M. H. Spielmann, *The History of "Punch"* (New York, 1895), p. 330. Spielmann discusses Hood's contributions to *Punch* (pp. 330–36) and gives a complete list in "Thomas Hood and *Punch*," *Bookman* (New York), X (1899), 151–52; Tom Hood gives a slightly different list in *Memorials*, II, 181–82 n.

24. *Works*, IX, 24, 26. The poem was written in connection with two illustrations by Kenny Meadows, "The Water Drop" and "The Gin Drop," and a humorous temperance article by "Q" (Douglas Jerrold), "Father Mathews's Polly-Put-the-Kettle-on-Icon" (*Punch*, V, 220–23). Hood used the expression "brutal monsters" in "The Forge" (*Works*, VIII, 298).

25. Jerrold, p. 365. The *OED* gives, however, two earlier uses of "Gin Palace."

26. *Works*, IX, 24, 25.

27. Cuyler, p. 411.

28. Whitley, "Thomas Hood," p. 181.

29. Reid, pp. 214, 206.

30. *Works*, IX, 31.

31. *Ibid.*, p. 32.

32. Hood collection, UCLA.

33. Spielmann, p. 332.

34. *Memorials*, II, 182.

35. *Works*, IX, 27–28; *Punch*, V, 260. Lemon omitted one stanza (easily the weakest) from the original MS (published in *Works*, IX, 30), and Spielmann conjectured, plausibly in my opinion, that he did so as "simply a matter of make-up" of the page (p. 334).

36. *Works*, IX, 29, 30.

37. Cf. Alvin Whitley, "Thomas Hood and 'The Times,' " *TLS*, May 17, 1957, p. 309. Other Victorian poets wrote topical poems—or poems which, though topical and inspired by accounts of happenings in the daily press, have not been traced to their origins. One wonders how many such poems there are—some of them perhaps familiar, some even by major authors. *Quellenforschung* in Victorian newspapers and periodicals has scarcely begun.

38. In *The Condition of the Working Class in England* [in 1844] (1845) Friedrich Engels pointed out that seamstresses earned from 1 1/2d. per shirt up to a rarely attained maximum of 6d. Engels states that it took eighteen hours to sew together "fine or fancy shirts"; but it was possible for a seamstress to sew together as many as three per day of the "ordinary" kind. If Biddell could, making trousers, earn 7s. a week, she was indeed, as Moses's foreman claimed, making a "good living." Cf. the recent translation of Engels's classic study by W. O. Henderson and W. H. Chaloner (London and New York, 1958), pp. 237–40, and also Emil Oswald, *Thomas Hood und die soziale Tendenzdichtung seiner Zeit* (Wien and Leipzig, 1904), p. 99.

39. Biddell's room, too, a person in the court observed, was the "very picture of wretchedness. It was almost without a vestige of furniture of any sort, and quite unfit for the residence of human beings" (*The Times*, Oct. 26).

40. *Works*, VII, 373.

41. *Ibid.*, VIII, 370.

42. Walter Jerrold, in a 1929 letter to Bertram Dobell (Hood collection, UCLA), points out that the MS of the "Song," unlike those of Hood's comic poems, is full of crossings-out and revisions. But cf. the *Eclectic Review* for March, 1846, p. 289.

The paragraph quoted from "The Defaulter" has little connection with the rest of the story. A guess would be that Hood inserted it at the last moment before sending the January *New Monthly* off to press. And a letter to Hewlett, dated "Dec 24th 1842," seems to confirm this guess: he mentions he had "written more than usual this month—an Etching Poem ["Etching Moralised"]—& The Defaulter, a prose story—& yet am done today as far as I am concerned!" (Brooke collection). In the story Hood mentions the woman's "perhaps . . . having to sue a shabby employer for the amount of her pitiful earnings," and that her plight was originally caused "by a breach of trust on the part of a banker" (*Works*, VIII, 370). He gives other details, so precise as to imply he had in mind a particular case, but after a search through *The Times* for November and December, 1842, I find none to which they fit exactly. The closest is an account, reprinted from the *Monthly Magazine*, in *The Times* of December 20, 1842,

about a seamstress who earned "1 1/2d. for making a sailor's shirt"—
the same price, apparently standard, that Hood's "respectable young
woman" is paid. Further: "The price of the cheapest quartern loaf
she can buy is 5 1/2d. A loaf of bread is 1d. dearer than her whole
day's work."

43. P. 210. Dodds notes: "All sensitive people were shocked by
the disclosures but no one knew quite what to do. The magistrate
had given [the foreman of] Mr. Moses a bad half-hour, yet official
action on the whole problem lagged. Sweated seamstresses continued
to sew 'a shroud as well as a shirt.' As late as 1859 the shirtmakers
were receiving only 4s. 6d. a dozen" (p. 148). The "Song" did have
one positive effect: "the initial meeting of the Society for the Protection and Employment of Distressed Needlewomen" (p. 149).

44. *DNB*, "Hood, Thomas."

45. *Memorials*, II, 183.

46. My aunt, Mrs. Alice Gauterin of Churton, Cheshire, speaking
for many of her generation, tells me it was required memorization
work in school in the first decade of the century.

47. Brooke collection.

48. Manuscript Division, New York Public Library.

49. *Works*, IX, 37.

50. Brooke collection.

51. *Ibid.*, a different letter.

52. Whitley, *HLQ*, p. 410.

53. First published in Dilke, *The Papers of a Critic* (London,
1875), I, 60. MS, Harvard.

54. Brooke collection.

55. *Ibid.*, a different letter.

56. *English Literary Periodicals* (New York, 1930), pp. 365–66.
Graham's judgment holds true for the magazine during its term of
publication. For a writer usually identified with comic writing, Hood
contributed surprisingly little humor; in *Hood's Magazine*, except for
the epigrams, most written to fill out a page, only Hewlett's whimsical
sketches (presumably) tickled readers' wits.

57. *Memorials*, II, 191.

58. *Works*, IX, 39–40.

59. Cf. Curtis Dahl, "The Victorian Wasteland," *CE*, XVI
(1955), 341–47; (reprinted in Austin Wright, ed., *Victorian Literature: Modern Essays in Criticism* [New York, 1961], pp. 32–41).
Browning wrote that "Childe Roland" "came upon me as a kind of
dream."

60. *Works*, IX, 40–42.

61. *A Quiet Corner in a Library* (Chicago, 1915), p. 45.

62. *Works*, IX, 45. J. Cousen's engraving, taken from a painting by Thomas Creswick and used as frontispiece for the January *Hood's Magazine*, either suggested or was specially engraved for "The Haunted House." A few months before Hood had visited Edinburgh Castle; he may have recalled the mystery that surrounded the gory murder of Queen Mary's secretary, David Rizzio, and blurred it into the poem's "BLOODY HAND" and unnamed "weighty crime."

63. *Works*, IX, 133–34, 135, 136.

64. *Ibid.*, pp. 137, 138.

65. *Ibid.*, pp. 138, 139.

66. *Christmas Stories* (London, 1954), p. 57. New Oxford Illustrated Dickens. Hood's review of Dickens's story is in *Works*, IX, 93–103.

67. *Charles Dickens: His Tragedy and Triumph* (New York, 1952), I, 489.

68. Brooke collection.

69. ALS, University of Rochester Library, to the publishers Smith and Elder (dated "Tuesday" [February, 1844])—Whitley, "Thomas Hood," p. 417; Hood collection, UCLA.

70. Brooke collection.

71. *Memorials*, II, 195. On Hood's relations with the Flights, see also his unpublished correspondence with Ward at UCLA and in the Fitzwilliam Museum, Cambridge, as well as Hannah Lawrance's article in the *British Quarterly Review*, XLVI (Oct., 1867).

72. Brooke collection.

73. *Memorials*, II, 195. Amidst the various suits and threats of countersuits, Hood eventually entered an action against Flight for the amount he claimed was owed him—£100.

74. Brooke collection.

75. Hood collection, UCLA.

76. Whitley, *HLQ*, pp. 410–11.

77. Hood collection, Harvard.

78. Brooke collection.

79. *Autobiographical Recollections* (London, 1877), p. 63.

80. *Memorials*, II, 196. Cf. P. F. Morgan, *TLS*, June 7, 1957, p. 349, and the *Eclectic Review*, March, 1846, p. 290.

81. Hood collection, National Library of Scotland. Letter dated October 8, 1844.

82. *Memorials*, II, 226–27.

83. Hood collection, UCLA.

84. *Memorials*, II, 200.

Notes to Chapter 5: *The Cheerful Philosopher*

1. *Works*, IX, 146–47. Perhaps Hood was influenced by Tennyson's "Lady Clara Vere de Vere," first published in 1842. Tennyson admonishes his heroine, time heavy on her hands:

> Are there no beggars at your gate,
> Nor any poor about your lands?
> Oh! teach the orphan-boy to read,
> Or teach the orphan-girl to sew.

2. *Ibid.*, pp. 147, 148.
3. *Ibid.*, pp. 198–99.
4. *Ibid.*, pp. 199, 200, 200–1.
5. Whitley, *HLQ*, p. 410.
6. ALS, John Rylands Library. To Hewlett he wrote he had "done a Poem . . . that some say beats the 'Shirt,' but I don't think it" (Brooke collection). Hood's saying he has "done" a poem recalls Heine's assertion that he "made" poems; while both poets—down-to-earth in their conception of their art—felt an emotional longing for the romanticism of their youth, both knew it did not meet life's reality as seen through the eyes of maturity.

Interesting (though no literary derivation is involved) is the similarity of situation in Hood's "The Song of the Shirt" and in the stirring revolutionary manifesto "Die Schlesischen Weber," which Heine published seven months later in *Vorwärts* (July 10, 1844), after a revolt by Silesian weavers had failed (*Gesammelte Werke* [Berlin, 1951], I, 469). Heine, like Hood, enjoyed in later years a *succès de moribond*. On Heine's poem see E. M. Butler, *Heinrich Heine: A Biography* (London, 1956), p. 177.

7. Chap. xvi. "The Gadshill Edition," ed. A Lang (New York, 1897), I, 251.
8. Chap. xlvi. New Oxford Illustrated Dickens (London, 1949), p. 354.
9. *Works*, IX, 204, 205.
10. Harrison, ed., XIV, 287.
11. *Works*, IX, 206.
12. Cf. his full account, "Thomas Hood and 'The Times,'" *TLS*, May 17, 1957, p. 309. *The Times* carried reports of the case on March 26, April 1, 17, 19, 20, 27, and 29, May 2 and 15. My narrative quotes from these reports.
13. *Hood's Magazine*, I, 5, 409. For *Punch* Douglas Jerrold wrote "The Case of Mary Furley" (VI, 223). Bertolt Brecht may have known of Hood's poem. Cf. his "Ballade vom ertrunkenen Mädchen"

(*Hundert Gedichte* [Berlin, 1958], p. 69) and Christian Enzensberger, "Die Fortentwicklung der Romantik an englischen Beispiel: Thomas Hood," *Deutsche Vierteljahrsschrift*, XXXVIII (1964), 560.

14. *Roundabout Papers* (Boston, 1883), p. 65.

15. *Works*, IX, 208.

16. J. C. Reid rightly dismisses (p. 216) John Hennig's attempt to trace "The Bridge of Sighs" to Goethe's *Faust* (in "The Literary Relations between Goethe and Thomas Hood," *Modern Language Quarterly*, XII, i [March, 1951], 57–66).

On the assumption that Hood could read German poetry in the original well, Hennig derives most of "The Bridge of Sighs" from passages in *Faust I* and *II*; he points out supposed resemblances in imagery, stanzaic pattern, and rime scheme; and, in particular, he compares the depiction of the mother and her illegitimate child in Hood's poem to the "Gretchen" episodes in *Faust I*. Hennig rests his assumption on a passage in *Up the Rhine*, viz., "To my own fancy, sundry passages of the 'Faust,'—*read aloud in the original language . . .*" (*Works*, VII, 80 [my italics]). Hennig assumes that, as far as Hood's knowledge of the German language is concerned, the passage is "historical." Quite aside from the possibility that Hood did not read the passages from *Faust* aloud and that perhaps he did not understand well what he read or heard, or that a passage in a travelogue meant to amuse risks not being "historical," the argument lacks conviction from other standpoints. Statements in Hood's letters, as noted earlier, indicate clearly that his knowledge of the language was inadequate for the reading of literature. In any event, he would hardly seem the man to whom one would intrepidly assign, as does Hennig, line-to-line parallels. We may assume, then, that Hood read *Faust I* in English.

Hennig prefaces his argument: "it could be generally assumed that during the nineteenth century the subject of the illegitimate mother has scarcely been treated without at least subconscious reference to Goethe's work" (p. 63). Although there is a general resemblance of theme, and occasionally of meter, between "The Bridge of Sighs" and parts of *Faust I*, I find in Hood's poem, if perhaps "subconscious reference" to *Faust I*, certainly no direct imitation or paraphrase, no "relationship . . . so obvious that it scarcely requires further exposition." To prove his claim Hennig wrenches lines radically out of context, and the "parallels" he quotes (pp. 63–64) can convince no reader who examines the two works honestly.

In regard to Hood's plea that humanity extend forgiveness to the girl, Hennig writes: "The end of *Faust II* is concerned with the salvation of Faust, while 'The Bridge of Sighs' is meant to be a vindication of the girl. Still, the parallelism is obvious." And we are treated to another series of "parallels" (pp. 64–65) as "obvious" as those quoted from Part I. Both sets are, in my reading, meaningless, and convey the impression of imitation-hunting at its silliest. At best, there is between "The Bridge of Sighs" and *Faust I* a general resemblance of tone and theme, but no evidence of direct imitation. Hood's line lengths of irregular dimeters and trimeters, and the rime schemes, housed in stanzas of uneven length, are often quite close to the ones Goethe used in the passages quoted, but as both poets were technically proficient in a wide range of meters, this cannot be taken as evidence of direct imitation.

Hood, in fact, was strongly critical of Goethe's masterpiece. In "Diabolical Suggestions" (1842) he associated it with "German Romances," and found fault, above all, with God's indifference to Gretchen before Satan's attacks:

> Youth and Innocence, personified in poor Margaret, have no chance. She has no fair field, and assuredly no favour. The fight is too unequal. She has to contend single-handed against Man and Mephistophiles [*sic*], the witchcraft of human love and the sorcery of Satanic hatred. The Prince of Hell in person acts supernaturally against her—but Heaven is passive, and works no miracle in her behalf. There is no help on earth—no pity in the skies—the guardian spirits and ministers of grace supposed to hover around, and to succour oppressed innocence, keep far aloof—the weak is abandoned to the strong—and the too tender and trusting nature is burdened, through a sheer diabolical juggle, with the un-natural murder of a Mother. The trial is beyond Humanity. The seductions of Faust are backed by the artifices of the subtle Spirit that overcame Eve; and Margaret falls as she needs must under such fearful odds—and seemingly un-watched by that providential eye which marks the fall of a sparrow. There is indeed the final chorus from Heaven, that "She is saved!" but was any mind ever satisfied—were *you* ever satisfied with that tardy exhibition of the Divine Justice—just as Poetical Justice is propitiated at the end of some wretched melo-dramatic novel, wherein at the twelfth hour the long persecuted heroine is unexpectedly promoted to a state of happiness ever after? (*Works*, VIII, 216–17)

If Hood had read *Faust II*, he would not have interpreted the character of Gretchen as he does here. And if he had not, it hardly needs mentioning that Hennig's whole case for the parallel salvation

of the girl in "The Bridge of Sighs" and of Gretchen in *Faust* collapses. Hood and Goethe are not really talking about the same thing;
moreover, the sections of the poem admittedly not derived from
Faust are scarcely different in form and expression from those that
supposedly are. Perhaps most relevant is, as Barker Fairley points out,
"how little it [the Gretchen tragedy] lends itself to analysis in terms
of social justice" (*A Study of Goethe* [London, 1947], p. 236).
Hennig takes a common theme—the fallen woman—and assumes
derivation, overlooking the possibility that Hood may have had, as
was the case, other "sources" of more telling importance.

17. *Thomas Hood*, p. 27. That the twins, newly born at the outset
of the narrative, tell the story also indicates that they survived to
happy maturity.

18. In an *Athenaeum* review (Nov. 7, 1840) of *The Old Curiosity Shop* (*Works*, VIII, 99).

19. *Works*, IX, 396–97.

20. *Ibid.*, p. 298.

21. ALS, University of Illinois. Accompanying this letter is a note
dated 1886, in which a past owner mentions having owned other Hood
letters, including a second on the Hoods' near-separation: "The 2 I
allude to were both on the same distressing subject & their publicity
would throw a shadow which I do not care to see thrown, over the
married life of the Hoods...." Though Fanny [Hood] Broderip had
once owned the letter, no suggestion of this discord appears in the
Memorials. Both internal and external evidence support a date of
June, 1844.

22. *Works*, IX, 224.

23. Maggs Bros. catalogue, Autumn, 1918, pp. 77–78.

24. This and the following quotations from the Hood-Ward correspondence are taken from typed transcripts of the letters in the Cameron collection. Although the *"Comic Miscellany"* part of the title of
Hood's Magazine was printed in increasingly smaller type, it never
disappeared, even though Ward would have liked it to. Hood, for the
reasons he gives in his letter, insisted it remain.

25. Fanny Hood in *Memorials*, II, 239, cites as also instrumental
"the late Lord Wharncliffe," probably James A. Stuart-Wortley-Mac-
kensie, first Baron Wharncliffe (1776–1845).

26. ALS, to Elliot, July 26, 1844 (Cornell University Library).

27. The Earl of Lytton, *The Life of Edward Bulwer* (London,
1913), II, 63–65.

28. Both the "Case" and the "Medical Certificate" are in the
British Museum. The certificate is reprinted in Reid, pp. 236–37.
A doctor associate of the author has kindly reviewed various of the

letters and other written statements pertinent to Hood's illnesses after 1835 and has the following comments on how modern (1968) medicine would, on the basis of this information, tend to diagnose his condition:

The most significant symptoms disclosed in this material were the coughing up of blood in considerable quantities and the heart complications centering on certain abnormalities in the upper circulatory system.

As to the first, although tuberculosis cannot be positively ruled out in the absence of information as to other symptoms that customarily are used to confirm this condition, it seems more likely that Hood suffered from an increasingly severe case of what is known as "pulmonary edema," which admittedly resembles tuberculosis in some respects but is usually more protracted in duration (ten years elapsed from the first observation of spitting of blood to the time of his death—tuberculosis would almost certainly have taken his life sooner) and also appears to subside for brief periods, whereas tuberculosis, once contracted, is virtually unremitting (one gathers from the correspondence that although the suffering was more or less continuous the spitting of blood was not so).

The suggestion that rheumatic heart disease was the basic cause of Hood's circulatory difficulties as well as of the troubles he (and, to some extent, Dr. Elliot) would ascribe to the stomach and/or liver is characteristic of 19th century thinking about such matters. A diagnostician nowadays—125 years later—would see in this constellation of symptoms (including the lung condition referred to above) a strong likelihood of syphilis as the basic disease. Pasteur's work, forty years after Hood's death, first brought to light the bacterial nature of many illnesses, and although a few of the external manifestations of syphilis had been recognized for centuries, twenty years more were to pass before this disease was really understood, both as to its causal factors and how it is transmitted. In view of Hood's long record of poor health, it is possible he may have contracted the condition pre-natally, since it is now known that a syphilitic mother often transmits the infection at some point during pregnancy.

This would not however invalidate Dr. Elliot's conclusions (as recorded in the Medical Certificate drawn up less than ten months before Hood's death) as to the terminal diagnosis and probably a medical coroner today would give congestive heart failure as the cause of death. One thing is certain: Hood must have been in constant pain for at least the last seven or eight years of his life. The detailed reports he wrote on his condition attest to a continuing awareness of his deteriorating health, but the fact that even in the face of what must have seemed imminent death he was nevertheless able to carry on his creative activities marks him as a man of unusual determination and fortitude.

29. Hood collection, British Museum. Though a few letters from this correspondence are reprinted (incorrectly) in *Memorials*, II, I quote from the originals, all of which are in the British Museum.

30. ALS, Columbia University Library (Whitley, "Thomas Hood," p. 430).

31. Hood to Ward, November (?), 1844, Columbia University Library (Whitley, "Thomas Hood," p. 434).

32. Cf. the four letters to Ward in the Columbia University Library (reprinted in Whitley, "Thomas Hood," pp. 430–37), and *Memorials*, II, 244–46.

33. *Memorials*, II, 227.

34. Hood collection, National Library of Scotland.

35. Hood collection, British Museum (*Memorials*, II, 230).

36. *Works*, IX, 227.

37. *Ibid.*, pp. 230, 235.

38. *Ibid.*, pp. 233, 232.

39. *Ibid.*, p. 238.

40. *Ibid.*

41. *Memorials*, II, 234; *Works*, IX, 247.

42. *Memorials*, II, 234. During October and November *The Times* frequently carried reports and letters attesting to the agricultural crisis, but, so far as I can discover, made no direct reference to Hood's "Lay."

43. ALS, Yale (*Memorials*, II, 243). To Dr. Elliot.

44. *Works*, IX, 235.

45. *Ibid.*, p. 237.

46. *Memorials*, II, 232–33.

47. *Works*, IX, 77. In a review of Harriet Martineau's *Life in the Sick Room* in *Hood's Magazine* (Jan., 1844).

48. Harrison, ed., XII, 217.

49. *Works*, IX, 237.

50. Brooke collection.

51. Cameron collection.

52. *Memorials*, II, 244.

53. Brooke collection.

54. *Memorials*, II, 251.

55. Sotheby catalogue (Feb. 10 and 11, 1964), p. 39.

56. *Works*, IV, 80.

57. *Memorials*, II, 262. F. A. Heath's engraving of the bust forms the frontispiece to the March *Hood's Magazine*.

58. Lytton, *Life of Bulwer*, II, 68.

59. March, 1846, p. 293. Several fragments of this "series of poems" exist, among them "The Lay of the Lark," whose final lines run: "His heavy eye was glazed and dull, / He only murmur'd 'bread!' " See *Works*, X, 477–79.

60. *Memorials*, II, 257. Cf. also Ian Jack, *English Literature 1815–1832* (Oxford, 1963), p. 153.

61. *Works*, X, 519.

62. *Ibid.*, p. 583.

63. Lytton, *Life of Bulwer*, II, 68.

64. In the *Literary Gazette*—quoted from *Hood's Magazine*, III, 6 (June, 1845), 615.

65. *Hood's Magazine*, p. 312.

66. *Memorials*, II, 273.

67. Alexander Elliott, *Hood in Scotland* (Dundee, 1885) p. 161.

68. Brooke collection.

69. ALS, in my possession.

70. *Memorials*, II, 260.

71. *Ibid.*, p. 264.

Notes to the Epilogue

1. In a letter to W. H. Ainsworth, Hood collection, UCLA; see also *Memorials*, II, 270.

2. In a letter, dated May 25, 1845, to the Literary Fund (Lane, "A Chord in Melancholy: Hood's Last Years," *K-SJ*, XIV [Winter, 1964], p. 60).

In May Charles Rowcroft assumed the editorship of *Hood's Magazine*, which continued publication until 1848. Under his direction it took a stand on political and social issues that would have pained Hood—not because of its liberalism but because a magazine that still bore his name was being used for political purposes.

3. Reid, pp. 226–27.

4. Hood collection, UCLA.

5. K. J. Fielding, "The Misfortunes of Hood: 1841," p. 536; Lane, "A Chord in Melancholy," p. 58.

6. Hood collection, UCLA.

7. Jerrold, p. 397.

8. *Ibid.*, pp. 399, 400.

9. Reid, p. 232.

10. See Jerrold, p. 401.

11. *Retrospect of a Long Life* (London, 1883), I, 67; cf. similar testimony in William Tegg, "Thomas Hood," *N & Q*, 8th s., VII (1895), 85. Both Hood children are in the *DNB*.

12. In "Poor Hood (written at Kensal Green Cemetery)" Miss Cook expressed shock that Hood had no tombstone (*Poetical Works of Eliza Cook* [London, 1869], pp. 576–78).

13. *Memorials*, II, 275.

14. *The Letters and Private Papers of William Makepeace Thackeray*, coll. and ed. Gordon N. Ray (Cambridge, Mass., 1946), III, 103.

15. *Memorials*, I, xvii.

16. *The Times*, July 20, 1854, p. 10.

17. *Memorials*, I, xvi. Photograph in Jerrold, *Thomas Hood*, opp. p. 396.

Bibliography

1. Manuscript Material

I wish to acknowledge permission to quote from Hood letters held by the following libraries:

Bristol Public Library
Bristol University
British Museum
California, University of, at Los Angeles
Cornell University
Harvard University
Illinois, University of
The Pierpont Morgan Library
National Library of Scotland
New York Public Library, Manuscript Division and Henry
    W. and Albert A. Berg Collection
Oxford University, Bodleian Library
Private Collections: Jocelyn Brooke; Robert C. Cameron
Yale University

When I have cited a library as source, I have consulted the MS text. As some of the letters in the above libraries are included in the unpublished Harvard dissertation, "Thomas Hood" (1950), by Alvin Whitley, I have used the text there given. Whitley also includes Hood letters held by the following libraries:

Boston Public Library
Columbia University
Folger Shakespeare Library, Washington, D.C.
Huntington Library
Maine Historical Society Library
Massachusetts Historical Society Library
Pennsylvania Historical Society Library
University of Rochester

In addition, the following libraries hold letters by or concerning Hood not cited in the footnotes to this dissertation:

Cambridge University, Fitzwilliam Museum
Dundee Public Library

Edinburgh, University of
Free Library of Philadelphia
Indiana University
Iowa, University of
Liverpool Public Library
Liverpool University
Manchester Public Library
New York University
Princeton University
The John Rylands Library

Lastly, there are Hood letters in the files of *Punch* and of the Royal Literary Fund.

2. Unpublished Material

Cuyler, Cornelius M. "Thomas Hood: An Illustration of the Transition from the Romantic to the Victorian Era." Unpublished Ph.D. dissertation, the Johns Hopkins University, 1943.

Davies, R. E. "Thomas Hood: a Critical Study." Unpublished Ph.D. dissertation, University of London, 1937.

Goodrich, Constance. "A Bibliography of the Works of Thomas Hood." Unpublished Ph.D. dissertation, Yale University, 1934.

Hughes, Bertram Lucius. "The Social Protests in Early Victorian Poetry." Unpublished Ph.D. dissertation, Cornell University, 1936.

Morgan, Peter F. "The Career of Thomas Hood, in Relation to the World of Letters of his Time." Unpublished Master's thesis, University of London, 1956.

_____. "Thomas Hood's Literary Reading as Shown in His Works." Unpublished Ph.D. dissertation, University of London, 1959.

Murphy, Daniel J. "The Journalistic Verse of Thomas Hood." Unpublished Master's thesis, Columbia University, 1951.

Whitley, Alvin. "Thomas Hood." Unpublished Ph.D. dissertation, Harvard University, 1950.

3. Articles and Books

With the exception of a few works of general interest, I have limited this bibliography to the more important articles and books on Hood that I have consulted and found helpful. Contemporary periodicals are not listed, nor are all the works cited in the footnotes. The dissertation by Alvin Whitley, cited above, has a thorough bibliography to 1950 of secondary works relating to Hood, his contemporaries, and the age; briefer lists may be found in the *Cambridge Bibliography of*

English Literature (1941), the *Supplement* (1955), and in J. C. Reid, *Thomas Hood* (1963). The yearly bibliographies of the romantic movement in *English Literary History* (1937–49), in *Philological Quarterly* (1950–64), and now in *English Language Notes* (1965–), as well as the "Current Bibliography" in the annual *Keats-Shelley Journal* are reasonably complete and mutually supplementing. That in *K-SJ* from July 1, 1950, to June 30, 1962, has been conveniently published in volume form, *Keats, Shelley, Byron, Hunt, and Their Circles*, ed. David Bonnell Green and Edwin Graves Wilson (Lincoln, Neb., 1964). Every student of Hood acknowledges with gratitude the nearly complete bibliography of editions of Hood's works assembled by Constance Goodrich in her dissertation cited above.

Adrian, Arthur A. *Mark Lemon: First Editor of "Punch."* London, 1966.

Ainger, Alfred, ed. *Poems of Thomas Hood.* Vol. I: *Serious Poems.* London, 1897.

Annan, Noel Gilroy. *Leslie Stephen.* Cambridge, Mass., 1952.

Anonymous. "Hood: The Poet Behind the Jester's Mask." *Times Literary Supplement*, May 5, 1945, p. 210.

————. *Eclectic Review*, n.s., XIX (March, 1846), 285–95.

————. *The Bookman* (London), LXIV (September, 1923), 276–78.

Auden, W. H., ed. *19th Century British Minor Poets.* New York, 1966.

Balmanno, Mary. *Pen and Pencil.* New York, 1858.

Bianquis, Geneviève. *La Vie quotidienne en Allemagne à l'époque romantique* (1795–1830). Paris, 1958.

Blunden, Edmund. *Votive Tablets.* London, 1931.

————. "The Poet Hood." *A Review of English Literature.* I, 1 (January, 1960), 26–34.

Bowring, Sir John. *Autobiographical Recollections of Sir John Bowring.* London, 1877.

Boyd, James. *Goethe's Knowledge of English Literature.* Oxford, 1932.

Brander, Laurence. *Thomas Hood.* ("Writers and Their Work, No. 159.") London, 1963.

Buckley, Jerome Hamilton. *The Victorian Temper.* New York, 1964.

Chew, Samuel C. "The Nineteenth Century and After (1789–1939)" in *A Literary History of England*, ed. Albert C. Baugh. New York, 1948.

Chorley, Henry. *London and Westminster Review*, XXIX, I (April, 1838), 119–45.

Clark, G. Kitson. *The Making of Victorian England.* Cambridge, Mass., 1962.

Cohen, J. M. *Robert Browning.* London, 1952.

————. "Thomas Hood: The Language of Poetry." *Times Literary Supplement*, September 19, 1952, pp. 605–6.

Davies, R. E. "Thomas Hood as Playwright and Prose Writer." *English Studies in Africa*, II (March, 1959), 73–89.

Dilke, Sir Charles Wentworth. *The Papers of a Critic*. 2 vols. London, 1875.

Dodds, John W. *The Age of Paradox: A Biography of England 1841–1851*. New York, 1952.

Eden, Helen Parry. "Thomas Hood." *The Catholic World*, CXXIII (September, 1926), 731–38.

Elliott, Alexander. *Hood in Scotland: Reminiscences of Thomas Hood, Poet and Humorist*. Dundee, 1885.

Elton, Oliver. *A Survey of English Literature, 1780–1830*. 2 vols. London, 1912.

Empson, William. *Seven Types of Ambiguity*. London, 1930.

Enzensberger, Christian. "Die Fortentwicklung der Romantik an englischen Beispiel: Thomas Hood." *Deutsche Vierteljahrsschrift*, XXXVIII (1964), 534–60.

Fielding, K. J. "The Misfortunes of Hood: 1841" *Notes and Queries*, CXCVIII, 12 (December, 1953), 534–36.

Forster, John. *The Life of Charles Dickens*, ed. J. W. T. Ley. London, 1928.

Garnett, Richard. "Hood, Thomas." *The Dictionary of National Biography*, ed. Sir Leslie Stephen and Sir Sidney Lee, IX. London, 1921–22.

Gilfillan, George. *A Second Gallery of Literary Portraits*. New York, 1850.

Graham, Walter. *English Literary Periodicals*. New York, 1930.

Gray, Donald J. "The Uses of Victorian Laughter." *Victorian Studies*, X, 2 (December, 1966), 145–76.

Green, David Bonnell, and Wilson, Edwin Graves. *Keats, Shelley, Byron, Hunt, and Their Circles. A Bibliography: July 1, 1950–June 30, 1962*. Lincoln, Nebr., 1964.

Grierson, Sir Herbert. *The Background of English Literature*. London, 1925.

Hall, S. C. *A Book of Memories*. London, 1871.

————. *The Book of Gems*. 3 vols. London, 1836–38.

————. *Retrospect of a Long Life*. 2 vols. London, 1883.

Harvey, Sir Paul, ed. *The Oxford Companion to English Literature*. 3rd ed. Oxford, 1947.

Head, Sir Francis. *Bubbles from the Brunnens of Nassau*. London, 1834.

Heath-Stubbs, John. *The Darkling Plain.* London, 1950.

Henley, William Ernest. *Views and Reviews: Essays in Appreciation.* Vol. I: *Literature.* London, 1908.

Hennig, John. "The Literary Relations between Goethe and Thomas Hood." *Modern Language Quarterly,* XII (1951), 57–66.

Hewlett, H. G. *Henry Fothergill Chorley.* 2 vols. London, 1873.

Hood, Thomas. *The Complete Poetical Works of Thomas Hood,* ed. Walter Jerrold. London, 1906.

————. *Memorials of Thomas Hood,* edited by his Son [Tom Hood] and Daughter [Frances Freeling Broderip]. 2 vols. London, 1860.

————. *The Works of Thomas Hood,* edited by his Son and Daughter. 10 vols. London, 1869–73.

————. *Tylney Hall.* London, 1883.

Horne, R. H. *A New Spirit of the Age.* New York, 1844.

House, Humphry. *The Dickens World.* 2nd ed. London, 1960.

Hudson,William Henry. *A Quiet Corner in a Library.* Chicago, 1915.

Jack, Ian. *English Literature, 1815–1832.* Oxford, 1963.

Jerrold, Walter. *Douglas Jerrold and "Punch."* London, 1910.

————. *Thomas Hood and Charles Lamb: The Story of a Friendship.* London, 1930.

————. *Thomas Hood: His Life and Times.* New York, 1909.

Johnson, Edgar. *Charles Dickens: His Tragedy and Triumph.* 2 vols. New York, 1952.

Kaufman, Paul. "The Reynolds-Hood Commonplace Book: A Fresh Appraisal." *Keats-Shelley Journal,* X (Winter, 1961), 43–52.

King, R. W. *The Translator of Dante: The Life, Work and Friendships of Henry Francis Cary.* London, 1925.

Kroeber, Karl. *Romantic Narrative Art.* Madison, Wis., 1960.

Lane, William G. "A Chord in Melancholy: Hood's Last Years." *Keats-Shelley Journal,* XIII (Winter, 1964), 43–61.

Lawrance, Hannah. *British Quarterly Review,* XLVI (October, 1867), 323–54.

Lytton, The Earl of. *The Life of Edward Bulwer.* 2 vols. London, 1913.

MacFarlane, Charles. *Reminiscences of a Literary Life.* London, 1917.

Maggs Brothers Catalogue. Autumn, 1918.

Marchand, Leslie A. *The Athenaeum: A Mirror of Victorian Culture.* Chapel Hill, N.C., 1941.

————. *Letters of Thomas Hood, from the Dilke Papers in the British Museum.* New Brunswick, N.J., 1945.

Milnes, Richard Monckton. *The Poetical Works of Thomas Hood with a Memoir of the Author.* New York, 1873.

More, Paul Elmer. *Shelburne Essays, Seventh Series.* New York, 1910.

Morgan, Peter F. "John Clare Again." *Times Literary Supplement,* February 7, 1958, p. 75.

————. "Thomas Hood." *Times Literary Supplement,* June 7, 1957, p. 349.

————. "John Hamilton Reynolds and Thomas Hood." *Keats-Shelley Journal,* XI (Winter, 1962), 83–95.

————. "Corrections in Some Letters of Thomas Hood." *Notes and Queries,* n.s., X (July, 1963), 261–62.

————. *Notes and Queries,* n.s., X (October, 1963), 385.

————. "Charles Lamb and Thomas Hood: Records of a Friendship." *Tennessee Studies in Literature,* IX (1964), 71–85.

Oswald, Emil. *Thomas Hood und die soziale Tendenzdichtung seiner Zeit.* Wien and Leipzig, 1904.

Poe, Edgar Allan. *Complete Works of Edgar Allan Poe,* ed. James A. Harrison. 17 vols. New York, 1902.

Quinlan, Maurice James. *Victorian Prelude: A History of English Manners, 1700–1830.* New York, 1941.

Redding, Cyrus. *Fifty Years' Recollections.* 3 vols. London, 1858.

Reid, J. C. *Thomas Hood.* London, 1963.

Reid, T. Wemyss. *Life, Letters and Friendships of Richard Monckton Milnes.* 2 vols. London, 1891.

Rollins, Hyder E. *The Keats Circle: Letters and Papers.* 2 vols. Cambridge, Mass., 1948.

Rossetti, William Michael. *The Poetical Works of Thomas Hood,* edited with a critical memoir; illustrated by Gustave Doré. New York, 1873.

Sadleir, Michael. *Bulwer: A Panorama. I: Edward and Rosina, 1803–1836.* Boston, 1931.

Shelley, Henry C. *Literary By-Paths in Old England.* Boston, 1909.

Saintsbury, George. *Essays in English Literature, 1780–1860, Second Series.* New York, 1895.

Sanbrook, A. J. "A Romantic Theme: The Last Man." *Forum for Modern Language Studies,* II (January, 1966), 25–33.

Sotheby Catalogue. February 10 and 11, 1964.

Spielmann, M. H. *The History of "Punch."* New York, 1895.

————. "Thomas Hood and 'Punch.'" *Bookman* (New York), X (1899), 151–52.

Stedman, Edmund Clarence. *Victorian Poets.* Boston and New York, 1888.

Super, R. H. *Walter Savage Landor: A Biography.* New York, 1954.

Sutton, Max Keith. "Inverse Sublimity in Victorian Humor." *Victorian Studies,* X, 2 (December, 1966), 177–92.

Symons, Arthur. *The Romantic Movement in English Poetry*. London, 1909.

Tennyson, Hallam. *Alfred Lord Tennyson: A Memoir*. 2 vols. London, 1897.

Thackeray, William Makepeace. *Roundabout Papers*. Boston, 1883.

Trevelyan, G. M. *English Social History: A Survey of Six Centuries, Chaucer to Queen Victoria*. London, 1944.

Walker, Hugh. *The Literature of the Victorian Era*. London, 1910.

Wallis, N. Hardy. "Thomas Hood (1799–1845)." *Essays by Divers Hands*, ed. Harold Nicolson. N.s. XXIII. London, 1947.

Whitley, Alvin. "Hood and Dickens: Some New Letters." *Huntington Library Quarterly*, XIV, 4 (August, 1951), 385–413.

————. "Keats and Hood." *Keats-Shelley Journal*, V (Winter, 1956), 33–47.

————. "Lord William Lennox and *The Tuft-Hunter*." *Harvard Library Bulletin*, VI, 1 (Winter, 1952), 125–33.

————. "Thomas Hood and 'The Times.'" *Times Literary Supplement*, May 17, 1957, p. 309.

————. "Thomas Hood as a Dramatist." *University of Texas Studies in English*, XXX (1951), 184–201.

————. "Two Hints for *Bleak House*." *The Dickensian*, LII, No. 320 (September, 1956), 183–84.

Wilson, John. "Hood's *Whims and Oddities*." *Blackwood's Edinburgh Magazine*, XXI, cxxi (January, 1827), 45–60.

Woodring, Carl Ray. *Victorian Samplers: William and Mary Howitt*. Lawrence, Kans., 1952.

Woodward, E. L. *The Age of Reform, 1832–1870*. Oxford, 1938.

Wright, Austin, ed. *Victorian Literature: Essays in Criticism*. New York, 1961.

Index